To Dani
all the memories!

BEYOND AND BELOW THE WATERLINE

by

JOE CASEY

PublishAmerica
Baltimore

First printing

ISBN: 1-60610-932-4
PUBLISHED BY PUBLISHAMERICA, LLLP
www.publishamerica.com
Baltimore

Printed in the United States of America

Dedicated to

THE STAR OF THE SEA

Acknowledgments

To all those whose stories found their way into
these pages, and to those who were patient
enough to review and encourage their publication.

Chapter 1
Early Days

We were a family from the Great Plains, city raised but with strong ties to the farm communities that had begot both our parents and had given us children a deep love of animals, especially dogs and horses. My childhood was not exceptional in terms of the contemporary world. I had a stern and successful father and an industrious and loving mother; a brother who was three years older than me and had taken much of my parents' experimental efforts in child rearing, and a younger sister who came along when they were veterans and had stopped trying to produce exceptional children. The extended family was large on both sides, so much so, that as a young child I believed that everyone in the world was somehow related to us.

My mother's sister, our Aunt Liz, was a powerhouse and when uncle Mac died suddenly just after the birth of their sixth child she took over the running of his insurance business and persuaded my father to leave the bank where he was a junior clerk and go into a partnership with her. It didn't take long for my father to realize that he had found a 'calling' in life insurance. It was the 1920's and there was no social net to help a family out if the breadwinner suffered an early death, leaving a destitute widow and small fatherless children. He became as devoted to the value of life insurance as any preacher was to the souls of his parishioners, and as a manager sold the idea of social salvation to all his agents so well that by the 1940's he was being groomed for the position of CEO of the whole company.

Some people never seem to be aware of themselves. Life just happens to them without their being aware of its passing, while others are aware of themselves from the time they are small children and wonder in varying degrees what makes them distinct from the rest of the people with whom they come in contact From the time of my youngest memories there was a real awareness of being distinct from others, not better or worse necessarily, but rather an awareness of being alive as a separate person.

We lived in the foothills of the Rocky Mountains where the Chinook winds often made light of winter and brought the promise of spring. Mornings in the foothills carried a touch of the first day of creation; the evenings were beautiful but it was the dawns that called the spirit to look upward and tremble with expectation. The rising sun seemed to bring a promise of new wonders to old greenery met casually on the sides of hills or in small valleys not yet fully awake. By noon the magic had all but vanished but the memory of Earth's early breath lingered through the tasks of school and home and there was always the certainty that a new phoenix would arise the next day. We ran at everything we did and in school fidgeted irrepressibly while constrained between recesses. To our bright young eyes the gophers of the hillsides and the hawks of the air taught us things unable to be captured within the tedium of the classroom. Both the land and the sky spoke a new language, filled with feeling and meaning but void of words and explanations. We belonged; it didn't matter what else there was as long as we were facing the hills.

We didn't know who Adam was or what Nature meant and we didn't have to know; we flowed outward as water does from a burst dam and we soaked into the hills and the valleys and the sky without ever diminishing the excitement from within. We rang with the laughter of discovery as we climbed down through the ripples of land that led to the river behind the school. It was a flat river of round white stones and water beetles and minnows and crustaceans and other wonders that belong to the unity of fantasy and reality. We were the children of light and for a time we named the creatures of the earth, as the first Adam had done. Some of us have never outgrown that early promise of life and we can still be seen moving in the fresh light of dawn, looking without thinking, feeling without awareness, sensing the waves of eternity flowing out from the centre of our existence.

As we got older we were always ready to ride off on our bikes, or go swimming in the polluted waters of the local rivers, or chase ground squirrels with our small bore rifles. In the long winters there was hockey or swimming at the "Y", or dances, or looking for some small hill to ski on in the flat expanse of the prairie. We managed with school, because we had to, even though the discipline was swift and the punishment hard. Once, after being 'strapped' at school for some rule infraction I jokingly told my father, which earned me another. It was the last time I ever told him. But the sun came up in the morning and there was always a sense of excitement about what the day would bring, and if nothing exciting had happened, we would go out in the early evening and ring doorbells and run, or grease the trolley tracks, or dare each other to go up to some girl's house and ask her father if she could come to the door. But always there was a sense that we were alive and life was to be lived.

These were not always the same friends, for as time and growth moved on new faces and new voices often replaced the ones of the years before. But we were all alike: alive, daring, curious, bonded and enjoying each other's company. As adolescence passed into the later teen years we began to experiment with liquor and girls, and found both were better than we had expected. The booze, even when it was bad, was so good, probably because it was so adult and so forbidden; and so were the girls. But girls were not real persons, at least, not real the way we were. We went out with them occasionally, and talked of them always but we were the ones who were really alive, got together and roared around in our fathers' cars, and drank and played football and joined clubs, and later, fraternities, and swam and laughed, simply because we were alive.

In grade 10 my next door neighbour was a boy my age who was called Boo for no apparent reason except that his mother had given him that nickname when he was a baby and it had stuck. We were close friends and spent a lot of time together. His mother had created a dessert to die for, made with cooked rice, raisins, pineapple, shredded coconut and tons of real whipped cream. Because he was an only child his mother doted on him and he was always permitted to invite me over whenever the special dessert was on the menu. His father, Archie, often took us fishing on the Netley Marsh where they owned an old farmhouse that was used as a summer retreat. Archie owned an electrical manufacturing company and was a member of all the right clubs and a successful man-about-town, and when Boo began to run with our group of River Heights boys, Archie grew increasingly uneasy. When we started to get in trouble with the Law because of our pranks, Boo's father decide to send him to a prestigious boarding school in the other end of town.

That April my parents had to fly to the capital to attend an insurance underwriters' conference and had asked Aunt Liz to watch over us while they were away. By this time Liz had sold her insurance business and had become a police matron, and didn't like to drive a car in the city unless it was absolutely necessary, which meant that Dad's new Mercury sat alone and unused in the garage at the back of the property. I had driven farm tractors and trucks since

I was thirteen but had never had the opportunity to try a real car on a real city street. The temptation was just too great and with the help of two friends we rolled the car out of the garage and down the lane on a Sunday morning. When we were far enough away from the house not to be betrayed by the sound of the starter, we set off to offer freedom to Boo from his 'prison' in the West End.

We parked outside the north wall of the campus and slunk into the old building, having previously devised a story about returning a book to Boo if some prefect should suddenly appear on the scene. The building was quiet except for the faint sound of choral voices coming from the chapel at the end of the long hall. One door was partly open at the back of the chapel and we crept in on our hands and knees up to the back pew and whispered to the occupants that we were there to rescue Boo. Teen age boys quickly enter into any such subversive activities and the message was quietly sent, pew by pew, to the second front bench where Boo sat. Within minutes he had crawled under the pews all the way back to where we waited, then led us out a side door and over the wall to our get-away car. We drove all day, laughed, told dirty jokes, ate hamburgers and chips, drank pop and called on several girls, none of whom trusted us enough to enter into our adventure.

Boo had to be back by five o'clock when Sunday supper was eaten in the presence of the dorm prefect, and so by five-thirty we had rolled the Mercury down the lane and back into the garage and my two friends had departed. When I entered the house Aunt Liz was standing in the hall with a terrible look on her face. Not everything had gone as well as we thought, for one of the Teaching Masters had seen us go over the wall and had taken down my father's license number and reported the incident to the Headmaster. From there it was a brief call to the central police station and a longer call to Officer Aunt Liz. When she got over scolding me she said that she had been forced to make promises of serious corporal punishment to the Headmaster, which she couldn't, in all conscience, possibly keep. Because she had no real use for private schools and Headmasters, and knowing of the wrath my father would visit upon me if he found out, she had decided never to tell my parents. Boo ended up losing all his recesses and special privileges for three weeks but the next time I saw him he thanked me, for it had made him a celebrity among the boys who previously had thought him rather weird.

Chapter 2
Northern Exposure

Because there was too much to do and too little time, studies in my senior year of high school took second place to the excitement that abounded at every turn. My father finally sent me to a college day school, hoping that the smaller classes and more immediate teacher contact would get me through and on to university. This was the first school I ever attended where teachers treated students as if they were real people. These teachers fraternized with the students and could easily be led off topic to discuss the more immediate concerns of late adolescence, while still getting enough work covered to prepare their students for final exams. By the end of the year strong and lasting friendships had been established throughout our classes and especially between Jim and myself. There are times in life when a chance meeting results immediately in a life-long friendship, and it was that way with Jim and me.

Jim had come to the college on a junior hockey scholarship and although our sports were different, the bond between us was real and deep and still exists. Through Jim I got my first real summer job, working as a pantryman/waiter in the dining car on a major railway. He was a year older than I and had worked the previous summer on a similar job. He taught me how to carry a large tray and serve the diners in a cramped area, and how to make salads and clean dishes in a swaying train that shunted unexpectedly for no apparent reason, and he helped me modify my birth certificate so that it said 'eighteen', the minimum hiring age, and I was able to get the job. With his experience he got the main line runs while mine were mostly supper crowds that were taking a four-hour train ride down to their cottages in the lake area. Supper was a busy time and there was a lot of clean up to be done after the passengers departed, but when the work was done and we had eaten ourselves, we knocked down the tables and set up cots where the tables had been. Usually we laid over Saturday and worked the train back to the city on Sunday night, so the young waiter and I had time to fall in love with any of the lovely young things that we met down at the water's edge. These were daytime romances for we never dared to invite a girl back to the railway coach, which was the actual domain of the chef who had a temper to behold and who spent the day drinking and catching up on his sleep.

That summer only once did I get a main line run and it was on a full dining car with a maitre de and a head chef and two second chefs and the working pace was staggering; we served the whole train, about two hundred passengers and crew, in less than two hours, and by the time the run was over I never wanted to wash another dish or make another salad. One other time I ran as a cook on a 'milk-run' train that stopped at every hamlet; the cook apparently got drunk and didn't show up and so they drafted me into the role of salad-maker and chef. We had Canadian back bacon in the fridge and when a passenger ordered a ham omelette I thought the bacon was cooked ham and put it raw into the omelette. It must have tasted all right because he sent his congratulations to the 'chef' at the end of the meal.

At the beginning of that summer Jim and I had planned to go on to university but as registration time drew near the thought of having no money in our pockets and having to spend most of the time studying, caused us both to rethink our futures. Jim went on to play hockey in the small, semi-professional teams that were everywhere, and I went north to search for adventure by working in survey camps, which were a part of the federal government's continuous mapping of unoccupied forest lands in the north. It was exciting work; living in tents in virgin territory, where no evidence of humans was to be seen. In the late summer we traveled by canoes or by Norseman bush plane if the starting distance was too great for a quick canoe passage. The pilots would lash our canoes up against the fuselage between the pontoons and once they were unloaded they would be our means of transportation among the thousands of rivers and lakes that dot the northern tree line.

In winter we would always move by bush planes that were equipped with skis, although there was a time between the first snowfall and freeze-up when we flew out and stayed in more populated areas and caught up on the paperwork and mapping. On one of those occasions we were sent to find a permanent benchmark which was just outside of town in some farmer's field. Such benchmarks consist of a poured concrete post sunk about six feet into the ground and having a brass cap mounted on its surface that contains the actual longitude and latitude of the location. We looked all day and when we couldn't locate it, asked several farmers if they had ever seen such an object when ploughing. Apparently the word was quickly spread around the whole area for just after we had finished lunch in the town cafe the next day one of the farmers actually showed up with the concrete benchmarked in the back of his truck and wanted to be paid for the work he had done with his tractor in pulling it out of the ground. We thanked him, took the post back and simply plopped it in the hole. So much for exact mapping.

When freeze-up was complete the planes would drop us off on some designated frozen lake where we would begin to run the survey line through the bush for seven miles and when we reached that limit, after a week or so, the planes would return and fly us fourteen miles further on in the general direction of the line we were running. The reason for these distances was that seven miles was about the farthest we could go in the short days of winter-light, working on snowshoes in 25 degrees below zero temperature. After we set up camp in the new location we would travel to where we left the line and gradually work back toward our new camp until we reached it, and then in the second week, work another seven miles from the camp until we reached the limit of our endurance. Sometimes the surveyors were so good at estimating the direction of the survey line that it would run right through our camp. On one occasion we had to move the cook tent so we could see where the line ran after it left the camp.

The camp was merely a collection of large canvas tents, each with collapsible wooden sides, and a small tin stove placed on a green-wood cribbing and having a series of joined stove pipes that ran up through a tin-fortified hole in the top of the tent. Each tent could hold four to six persons with enough room for a sleeping bag and a duffle sack filled with personal clothing. There were no other amenities for we traveled light since we moved so often. Even the toilet was only a fallen log, which sometimes slipped and dumped its occupant into the snow, much to the glee of the other camp members, who hearing the cries and curses of the victim knew exactly what had happened. Tearing down and reassembling a winter camp was a day-long effort; everything had to be rolled up or collapsed so it would fit into the plane, then flown to the new location and unrolled and rebuilt. At the new campsite the snow had to be dug out of the area where each tent would sit, then great quantities of spruce branches were cut from the trees and laid out as flooring in the tents, and finally each tent was unrolled and erected, as was the larger cook tent, and all this in weather that ranged anywhere from zero to fifty below.

Each day except Sunday we climbed into our sleeping bags at about eight in the evening and were due in the cook tent for breakfast and a packed lunch for the trail, at five in the morning. In the really cold months every person in the tent had a week's duty of getting up around one in the morning and bank the tin stove with dry wood. It helped, but the nights were always cold. On one move the weather turned stormy and the plane was unable to deliver the stoves for the tents. They were usually the last item that got moved from the old campsite since they were not needed until everything had been put in place in the new camp. That night we put on every piece of clothing that was in our duffle sacks and climbed into the sleeping bags and shivered the night away. In the morning a lip of hoarfrost had to be broken off the top of the bags before we could crawl out, and from then on the men insisted that the stoves had to be sent even before the tents were moved. Experience is a great teacher, and the winter northlands are unforgiving.

On one remarkably cold day, a new surveyor was flown in to replace a member who had developed pneumonia. Fresh off the plane from Ireland he had never experienced the cold of the north and had dressed for his first day of work wearing almost every bit of clothing he had brought with him. It was impossible to tell how big a man he actually was for he looked like a large basketball with arms, and to make it even worse he waddled as he walked because he had never before worked wearing snowshoes. We set out for the working line, he carrying the heavy surveying instrument and me going on before, breaking trail for his uneducated snowshoes. We came down a small hill onto a frozen marsh and he stopped to rest while I climbed up the far side of the hill. When I looked back he had started across the marsh with his eyes fixed on the trail I had left. Then the bull moose appeared, coming in off the larger area of the frozen lake; it had likely never seen humans before and slowly advanced toward the plodding surveyor.

I called out to warn him but the layers of scarves about his head had made him quite deaf. He finally looked up when he had almost collided with the moose, and let out a remarkable cry of terror, dropping the instrument and attempting to run on the awkward snowshoes. After three or four paces he fell face down on the marsh bed, warbling what sounded like a primitive death chant, with his arms flailing about his head as if to ward off a drove of bees. The curious moose sniffed him and attempted to roll him over with its nose, but that only produced an increase in the flailing of his arms and the volume in the death song he was composing. The startled moose soon crashed off through the small trees that lined the lake, leaving a weeping surveyor and an assistant doubled over in laughter. He finally rose from the lake bed, as one might rise from the grave, looked around him and headed back to camp where he remained in the tent until the next plane came to carry him back to a more civilized existence. After reaching camp myself, carrying both my gear and his I went in to check on him.

"You can give this country back to the natives. I'm going back to Ireland where there are no such beasts!" was his only reply, and he sat there until the plane came for him.

Our head surveyor was not an easy man to work for; he believed that we didn't make enough effort to keep pace with the assurances he had offered to the Department and because of his insistence we often worked late even in a new area where there were few landmarks to show the way back to the warmth of our tented campsite. As the daylight faded it was often difficult to see the path our snowshoes had earlier trammeled through the virgin snow, especially since the packed Indian-file trail was never straight as it rolled around dead-fall trees looking for the easiest route. On one occasion we had spent part of the day pushing the survey line up to and through the camp and at three o'clock found ourselves breaking a new path northward from the camp with only an hour or two of light left.

As the Native axe men cleared the trees ahead the surveyor and myself measured the topography and 'chained' the distance. The actual 'chain' was a 100 foot measured steel line on a reel; the chainman would go on ahead holding the free end of the chain and waiting for the cry "chain!" from the surveyor when the end of the chain appeared on the reel. The chainman then placed a long steel pin in the ground marking the newly measured distance. Often the small bushes the axe men had not brushed out would snag the steel line, which could be freed by raising up the two ends of the line and shaking the tangle out of the undergrowth. The surveyor was angry on that occasion because the others had packed up their gear and already started back to camp in the darkening light and he had pulled so hard on the snag that the line actually broke near the end of the reel.

He immediately started back to camp himself, leaving the broken reel on the ground for me to gather up. The problem was that it had started to snow heavily and the reel was not visible by the time I had reached where he had stood. It took fifteen minutes to search through all the possible places where it might have been dropped, and when it was finally secured the light had faded and the trail had disappeared. Camp was only about half a mile away, but the direction was uncertain and since we had not originally thought we would work north of the camp that day we had left our tea tin, matches and tea bags in our tents. Without a fire and something hot to drink it was not likely a person could survive a whole night in those frozen woods without at least ending up with serious frostbite, and that was the brightest prospect.

With the snow blotting out the recent trail, soon one direction seemed as good as any other; to miss the camp meant that there was no other habitation for over 100 miles in any direction. Up until that time in my life I had never felt alone, even when I had chosen to wander away from the others in order to *be* alone. Home and family and friends were always there, at least in my mind, but on this occasion the possibility of being truly alone and perishing at first startled and then terrified me. It was the first time that the duality of life—to be alone or to be with others—tipped heavily in favour of an eternity of desolation. I hadn't prayed in years and really had no thought of God or a higher purpose in life, but since there was none other to turn to, a begging prayer of terror formed in my mind; within minutes I had fallen over one of the guy-wires of our own tent and although I had been wandering for a hour my absence had not been noticed. Had the wire not been there it is likely I would have passed by the tent, darkened because all the men were in the cook tent eating supper, and since our tent was the last tent in the line of tents in the camp it was the wire that had saved me. Next day, warmed, fed and with emergency supplies in a backpack it all seemed like a fortunate coincidence, but from time to time the sense of absolute desolation returned to haunt me.

Chapter 3
Winter's End

The pilots that flew for the survey parties were a breed unto themselves, capable of handling any situation as a normal part of a day's work. The first time this became apparent was on the first day of winter work; on take-off the plane was at about five hundred feet when the oil pump blew and spewed a thick, black jelly over the windshield. The pilot simply opened his door and wiped the continuous stream off a small patch of the windshield, turned the plane around and came back for repairs. Sometimes fate intervened and the pilot wasn't so successful. One summer the Norseman caught a sunken log on one of its pontoons as it was taking-off on our small lake. It turned the plane into the shore where it destroyed its propeller on the trunk of a northern pine tree, and then sat there forlorn for a week until a new prop could be flown in.

One of our pilots had been caught in a fire and his face was a white mask of skin grafts; a great flyer but moody and withdrawn and difficult to get to know, until the day we ran out of gas on the vast tundra of the north. First the belly tank went dry and the plane dropped a thousand feet before he grinned and turned to me.

"Quiet, isn't it." he said and then cut in the remaining wing tank which was only partially full.

We began to look for an unnamed lake where he had built a small dock and shed to keep a cache of 50 gallon gas drums for just such an emergency. The lake finally appeared but the plane ran out of gas just after we hit the water and before we could taxi to the dock, so he pulled a pair of paddles out of the back racks and with each of us straddling one of the pontoons we proceeded slowly to the makeshift wharf.

At the end of the dock was a rough shed made out of local dead-fall with a door hung by leather straps. Unfortunately a bear had pulled the straps off and eaten them and once inside had made short work of the rubber hose that was attached to the hand pump. There was no other way of pumping the gas from the drums into the wing tank of the plane. We talked then about how unfeeling the North was and how you always had to be prepared for any eventuality.

"A beautiful but harsh land," he said, "fit only for those who like to wrestle with nature."

The largest container we could find was the pilot's own ten-gallon cowboy hat and after we tipped the first drum over he opened the plug enough for the gas to run into the hat which I held. When the hat was full he closed the plug, got up on the wing of the plane and had me hand up the hat to him so he could begin to fill the tank. The work took hours and much of the gas spilled and made rainbow circles on the flat water of the lake.

"Don't make a spark! Don't make a spark!" he kept repeating both to himself and to me.

By the time we had emptied the 50 gallon drums into the plane there was so much gas on the water around the dock we had to paddle the loaded plane out into the middle of the lake to avoid the chance that the engine might backfire and ignite the painted water. We flew back to the home base and it was the last time I saw him. A few weeks later he was killed while trying to splash water with his pontoons on the fish dock where his girlfriend worked. One pontoon got too close to the piling on the dock and hooked under it sending the heavy plane down into sixteen feet of dark water and drowning this complex person. Some said it wasn't an accident, but I think it really was.

One winter day working on line with the surveyor it became apparent that the Native axe men, who cleared the trees in front of us, has stopped working and were involved in some sort of a game. They would rush together in a small circle and dance around a pole that was stuck in the snow. After we watched for some time and tried to guess the point of the game, the surveyor sent me forward to encourage them to get back to work. As I approached it became clear that the point of the game had to do with sticking the pole into a snow bank and then running away as quickly as possible; then from a distance, collapsing down on their snowshoes and laughing uproariously.

As I walked up they had gathered together and were slowly making their way to the central pole and soon jabbed the snow again with it. Almost immediately a hibernating young bear exploded out of the snow bank and took the quickest way out of the gathering, knocking me down in its haste to escape. It happened so quickly that it was over before any fear had developed. If poking the snow with a pole had caused the axe men to laugh heartily, the sight of a young surveyor's helper falling backwards as the bear stepped on and over him was too much for them. They lay in the snow and laughed until the pain in their sides forced them to stop. It was an hour before any of them were fit to work, and every time they looked at me they doubled over in more uncontrollable mirth. Finally, the surveyor, hoping to get some work out of them, sent me back to the camp early. By evening everyone in camp knew of the incident, and knew that the axe men had a new name for me in their language, roughly translated as 'He who is stepped on by baby bear.' After that they never called me anything else.

To win back their respect I began to spend all my spare daylight hours training to increase my speed on the snowshoes, an ability that did impress them. Within six weeks none of the party could match my speed and even when they had a head start I could beat them back into camp. At the end of one day's work, when we were six or seven miles from camp, one of the younger natives asked if I would give them a head start of ten minutes and race them back to camp. The prize was to be my dessert against his for a whole week, and the contract was soon made. They started off and were soon out of sight, while the ten minutes seemed to pass more slowly than it had all day. At the second it arrived I was off at top speed, racing along the top of the first hill that led to a frozen lake.

The hill ended on a cliff about fifteen feet above the ice and their tracks had led right to the edge; below it was just possible in the fading light to make out the imprint of their snowshoes in the snow on the edge of the lake. If they had managed that jump, then the snow must be soft directly below the cliff and there was no time to waste. But there was really no snow except what they had kicked onto the ice from the bank and when I landed one snowshoe broke right in half and the drop knocked the wind out of me. When I stood up it was apparent there was *another* set of snowshoe prints that led from my landing spot back along the bank and up the hill on an easy angle. They had walked to the edge of the cliff then carefully walked backward, stepped over a fallen tree and made their way down the hill to set up the false landing; with that done they set off toward camp at a leisurely pace, confident that the young chain-man would not catch up to them. During the following week my pie was passed around, with each of the combatants claiming that it was the best piece of pie he had ever tasted.

When spring came, or threatened to be on the way, we flew out while the ice on the lakes would still support the weight of the loaded plane, and returned to the windy city. We had a month or more to wait for the waterways to open up and submit to the attack of the canoes. But there was always work to be done and one of the jobs my father wanted done was to finish a small 'bunkie' down at our lakeside cottage some seventy miles away. It stood in a large beach area which in the early spring was absolutely deserted, and quite primitive. There was no electricity and no running water; just a lovely large cottage with room and path and a superb deep well a quarter of a mile away. Having loaded the truck with food, tools, lumber and kerosene for the lamps there seemed no need for further planning and a portable radio and books were left behind. The first few days were long and busy, and when the sun went down it was time for supper and then bed. As the week wore on and most of the heavy work was done, the nights seemed to become longer and sleep did not arrive as soon as the lamp was extinguished. Unfortunately the only book the cottage offered was a large volume entitled *Famous Ghost Stories*, an anthology of the great horror stories of the centuries. They were fascinating but while they were being read the spring wind took on a threatening note and the ordinary silence of a deserted landscape crackled with noises that hadn't earlier been noticed.

There wasn't another soul within ten miles and often the book would be laid aside when the tales became too real, only to be picked up later when the chilling silence continued to make sleep elusive. On one particular night at the crucial part of one of the most alarming stories a sudden squeaking resonated from the closest window. Pressed against the glass was a ghostly phantasm with great lips, a long throat and eyes that had rolled back in to its head. I screamed, the apparition gave a great sobbing groan and disappeared. It later turned out to be lost horse that had wandered away from its barn, and seeing the light in the window imagined that it had at last found its way home. As the cottage was raised on a stone foundation the horse had been forced to stretch its neck to see inside, which had caused its eyes to roll downward showing only the white tops of the orbs. Its "groan" was a frightened whinny caused by the figure inside suddenly jumping up screaming and throwing a book into the air.

We never met again, which was a blessing on both our lives. Soon after that I returned to the beckoning northern woods.

There was something almost sad about working survey lines in the summer; almost a deja vu sense of yearning for something intangible, as if we had walked the woods before and seen owls and deer and beaver and lived with them, and been a part of them at some time that memory could not recall. It was especially present in the evenings when the loons would cry their mournful song and the flat water of the lakes would suddenly be pierced by a young fish leaping after a passing insect. Life has a strange repetitiveness to it and because none of the birds or animals were domesticated, any creature that presented itself gave off the sense that it had always been there and that its life was somehow eternal. It is a sense of unity and eternity that does not present itself in the city or town, although occasionally some farmers can be seen leaning on a fence in the summer evening with the same far away look that we experienced in the northern woods. Summer work was less taxing and easier and more fun. We covered more ground in one day's work than would be covered in three or four days in the winter, and we were more alive to the movements of the woods around us. Sometimes we were too alive and took our environment for granted, such as the time we camped by a brown lake with strange tasting water. No one worked the next day for we spent the day running to the latrine until we became so weak that even that seemed an unnecessary activity. Whatever was in the water, some said it was an excess of iron, it caused us to pull up camp and move on as soon as some of our strength returned.

On another occasion we arrived at a place owned by the local blackflies, who had perfected a bombing maneuver whereby they could descend on any open piece of flesh, bite, inject and vanish before the victim could defend. After the first of these feeding frenzies we also were laid up for a whole day. Everyone looked the same, with round puffy faces and limbs that were smooth and nearly twice their normal sizes. Since the work in the area owned by the blackflies was to keep us occupied for several days, we had the Department fly in hats, gloves, raincoats and yards of green netting. We were then able to work, but it was hot and uncomfortable and the dye from the netting ran off from our sweat and stained every part of our body. Luckily it was only a vegetable dye, and after a week of scrubbing it went away. These are the memories of the north, but mostly we remember the evenings and the wild life, seldom seen in the winter, and the fish that would line up to sample our fish hooks, and always we remembered and talked about the sense of forever that was so present when the tall northern pines moved in the summer wind.

And I remember Luke, a Metis Native, who in those days were commonly called "half-breeds", and one of the gentlest and most unusual men I was ever to meet. Luke was about thirty-five years old and looked like Errol Flynn, a top Hollywood idol of the time. Although he was not exceptionally tall or heavy he had enormous strength and could dog-trot up a steep half-mile portage carrying a full eighty pound pack and a cargo canoe. These canoes were large—about fourteen feet long with cork-filled gunnels, and it took two of us to wrestle a single one up over the portage *without* any packs on our backs, yet he always came back to help the others with the supplies or their own gear.

As we passed the summer together he taught me many things about nature and when I told him about being lost on a winter survey he asked what it was that I most feared. I said it was that I might have frozen, and even if I had been able to build a fire, the greater fear was of wandering aimlessly and eventually starving to death. He laughed.

"How can you starve in your own kitchen?" he asked and proceeded to show where the food was in the woods—plants to eat, and small animals and birds such as ptarmigans.

"It's a feast fit for a king. Just hold out your hand and Mother Nature will feed you; all you have to know is where she keeps it hidden."

He had an uncanny sense of the weather also, and one fine warm day in July as the party camped by a small river he showed me how to build a bed out of spruce poles and fresh branches. Our summer tents had no floors in them and were much lighter to carry and so we built our cots of laced green branches with four poles driven into the soft earth. The three other men in the tent laughed at our efforts and asked if we were expecting a flood, but in the middle of the night a storm broke that would have made Noah envious, a storm that no one except Luke knew was coming. All the other members of the survey party had wet sleeping bags for the next week, and the next time Luke started to build a bed everyone followed suit. He had a family, a wife and two small children, and had come on the survey because the fishing was bad that year, but he was homesick and as soon as we had surveyed our section of the new rail line into Lynn Lake, a settlement sitting on the edge of a huge ore deposit, he was the first to fly out. He never even said 'Goodbye', but I knew he wouldn't, for he believed that lives touched one another in passing, and if you let them, each enriched the other.

Chapter 4
Tommy

I left the tall trees of the north in August and went to be with the family at our lakeside cottage before seeking further formal education. They were all enthralled by the stories of my wilderness exploits, but the most ardent listener was my thirteen year old sister who couldn't hear enough of such, "...marvelous canoe adventures!" and begged to be taken on one. Within two days we had borrowed a canoe, found an old tent, taken sleeping bags and food from the cottage and managed to locate everything that was needed for a two or three day camping trip up the lake along its virgin shoreline.

During the first day of the trip all went well until about four o'clock in the afternoon when we rounded a point of land and ran into a stiff breeze and fairly large waves. The equipment was tucked under a waterproof tarp and there was no real danger, but when a rogue wave cascaded over the outer gunnels and soaked our legs my sister's love for adventure suddenly evaporated and at her insistence we paddled to shore. Her considered view was that the wave was my fault, that I was no fit canoeist and that it was chance alone that had kept us from drowning. After that there was silence in the woods as she grabbed her sleeping bag and headed for the safety of the nearby trees. The silence continued as I built a fire, erected the tent and cooked a meal and only partially dissipated as she took her plate of food and dragged the sleeping bag into the tent.

Luckily the dawn of the next day was magnificent and I was partially forgiven, for she helped load the canoe to continue the journey as long as we stayed, '...close to shore.' That day we traveled many miles, often in mutual silence, breathless from the beauty of unspoiled nature. By evening we had established a campsite, set up our ancient A-frame tent in the woods not far from the beach, enjoyed a supper cooked over an open fire and were ready to crawl into our sleeping bags. In erecting the tent I had cut two poles, the shorter one to hold up the front of the tent and the longer one attached to it at one end and tied to the trunk of a tree at the other end, thus acting as a ridgepole along the whole top of the tent. The sides of this shelter were quite taut, held down by tent pegs driven into the soft earth, while inside there was enough room for our knapsacks, the two sleeping bags and my small bore .22 caliber rifle. Before long we were both fast asleep but by midnight the woods had lost the day's heat and the lake was too far away to share its remaining warmth with us and we were both awake and shivering. After a short discussion it was decided that we should return to the beach, rebuild the fire and doze by it until sunrise, rather than to remain in the tent and offer up our remaining heat to the night air.

Just as we began to wriggle out of our sleeping bags her side of the tent hollowed down as if a bear's paw had questioned what was within. Terror takes away the ability to perform voluntary respiration and by the time we had regained our breath the side of the tent had repeated its declination twice more. I grabbed a flashlight, fired a couple of .22 shots out the flap of the tent, pushed my sister ahead of me, ran terror-stricken for the beach, launched the canoe and sat for over an hour some two hundred feet from shore. We had been cold in the tent but now we were becoming hypothermic, sitting in the canoe in the middle of the night dressed only in our skivvies. After an eternity, gun in hand (although too small a firearm to do any significant damage to a bear), I *crept* up the path and stood looking at our tent-of-horror in the beam of the flashlight, then softly called my sister to come and share my amazement. A small otter was repeatedly climbing the tree to which the ridgepole was attached, walking along the pole to its centre and using the slope of the tent as its own personal slide. We watched fascinated until the cold night air drove us back into the tent and into our clothes. He slid until dawn and later as we left his playground with the tent and started to paddle homeward he entered the water and made a slow circle around the canoe as a gesture of gratitude. Some things you never forget.

When summer was over I began my first year of Science at university. After two years in the northern woods it seemed like a good time to plan a permanent career. Once registered there was the usual round of fraternity parties at which prospective candidates were 'rushed', a traditional method of choosing new members. One particular frat was known for its ability on the football field and for the parties that it threw, an attractive duality for a person ready for the next adventure. There was great secrecy about how the initiation was done but in spite of the scare stories about former candidates going insane or disappearing, we candidates believed that it was just a moderately challenging endurance test. It turned out to be more than that.

My phone rang late on a Friday evening and a disguised voice said that early the next day I was to walk into the countryside and take a deserted farm road for several miles to a point where a small lake appeared and to wait until the 'assessment committee' arrived. It didn't take long to reach the spot the next morning but the 'committee' didn't arrive until after dark. After I spent most of the day wondering if the directions had been misunderstood, the headlights of a car appeared in the distance and slowly advanced, until the car stopped just in front of where I stood. After making sure I was the candidate they had been sent to get, they told me to turn around, kneel down and not to attempt to converse with any of them. A blindfold was put over my eyes and I was led back to the car and placed on the floor of the back seat.

They stopped at a burger stand to order food and as we drove around they said how sorry they were that they couldn't share the burgers with me, especially since they were so tasty. Later we stopped again and I was told we had come to the city park, an area of open fields and stout oak trees. Could I follow instructions? Would I trust them? I was to run at top speed until one of them yelled 'Right!' or 'Left!' and then immediately turn sharply to avoid being splattered on the trunk of a fifty year old oak. It's odd how we place our trust in others under stressful conditions, and it really felt as if I was missing those majestic old trees by a hair's breath, while in reality I ran in a large square around an empty field. Because I was so into the spirit of the test and because I was running so hard I couldn't hear them laughing.

"Right! Now left! Faster! Look out! Left! Left!" they shouted out in unison and I believed them.

The next step was to return to the frat house where all the candidates had been assembled, still blindfolded, and allow the 'brothers' to test our powers of endurance as they took turns trying to find out which candidate had the highest pain threshold from the spanking paddle. Then, one at a time we were then led down into the basement and placed in a wooden coffin while black robed figures stood around and loudly hummed the funeral march. The coffin was closed and lowered into a hole in the floor and as the humming got quieter the impression was that you really were being lowered into a grave. A period of absolute silence followed while the enclosed candidate, starved, beaten and exhausted, at last achieved a few moments of peace. Suddenly the coffin was yanked upward and stood on its end. The lid was removed and black robed figures, each with a torch in his hand, chanted in unison: "Let the stranger be branded!" The candidates' right forearm was grabbed, held tightly and a red-hot poker with the Greek letters of the fraternity was pressed against his yielding flesh. A drink of rum was forced upon the new 'brother' and a bandage was placed over the second-degree burn. After that, events became a little garbled; everyone offered congratulations, hot food was served and the party began. Late that night they took me home and my mother poured me into bed.

Next day, and for two weeks after that, the only clear part of the initiation was the memory of the branding. But it seemed all worth it for the initiated were now accepted into an elite group, could wander in and out of the house at any time, could join in a constant round of parties with the local sororities, and best of all, play on the winning inter-fraternity football team. They were halcyon days, but for many of us they were bought at the price of failing grades.

One of the sorority girls had been dating my brother for some time and since they were serious about the role of financial success in the meaning of life they had decided to marry as soon as both had secured good jobs after graduation. Both were dedicated and enthusiastic and so by the following February after their spring graduation they were ready to begin the eternal cycle of family formation. Mother had not trusted either his friends or myself anywhere near the marriage preparation for fear we would play some memorable prank that might dampen their magic moment, and she had been eminently successful. She was one step ahead of us at every turn and defeated all our attempts at sabotaging their luggage or interfering with their honeymoon travel plans. The ceremonies had gone off without a hitch and when we accompanied the party to the train station my brother had gloated at all our failed attempts, and then he made a fatal error.

"We got you guys, didn't we! No one knew we were going to Minneapolis for the honeymoon. We'll tell you all about the big city when we get back."

However, he should never have underestimated the power of resolute, inebriated people; once we were back at the home of one of the married ushers it was not difficult to phone the major hotels in Minneapolis to find the one at which they were registered. Collectively we composed a telegram to the hotel stating that the girl was under age and that her parents had already left by plane to confront the couple when they arrived at the hotel. Since the telegram had to be charged to a specific name and address we had used mine.

At 5:30 in the morning I was roused out of bed by a call from the assistant manager who asked permission *to call in the Minneapolis police*. It took some talking to assure him that her family would straighten everything out when they arrived and that police intervention was not necessary, but he was finally convinced and I went back to bed happy with the way the situation was progressing. At 7:30 the manager himself phoned to say that her parents had not arrived but that the couple had, and were angry when they were told that their registration had been misplaced and that no room was available. They had been placed in the dining room while the hotel, supposedly, rechecked the registrations, but that now, the manager insisted, the hotel had no option except to call in the police. Suddenly my mother's voice came over the telephone extension and the whole plan unraveled. Both were scathing in their condemnation of the foolishness of young people in general and myself in particular, with all expenses incurred in this Faustian comedy to be sent directly to me. But the story doesn't end there: the following summer when my brother and his new bride were down with the family at the cottage and we were all sitting around the breakfast table with our second cup of coffee he began to reminisce.

"That hotel was sure staffed by strange people. When we arrived they said they had no room for us, though I had made the reservation a month before. They put us in the dining room and then all the waitresses one by one walked by our table and looked at us strangely. I thought there might still be some confetti on us but there was none. Then after about forty minutes we were called to the front desk where the whole staff was assembled to wish us well and to present flowers to the bride; but how did they know? I hadn't registered as a honeymoon couple. And when we went upstairs they had given us the honeymoon suite at the same price as a room and treated us royally during our whole stay."

My brother and his wife listened carefully to my confession and didn't seem at all pleased until they found out that the honeymoon suite had actually been paid for by me, as were the flowers and the fruit in their suite. They thought that part was funny.

I had kept in touch with Jim, my close friend from our college school, who had really wanted to play professional hockey and nothing else. However, he had moved on to the world of work after the National Hockey League had dropped him following the summer try-outs and had found a job in sales for a large meat packing company. The thing that pleased him most was the country territory that had been given to him for it included several small rural towns where hockey was the reason for life in the long dark winter days. He moved into a central town, joined the town hockey team and became an instant hero after the first game of the season.

Most of the players on the team were young farm boys who had little to do in the winter and spent their time dreaming of a huge payday in professional hockey, but who were not really very talented. Jim said they were the kind of players who needed the hockey stick for balance on the ice and were more skilled at fighting than at skating. The one skill that all of them seemed to have developed was the art of 'boarding' an opposing team member up against the low boards of the town ice rink. In those days there were no extended barriers between the rink and the spectators in the front seats, and if a player could check his opponent just right, the victim went over the boards, head down and feet up into the lap of some spectator. Since the young ladies of the town always came early the prospect of having some young healthy farm lad ending up in their lap was worth leaving the family dishes in the sink until after the game. Jim said that both the home-town girls and the next-town ones always kissed you when you went over the boards early in the game but as the game wore on and feelings began to run high you only got kissed by your own girls; the other ones changed their attitude and either tried to pull the hockey jersey over the player's head or slapped him in whatever part of the anatomy was easily available.

By the end of the first season everyone knew and liked Jim; he was charming and a great athlete and the store owners bought all their meat from him. Every time I visited him his phone rang off the hook from the calls of young things who had either just baked him some delicious dish or were inviting him to a party or a dance.

"This is Nirvana," he once said. "I've died and gone to heaven!"

Naturally with all that feminine attention it wasn't long until one of them actually led him down the aisle, and then as far as the other girls were concerned he had come down from Mount Olympus to the realm of ordinary mortals.

My sport was definitely not hockey, although like all northern boys I could skate well enough and knew the art of boarding, but I had never conquered those sudden right turns so essential for fighting for the puck in the corner. I was a strong swimmer and had become a Life Guard and Water Safety Instructor by the time I was sixteen and was good enough to swim for the college team. Tommy was also a member of the team and one of the outstanding swimmers in local area competitions. His specialty was the butterfly and he had set a junior record for the stroke while he was still in high school. We would often practice together, but there was no way I could keep up to him in any of the individual medley strokes—he literally burned up the water and had he lived he would have indubitably gone on to the Olympics.

One day in the winter he asked if I would train at the Y with him the next Saturday, but I had already made plans to spend the day hunting on the prairie just outside the city. He was instantly interested and asked if he could come along, which at first didn't seem like a good idea. Winter hunting of rabbits and small game was done on cross-county skis and a hunter had to know where it was safe to hunt and how to avoid getting lost in the bitter cold. For me it was easy to combine the skills I had learned on the winter surveys with those of hunting. I had owned a couple of 22 rifles for a long time, and when Tommy pressed the issue with promises of helping me improve my swimming strokes I finally consented.

He came over to our place and learned quickly the basic rudiments of handling a firearm safely, how to judge distance in aiming and how to squeeze off a shot from a steady position, both standing and lying down. He knew something about skiing on the flat prairie and had a set of his own skis, so when we went out that weekend he seemed ready to begin. We skied for an hour once we were out of the city, and found a place to set up the tin cans we had brought for practice. Tommy was a natural; within an hour he was able to knock down more cans than I could and was ready to go rabbit hunting. Since we were to be out for most of the day the plan was to hunt for two hours, stop and build a fire and eat the lunch we had brought and then hunt for another two hours before turning homeward.

At noon we found ourselves in a small clump of trees where we could clear away the snow and built a fire-pit, but the tinder we found was damp and it took all of our matches to get a good sized fire going. Even then we needed more dry wood to thaw out the sandwiches and make the tea so I skied some distance away to get a large old branch that would keep the fire going for an hour. When I returned Tommy was crouching by the fire staring at some object in the flames.

"What is that Tommy?" I asked.

"It's my soup to warm us up." he replied happily as he stared into the fire.

But when I looked again at the tin it seemed to be an odd shape, bulging out both on the ends and the sides. Tommy had never made soup outside his own kitchen and since he had no pan for the soup he had just placed the large tin in the fire without opening the top. It suddenly exploded showering hot condensed tomato soup all over us and sending the flattened tin almost into orbit. Worse still, it had blown the fire completely out and ended any thought of a hot lunch. Sometimes you plan so carefully that the simplest things are overlooked and when Tommy had asked the day before what he should bring for lunch I had told him to bring whatever he liked. I had brought some sandwiches and a can of baked beans, and while I gnawed on the frozen sandwiches. Tommy ate cold baked beans all the way home, and said they were delicious.

Tommy and I were in different courses at university; he was in Physical Education and I was taking Science, but we saw one another frequently on campus but not any longer in the swimming pool. My father was doing well in the business world and took out a family membership in the Winter Club which had an excellent swimming pool that I frequently used, while Tommy went on training at the city Y. One weekend in the Spring he and three other students decided to drive down to Minneapolis to watch some sporting event and on the way back had a flat tire on the road after dark. They had pulled off onto the shoulder as far as they could and were changing the rear passenger-side tire. Tommy was standing in front of the car trying to wave off other cars that came too close when a inebriated driver ploughed into the back of Tommy's stationary vehicle. The impact moved the car ahead and knocked Tommy out into the centre of the road and before he could get to his feet another car, traveling in the opposite direction, ran over him.

Tommy was rushed to the nearest hospital where the doctors worked for the rest of the night setting his broken bones and monitoring his condition. Later he was sent to the hospital nearest to his home and when I visited him there his doctor remarked that if he hadn't been in such great physical shape he wouldn't have survived the accident. Tommy spent months in therapy and I often visited with him. He wasn't able to return to the university in the Fall, but he was a champion and worked at his therapy every day until he was almost well just before Christmas. During his convalescence he had become interested in photography, and for Christmas his mother gave him a new camera with a wide angle lens.

He phoned me and asked if we could go out ski-hunting on the day after Christmas so he could try out the new camera but I was already committed to a date with a girl and couldn't make it. I suggested we go on another day and he agreed, but on the day he had mentioned he went alone. Outside the city where we used to cross-country ski there was a busy perimeter double set of railway tracks that we often used as our turn-around point in hunting. He apparently crossed the first set of tracks to get a shot of a westbound freight train and was standing on the eastbound tracks waiting to get the perfect shot of the onrushing westbound train. He never saw the eastbound train until it was almost upon him and must have thought the whistle was just from the other train. At the inquest the engineer said he never turned to see the screeching engine bearing down on him until he turned to get another picture of the passing train and then there wasn't time to ski off the tracks. The brakeman ran back to Tommy's broken body as soon as the train had slowed sufficiently to get off, and cradled Tommy in his arms as he died.

"Tell my mother not to worry." were the only words he said.

Chapter 5
Changes

Tommy's death shook me to the marrow of my bones and unanswerable questions flooded my mind.

"Why had he died when he had almost recovered from the first terrible accident? Why had he gone out alone? How could such an impossible scenario of passing trains ever happened just when he was standing on the track? Why wasn't I there with him? Why had I taught him to hunt?"

But mainly the question was, "Of all of us why was it Tommy who died?"

Tommy was the *good* guy; he didn't drink or smoke or chase girls or party into the early hours. He was doing well at university because he studied diligently and he was a top athlete who had a great future in store for him. All his friends envied his dedication and his natural ability and the zest he felt for the value of life. Any one of the others of us should have gone first, for we drank and drove, stayed up all night, studied little if at all, didn't take life seriously and were always ready for one more risky adventure.

The shock I felt didn't go away even after the funeral and for the second time in my life, the fear of death touched me, only this time it stayed. I couldn't get over his impossible death and guilt kept me awake most nights for a long time. Later I learned that what I had was called free-floating anxiety, but all I knew was that I was not the same person anymore. Sleep avoided my bed and my weight fell. I tried to be with my friends but Tommy's handsome, unmarked face that I had last seen in his coffin kept returning like Banquo's ghost. My parents eventually became alarmed and sent me first to our family doctor and later to a psychiatrist, but even the therapy and the tranquillizers didn't help much, although I did begin to get some troubled sleep. I had never before thought of the purpose of life or even wondered if it had any purpose at all. Life was there and I was part of it and knew I was part of it, and that was as far as my philosophy went. Although I had never tried to put it into words, my acceptance of life was based on whatever the daily environment presented.

Now I was often on the edge of panic because it had suddenly been brought home that life could end without warning and there was nothing a person could do about it. It was here now but could be gone as quickly as had Tommy's. All grief results from the loss of a part of a symbiosis, that is, the loss of a perceived mutual sharing, whether the loss involves a person a place or a thing. If, as John Donne noted, a piece is washed away, we are the less. And grief is intensified, as the investment was the greater on the part of the one grieving. The mother whose child dies cannot be easily comforted; her loss is too great. Without my realizing it, Tommy had become my model. He was what I was not: a natural athlete, a fine student, a person with a goal and someone respected by everyone who met him. Unconsciously, when Tommy died the best part of me had died with him. Although I didn't know it, I was really grieving for my own death.

My final grades at university were dismal and as soon as it became possible I headed back to the northern forests in search of the peace and joy that had once existed there for me. But it wasn't there and after a month I left and went west to the mountains where we had once lived and found work in the dining hall of one of the large hotels. There the depression intensified, probably because the young students who worked there in the summer were as carefree as I had been and I envied their attitude. Work in the dining hall at least kept a person busy but days off were the worst, for then there was time to fear. To avoid this I frequently made plans to join with groups planning trips on such days. I heard that a group I knew would be going on an excursion on my next day off, up a nearby small mountain with an easy trail to follow.

The group was to gather at 9:00 o'clock in the morning but since sleep was still minimal I arrived at 7:30 and after waiting for forty minutes began the climb alone. It was so still and peaceful on the trail for the sun had not yet climbed over the larger mountains and there was a hush over all of nature. And as I climbed I wished with all my heart for such a peace for my troubled mind. At the top there was an observation point, fenced off, on a cliff that fell away to the valley six hundred feet below. As I stood there I realized that the answer was so simple and so quick. I stepped over the railing and stood on the edge...and then the sun suddenly appeared over the mountain top and the darkened valley was bathed in beautiful light. It seemed I stood there for an eternity as the mountain exploded in a rush of rainbow colours that kept increasing moment by moment. It was, I realized, too fine a day to leave this world and I stepped back over the railing. In later years, as a professional counsellor, I always understood the sense of flight from agony that is present in those who consider suicide.

But that morning some of the sunlight penetrated my darkened soul and a spark of hope entered where none had been before. By the end of the summer life was manageable if not enjoyable and I returned home and found a job in advertising on one of the large city newspapers. I began a relationship with a girl I had met while at university and found myself enjoying her friendly company and the acceptance her parents offered. Our families had known one another for years and the dating seemed to please both her parents and mine. We saw each other only on weekends; I was learning a new job and she was completing her studies, but our relationship deepened as the weeks passed.

Working downtown I'd often walk and shop at lunchtime and one Fall day, when the pressure of advertising deadlines had caused some of the anxiety to resurface, I noticed a sign that invited passers-by to enter and rest in the nearby church. The church was warm and welcoming with votive lights and muted colours, and at first I thought that it was the Anglican Cathedral, but soon realized that the hymnals in the pews were Catholic, filled with Latin hymns and rubrics. The church with its central alter and numerous statues was strange to the eyes of an Irish boy from a Protestant heritage and although I stayed only a few minutes its peacefulness brought me back repeatedly. Our family was not particularly religious, my father taking pride in the fact that he was a self-made success, but we said 'grace' at meals and as children attended Sunday service with our parents. The general attitude, if one existed, was that cultural religion was good for a stable community, but that becoming too interested in religion would lead to a false sense of dependency that excused any real effort that was necessary to get ahead in life.

I hadn't been in a church for years and since becoming an adolescent had never really thought about God in any way, but after a few of these visits the dichotomy of accepting a church-generated feeling of peace without any faith began to worry me. I spoke to my mother about her faith and why she believed in God and at first the question seemed to embarrass her, but she finally said that her belief had worked for her: whenever she had a serious problem she would pray and then open the family Bible randomly and seek to find consolation in the first verse she read. Later that night I thought over what she had said and would have tried prayer except that it still seemed like a form of self-delusion—simply a way of wishing—merely another way of talking to one's self—another pill to reduce anxiety. Yet as the weeks went by there remained the peacefulness found in the frequent visits to the downtown church.

Finally one day, perhaps out of the same curiosity that one might have with an Ouija board, I took up the family Bible and prayed.

"God, if you *are* there, please hear me," and opened the Book.

It opened in a section of the New Testament, at Matthew's account of the Beatitudes, which is a summary of Christ's teachings and the only place in the Bible that such a full condensation exists. Was it just a coincidence that out of the hundreds of pages of text it should open right there? Perhaps, but whatever the reason it brought a complete sense of peace and for the first time since Tommy's death I felt alive again. Who cares whether it was real or self-delusional. Humans from time immemorial have believed that if something works they should use it. And so, at twenty years of age, a quest for the Holy Grail was accepted.

As time went on I tried various recommended prayers in different churches and all of them worked, more or less, in making life come alive. With the sense of renewed life also arrived, quite unexpectedly, a sense of shame over a former life of self-fulfillment and when my mother took me to hear a young preacher named Billy Graham who was using our city's auditorium to conduct a Crusade, the sense of shame was intensified, but neither my mother or myself were able to bring ourselves to 'accept Christ' at the end of the program. The road to faith had been found but it was still a narrow trail with many obstacles to overcome.

Back in the middle part of the 20th century in our area there was a lot of animosity between Catholics and Protestants, and both groups tended to stay to themselves, each with grand untruths about the other's Faith. When I found an abandoned copy of *The Annals of the Propagation of the Faith* in a neighbour's driveway I was surprised to see how much effort the Catholic Church was making among the people of the poor countries, and it raised questions in my mind especially about the dedication of the priests and Sisters that worked among these people. There was no one that I knew in our circle of friends who could supply any information about Catholicism. The only Catholic person I knew even slightly was a woman who had tutored me in high school and when I asked her out for coffee she thought it was to set up another tutoring session. Margaret was surprised when I asked her about her faith and when she couldn't answer all my questions she suggested making an appointment for me to see a priest she knew, who was a convert to the faith himself and could understand the background to my curious questions.

Father Bill McWalter was a Jesuit priest and the bursar at a Catholic Boy's School. As a young Commerce graduate he had made a name for himself in the banking business and when a revolution took place in South America his bank sent him down to secure its assets with the new radical government. He saw a mob drag a priest out of downtown church and offer him the chance of renouncing his faith and joining the revolution. When he refused they hung him from a lamppost and posted a guard to make sure no one cut the body down. Bill returned home wondering how anyone could be so devoted to a religion that he would die for his beliefs. He himself had no such beliefs and had moved in a fast crowd of talented people, artists, singers and writers, but when he returned he found their attitude shallow and merely cosmetic. Eventually he had approached an old Jesuit priest at a small parish church and began to take instructions in Catholicism. At thirty-two years of age he started on the thirteen years of training that led to his ordination when he was forty-five.

He taught advanced mathematics in the college and always took the toughest classes, and the boys worshipped him. He had come to St. Paul's after a particularly tough group of grade 12 students had sent two other math teachers off to reconsider their vocation to teaching. When he arrived at the class the first day he entered and assigned a set of problems from the textbook, then began to busy himself with work at his desk. He waited until the grumbling and muttered comments had reached a crescendo, then picked out the biggest boy in the class and told him to stand up. The boy slowly got to his feet and with a smirk on his face leaned against the desk. Father then casually walked down to where he stood and knocked him out with one punch. When I heard this story I asked him what had become of the boy and the class after that and he laughed.

"They turned out to be one of the best math classes I ever taught and the boy became one of my friends. He still writes and comments about 'the good old days.'"

He was an uncommon man and it was easy to see why he was liked so much; he was absolutely down to earth and had a fund of knowledge that was truly remarkable. He could hold his own on sports, business, philosophy, literature, theatre, music and the possibility of alien life forms. It was often difficult to get to see him for not only was he busy with his classes and his priestly duties, he was also the Bursar of the college. Still he made time for me and he patiently listened to and discussed all my worries and questions.

He kept saying, "We don't want you just yet. Take your time and think about it. The last thing we need is another bad Catholic. If you become a Catholic it's only because you want to be a good one, and that's not easy."

There were several concepts that were very appealing about Catholicism; one was the concept of purity and self-control, which seemed so right in its appeal to the higher values of humanity. Another was the idea that Christ could inhabit physically the consecrated wine and host at Mass, and a third and most appealing at me time was the possibility that miracles could actually exist, a doctrine that the Church supported. Bill gave me a book on the shrine at Lourdes in France and I read it and a dozen other books on St. Bernadette. To this day she has retained an active role in my life. Her story led to other studies on the miracles other saints had manifested and the doubting attitude the Church had on all such unexplainable occurrences until they were scientifically examined, tested and not found to be frauds.

On one occasion I asked Bill if he had ever witnessed a real miracle and he said he almost had once when he was serving Mass at the shrine near the place where St John de Brebeuf was martyred. He was a seminarian then and in those days the people came up for communion and knelt at the altar rail and the priest placed the host on the tongue of each worshipper. The server's job was to hold a small golden plate under the chin of each person in case the host slipped from the priest's hand before he had placed it in the parishioner's mouth. Bill had been serving at the shrine most of the summer and was used to seeing sick people approach the sacrament hoping for some relief. He didn't pay any special attention to the man who had just opened his mouth to receive communion until the smell of decay reached him and made him gag. The man had only half a tongue, the rest having already been consumed by the cancer he endured. He commented to the priest afterwards about the frightful sight they had seen and hoped the man would not return, or pick a Mass at which he was not serving. The very next day at the same Mass there was an uproar at the back of the church with a man uninhibitedly shouting out in the stillness.

"I've been cured! I've been cured! Oh! Thank God! I've been cured!"

When the man came up for communion Bill could not bring himself to look at the man's tongue, although he realized that the stench was no longer present, and afterwards in the sacristy he asked the priest what the tongue looked like and was told that it was whole and intact but the part that had been missing was slightly more pink than the rest. Later the man was examined by physicians and the case was duly recorded and sent to Rome for consideration of its authenticity.

After six months of reading and asking questions I became a Catholic. While this was happening I was still working and seeing my girlfriend regularly, and for Christmas that year I gave her an engagement ring, much to the delight of both sets of parents for to them my conversion was just a stage in settling down to a normal life. Then one day Bill asked me if I had ever considered entering the priesthood, and the question stunned me for I was on the road to marriage and a future in advertising, and I asked if there was a role for a married advertiser in the priesthood, since we had become such good friends that we felt at ease in kidding one another. He was indeed a terrible kidder and at my adult Confirmation at the Cathedral with many other converts he whispered that we had to take off our shoes as we approached the Bishop and leave them in a pile at the front of the Church. He said it with such a straight face that I actually thought it was a part of the program. Then he smiled.

"At the of the end of the ceremony, when the Bishop says 'Go!' you all have to run back and put your shoes on again and the last one to finish has to clean the Church."

However, he wasn't kidding about a vocation to the priesthood and a small worry began to enter my stabilized world. Previously the thought of the priesthood had not crossed my mind but it slowly began to bother me, like an occasional toothache which is denied or dismissed as being symptomatic of nothing serious. I never mentioned it to my fiancée and instead began to think of gifts that she would like. She was fond of our family dog, Duke, a golden Labrador, and so for her birthday I bought her a black lab puppy. It pleased her immensely, and even her father and younger brother liked it, but it brought the wrath of the mother down on my neck.

"Who will clean up after it? Who will walk it? Who will feed it? They will all play with it and then leave all the work to me!"

I stayed away a week until I thought the coast was clear then went and saw the mother privately and told her I had found a good home for the puppy. It was too late; she had already fallen in love with it; it had all worked out just fine. One evening I came over and thinking the puppy had not been fed, mixed up a big bowl of pablum, but the mother had fed it just before I arrived. When it was through its small rear legs were not strong enough to support its weight and it sat on the floor wagging its tail with its rear legs stuck out on either side of its rounded belly. The pup was sitting there looking up as if to ask for thirds when my fiancée's mother walked in. From then on I was forbidden to feed the puppy or be in the kitchen alone with it.

The thought of being 'called' to the priesthood stayed with me in my prayers and reflective times, more as a fear than as a hope, and when I received a promotion at the newspaper we set the wedding date for the following year. The priesthood wasn't what I wanted out of life but I had read the *Confessions of Saint Augustus* and was painfully aware that 'man proposes but God disposes' in matters of importance. And so I began to close my daily prayers by saying, "If you want me in the priesthood, then You break us up, and if nothing happens by a year next September then we'll get married with Your blessing."

It was a confident and foolish prayer but I hadn't had much experience with the power of God. Within three weeks her father was out of a job as manager of the store where he had been for more than fifteen years, because the store had been sold to a larger chain that wanted only to close it and absorb its business. He was given a good severance package, which kept the family afloat until a firm that specialized in finding executive jobs found him a management position in a field close to his background, but it meant that the family had to move to the east coast as soon as possible. He left shortly after the placement had been secured, while my girl and her family stayed until the end of the school year, sold the house and packed up. Both of us were devastated by the sudden chain of events but her mother was far too busy to take our separation seriously.

"Something will come up." she said. "Don't worry. These things have a way of working themselves out."

The day they left was perhaps the saddest day in my life: we parted heartbroken at the airport and then I waited around for two hours to meet my neighbour Boo and his mother and take them to the mortuary. His father had died of a sudden heart attack while down east and they had gone down to bring the body home, and my father, who was out of town with my mother at that time, had asked me to offer our sympathy and be of any service they required. A few days later after some of the sadness had lessened I went to see Bill and discussed the possibility of entering the Jesuit Order. He told me that no convert could be accepted into the novitiate until a three year moratorium was observed and advised me to apply to the university and get some of my schooling done during that three year waiting period, especially since most Jesuits went on to get a Doctorate and early studies might indicate an area in which I could specialize.

My father was terribly upset when I became a Catholic, for the men of the family had been members of the Orange Lodge as far back as anyone could remember and therefore I was, "A turncoat, a Papist, a sheep, whose betrayal has set your dead grandfather spinning in his grave."

But once his Irish temper had run its course, he relented and offered to send me back to university in the fall if that was what I wanted to do. And that was what happened. I stayed with the newspaper until university began then enrolled again in a first year of science studies, this time no longer a welcomed member of a fraternity or a party animal but a student who began to trod the dedicated and difficult path set earlier by Tommy.

The lectures were not difficult to follow but learning how to review after each class was at first an almost impossible task, for it seemed that my mind could invent thousands of things that had to have immediate attention the moment I sat down to work on the assignments...phone calls that had to be made, letters that had to be written, appointments that had to be kept. It has been suggested that one of the tasks of the mind is to keep a balance in the person by using defence mechanisms to deflect situations that can cause anxiety, and new fields of endeavour in which a person will be tested certainly were filled with anxiety. Whatever the reason my first marks were not good and the final in chemistry eventually had to be rewritten at the end of the summer.

During that year my fiancée and I had written to each other but our workloads and the distance eventually slowed the writing almost to a standstill. When April arrived the university guidance department began to post summer job openings and I applied to work in a paper mill on the north shore of Lake Superior and was accepted. In late May I took a long train ride down to a town that was just starting up, with a new mill planned and built by the Kimberley-Clark Paper Company.

Those who have passed near a paper mill do not have to be told of the strange and pungent odours that results from the cooking of wood chips, the raw product from which paper is made. The afternoon I arrived at the personnel office the wind was blowing away from the town and it seemed like any other pine-wooded northern area. My shift started at eight the next morning and I was bunked in with another worker whose shift ended at midnight. I was asleep when he entered the room but about two in the morning I awoke because of the strong odour that was flooding the room.

"The man has not changed his socks for a month and now he hangs them over the radiator to dry them out!" I said to myself, and tried to go back to sleep.

But I was up by six and after dressing walked to the camp cafeteria, which was open twenty-four hours a day, and then shook my head in disbelief that anyone's socks could continue to pollute the atmosphere that far away from the radiator. Although the mill was four miles from the town as time went on we all learned to live with the smell, since it flooded the town almost all the time. But apart from the smell it was a wonderful place to live and there was a large variety of jobs that students could take over as summer relief while the regular workers went off on their holidays. Our crew of two students and one foreman started off putting in lawns for the new houses that were being built. We lasted only two weeks on that job because in the second week we cut down a large tree that was in the way while the foreman was off getting a coffee. The next day we were sent to the jack ladder, the lowest station in the mill. The tree hadn't fall the way it was planned but instead fell across the main hydro lines that fed the mill and knocked out all the power in the mill for several hours. Luckily we had joined the union as soon as we arrived for without its protection it is likely we would have lost our jobs on the spot.

The jack ladder was where the logs were first pulled sideways out of the river and sent through the saws. The saws cut them into four-foot lengths for transportation up the quarter-mile long conveyor belt to the upper part of the mill where they were debarked in large rotating steel drums before they were sent to the chipper. The bridge in front of the saws, where the men stood with their pike-poles, was only about four feet wide. If a worker missed his footing he fell forward or backward into the river and stood the risk of being picked up by the rough-toothed escalator that drew the logs up into the saws. If you could survive a week without falling into the river you were considered a part of the crew but until then the regulars would watch hopefully for a new man's icy plunge, for then the foreman would have to hit the emergency stop button and everyone would get a rest.

After a week of avoiding a splashdown some other summer students arrived and we were sent to the debarking room in the mill itself. Our job was to make sure the skinned four foot logs did not jam up at the end of the barking drums on their way to be sliced into quarter-sized chips that could then be cooked in the giant kettles in the main part of the building. It was easy work and often a mill-hand could take time off to lean against the frame of an open ventilation window and enjoy the view. My first view presented the sight of a red-headed seagull that was flying slowly around the window waiting for scraps from the workers. Soon I saw a blue-headed one, then a brown and a yellow and several others, sporting almost every colour of the rainbow. The impossible variation was explained when one of the workers appeared with half a sandwich hanging from a long piece of string. He threw the sandwich out to an uncoloured circling gull and reeled it in as soon as the sandwich was swallowed. Then holding the bird by its bill he painted the back of its head another colour, cut the string and let the gull fly away. Apparently it did them no harm for even the painted ones hung around the window and were always ready for the offered sandwich. Perhaps that's the origin of the old saying: 'No strings attached.'

It was sometimes dangerous work, although safety was a watchword in the new plant. They used caustic soda in breaking down the wood fibres and one worker accidentally swallowed some by taking a drink from a drain line that he thought contained water. He lived for only two years in spite of the best efforts of the specialists. Another man lost his arm when his hand got caught in the conveyor belt and only the quick thinking of the shift foreman who clamped the artery saved his life. One mill-hand, taking a shortcut on a steel beam above the rollers, slipped and had his legs broken before the automatic release plate stopped the presses. But I worked there for three summers and except for an occasional slip or tumble there were no other serious accidents. It was a good place to work and many long lasting friendships were formed including one with Josef.

Josef was from Russia and he and his mother had been captured by the Germans during WW II and put in a prisoner-of-war camp. He must have been very young when that happened for he was only nine when the Americans liberated the camp in 1945. He didn't remember his father and had stayed with his mother in her compound all those terrible years. One of his earliest recollections was a game the boys played in which a small stone was tossed a few inches beyond the high voltage electrified fence and the boy with the short straw had to carefully reach through the wire and retrieve it. He said they played it often while the guards watched and took bets on the outcome. He remembers that while the Germans were starting to retreat from the camp he and a friend had not doffed their caps to the Camp Commander when he passed. The Commander had shouted at them saying the Germans were still the Master Race and deserved respect and the boy had replied with an old Polish saying: 'You are as good as your shoes.', which at that time in the war were made of paper. The Commander took out his Luger and shot him on the spot.

After the Germans retreated the camp was liberated but there still wasn't much food, and the inmates were allowed to scavenge outside the camp for anything they could find. Josef's mother had told him that if he found a dead cat or rat or any other piece of meat he was to build a fire and cook it well before he ate it, saying that it was poison unless it was thoroughly baked or broiled. He and another boy found a dead rabbit, skinned it and put it on a spit over a fire. They roasted it for half an hour before the other boy demanded his half. Josef went on roasting his half for a lot longer and never got sick, but his friend had to be taken to the hospital the Americans had set up in the nearby town, and Josef never saw him again.

Josef's mother was a fine woman, gentle and hospitable, and with a great living faith but she didn't like Germans. When she found out I was Irish she had me over for supper with her son. She had made a cooked chicken, as well as some vegetable dishes, and gave half the chicken to Josef and half to me. She ate the chicken's *feet* in spite of my protests, saying that the one thing the war had taught her was not to waste food. She refused to talk about her camp experiences; they were too painful for her, but Josef had no end of stories about how some of the men had attempted to escape and had been caught and hung in the compound as a warning to others, about the brutality of the guards, the starvation rations, the boredom of imprisonment and how they watched the dead inmates being carried out of the huts every morning.

We worked on the same shift in similar jobs and our schedule was predictable: seven days at eight to four, then seven at four to midnight and a final set from midnight to eight in the morning. In between each week we had one day off and at the end of the three weeks each shift got four days off before starting the cycle again. Near the end of our first round there was a message left for me on the notice board that I was to phone Father Bill as soon as possible. When I called he asked if I could come back home for a couple of days since the Bishop had asked to see me. He wouldn't enlarge on the request except to say that it was something pretty serious, so I caught the first Greyhound bus available as soon as our time-off arrived. I remember thinking that they were going to kick me out of the Church because of my wild youth, and worried all the way back. As soon as I arrived at the College I went to Father Bill's office and was told that the Bishop would see me next day in the Chancery Office at nine in the morning. Apart from that all Bill would do was shake his head and tell me not to worry and in spite of my pleadings he gave no suggestion of what the meeting was about.

The next day I was ushered in to see the Bishop in the Chancery Office, which was right next to the Church that I had begun to visit a year ago. He shook my hand as if he knew who I was, although the only time I'd ever seen him was at the Confirmation ceremony and at a New Year's Day blessing I'd attended with Bill, and after some small talk he asked if I would like to work for him. The Dioceses had purchased an old estate they intended to turn into a new Chancery Office and Bishop's residence, just outside the city, with a swimming pool that was badly in need of repair and this was what I thought he wanted me to do. I thanked him for the offer but said I was already in a very good paying summer job and needed the money for the next year at university. Then he was specific: would I go to the seminary in the fall and begin to study for the priesthood? The question took me completely by surprise for of all the things I had worried about on the trip home, this idea had not even crossed my mind, and I blurted out, "Your Grace, I can't enter the noviciate until I've been a Catholic for three years!"

His voice had an edge to it when he replied: "We're not all Jesuits, you know! I want you to study to become a *diocesan* priest."

Some revelations are so unexpected that the mind just blanks out; there are so many things to consider that no path through them is obvious and the mind suspends its power to choose. After several minutes I asked if I could have some time to think this through since it involved my family, my university goals and most of all, my hopes of entering the Jesuit Order, the only group of priests I had ever known.

"Call me tomorrow before you leave, for if you decide to go I must make arrangements with the seminary; they only have a few spots left."

I don't remember leaving his office but I spent a long time in soul searching in the church next door before I went back to see Father Bill. When I entered Bill's office the shock had worn off a bit. I was nowhere near any decision and when he asked what I had told the Bishop the answer was,

"Nothing. What could I tell him? Why didn't you warn me? It's too much right now. You know I was hoping to enter the Jesuits." Bill sat quietly for a long time. Finally he spoke.

"Well, let's face life. You're older than most who ask to enter our Order. Most come right out of high school, and they come with very good marks since they'll end up teaching high school for several years before they go to advanced studies. You seem to have a vocation to the priesthood, all right, but our entrance standards might be too strict right now. Why not give the diocesan seminary a try to see if you really have a vocation? Most who enter leave before ordination and go on and become good, active lay people in the Church. They are the real backbone of our faith. Maybe you have a real calling and maybe you don't, but if you don't give it a try, how will you ever know? If after you're ordained for a few years you want to apply to the Jesuits your chances would be much better."

We sat together quietly for a few moment, then Bill said: "I have to make a phone call. I won't be a minute." He picked up the phone and called the Bishop and after a few moments handed me the phone and said, "Decide. It's the Bishop." So I said "Yes" and a new phase started in my life.

Chapter 6
Seminary Daze

The next day I went to see the Bishop and learned that the seminary was in another part of the country and that the studies there lasted seven years. There would be three more years of undergraduate studies and a final four years of theological courses leading up to ordination. It was a long road, he said, with no guarantee that the goal would ever be reached since less than half of the original candidates would end up becoming priests. It would be a difficult lifestyle, and different from any previous university experience, with a standardized Rule that covered all aspects of student life from sun up to sun down, but if I was willing to attempt it, then he was willing to give me a chance. When asked what clothing was needed the answer was: Black pants, black shoes and a soutane. I had no idea what a soutane was, but he told me not to worry for he would give me an old one of his, and before I left his office he had placed the garment in a shopping bag and handed it to me.

Earlier that day I had made an appointment to have lunch with my father since he was in the city alone, my mother and sister having gone down at the cottage. When I went into the restaurant with the bag the Bishop had given me its contents were his first question. I hadn't intended to tell him about my decision until the end of the summer, but there was no denying the long black cassock that he pulled out of its hiding place. I tried to explain but it was beyond his understanding and he only groaned in disappointment.

"Under these conditions," he said, "there will be no money ever for such a foolish venture."

And then he drove me in silence to the bus depot. I phoned Father Bill from the station to say goodbye and to tell him of my father's reaction and he said it was the same as he had received from his dad many years before.

"Just keep praying for him; he'll eventually come around." But then, he didn't know my Irish father.

Shortly after returning to the mill, near the end of June, a man came onto the wood handling room and asked me to drop in to his office at the end of the shift. He was the director of athletics for the town and made me an offer I couldn't refuse. The university student hired to run the swimming program for the children of the town had not shown up and couldn't be reached. In going over the application forms from the other students, he had seen that I was certified as a lifeguard and water safety instructor and that I had already taught some classes at a city pool. He had decided that he would interview me and if he thought I had potential would offer me the job. It was a great job; I loved teaching swimming and this gave me the opportunity to teach at every level, right from toddlers to junior lifeguard, and since the town was not yet incorporated, the wages would be the same as in the mill, except there would be time and a half for Saturdays and double time for Sundays.

The swimming area was not a pool but part of a lake that had been formed when a large dam was built to keep the river water high enough for the logs to be sent down from their cutting zone many miles north of the town. The east side of the swimming area was the dam itself while the south and west side were formed by floating boardwalks chained together and anchored to the bottom. The beach itself was a natural sand bank that was about a hundred yards long and thirty-five yards wide and rose at the back to a height of fifteen feet. There was a large changing room partitioned in the middle with entrances at each end; one for boys and a second for girls, and a second smaller building, also partitioned, one end being the lifeguard's office and the other a double seated outdoor toilet. Needless to say, not much time was spent in the office, especially on hot days.

The mill sent its maintenance crew to prepare the swimming area so it would be open the day after the school closed, and it also arranged to bring buses from the centre of town to the 'pool' every morning at nine-thirty and return for them at four-thirty. The distance to the town from the pool was about four miles by road and three if you cut through the forest. The problem with the forest route was that the place was home to a number of black bears, which were drawn to the area by the town dump a half-mile away. There was little doubt that some bears did roam these woods for occasionally one would show up on the road just behind the changing room and then a quick phone call to the nearby jack-ladder would bring several husky workers armed with pike poles to chase the bear away. However, we always worried that some young swimmer would miss the bus and attempt the forest route alone, with no friendly pike poles to offer defence and although we forbad the use of the forest route and watched diligently, occasionally one or several, would brave the dark woods and brag about it afterwards. Luckily we never lost one of them, but often enough they caused us serious alarm.

Once two sisters brought their five-year-old brother through the woods and he disappeared just before lunchtime. It was one of those days when every kid in town had decided to go swimming right after a breakfast of two bowls of sugar-packed cereal, and consequently all of them had lost the ability to sit quietly for longer than six seconds. Those who were not in the water splashing each other were racing up and down the sand banks laughing and screaming at the top of their lungs. In this terrible and wonderful mix of confusion and excitement the two sisters had suddenly realized that they hadn't seen their little brother for quite a while. The horrible fear of course, was that he had slipped under the water without anyone noticing and drowned.

Getting the children out of the water was a Herculean task and was only accomplished when one of the older boys yelled that he had seen a snake in the water. That emptied the pool in record time and the older swimmers and myself were able to search the grey water in a rehearsed pattern, and found it to be empty except for toys the children had brought with them. We scoured the surrounding paths and forest and found nothing. Finally, fearing the worst and being ready to call in the police and the search teams, the oldest sister was sent tearfully to call home from our emergency line. Her brother was sitting at the table with his mother eating his soup and hadn't even mentioned that he had found his way home alone through the woods. I often wonder what type of an adventurer he turned out to be when he grew up.

Since the children were at the pool from morning until late afternoon, unless one of their parents drove up to get them, it was necessary for them to bring their lunch and goodies for the whole day, which presented a problem. Some would arrive with what looked like old pillowcases stuffed with food and drink and suntan lotion and toys and towels and colouring books and some objects that boggled the mind as to their function. Others arrived with one poor little jelly sandwich and a small container of cool aid. Each group, or sometimes a lonely individual, would stake out a piece of beach which was then 'theirs' for the rest of the day and it was as seriously protected as any turf in New York City. Swimming lessons were taught in the morning as soon as possible and ended around noon just in time for lunch. The afternoon was then spent in settling complaints of theft or kicked sand or violated property lines or other serious matters, while at the same time attempting to keep a watchful eye on all those at 'free-swim' in one of the two pools, which were separated not only by depth but also by a heavy log boom.

On opening day I had caught the bus downtown with the children and acted as a monitor all the way to the pool, and had expected to take it back with them at the end of the day. Foolish thought! At the end of the first day when the bus appeared they dropped whatever they were doing and ran screaming to be first in line as soon as the driver opened the door. From that moment on I realized that my main job when the bus appeared was to keep them from pushing one another under its wheels before the bus had come to a full stop. The drivers often commented that during the school year they were relatively easy to control, but that as soon as summer arrived all their previous bus training was abandoned in a wild surge of freedom. One look at the beachfront that first day convinced me to send the driver on his way with his load of rollicking children. The place was a disaster. Everywhere there were lunch wrappers, bottles, empty bags, lost containers and countless sandy towels and wet bathing suits. There was more sand in the change rooms than on the beach and a brand new collection of graffiti on the freshly painted walls. Clean-up took an extra hour and established a pattern for the rest of the summer. Then there was always the lovely, quiet and a little scary, walk home through the forest.

It was a young town and a nice place to raise a family. The local doctors at the small hospital jokingly called it *Fertile Valley* and threatened to leave because they wanted to practice general medicine but were doing only obstetrics and gynaecology. On hot summer days some of the young mothers would bring their tiny babies up to the pool in the afternoon and if the water was warm enough they would swoosh them gently back and forth in the water until they either got tired or the babies began to cry. It was also a first introduction for many of us to watch babies actually swim for several seconds all on their own. Some of these mothers were good swimmers themselves and believed that babies had a natural ability to swim. In the many times over the next three years that I watched these baby sessions I never saw one that swallowed water or seemed to choke, and some could stay face down in the water making short, jerky swim motions for as long as a minute, which was often a lot longer than some of my beginners could manage when they first entered the program.

It seems that the fear of water is something that is conditioned into us, rather than an instinctive reaction.

Of course it was a joke to say that the doctors didn't get to practice general medicine; we constantly sent them cases of sunburn, poison ivy, cut feet, blisters, skinned knees, slivers and lacerated scalps, as well as a few black eyes and bloody noses. The one case that stands out in my memory is that of a four-year-old girl who was jumping off the sand hill onto the soft slope that led to the beach. She and her fellow playmates had been doing this for several minutes and seemed to be safe enough. Suddenly after another ordinary jump she began to cry and almost immediately a little friend came running up to say that Susy had lost her front teeth, and indeed she had. On the last jump she had gone higher than before and when she landed her knee came up just as her head went down. Such tears from both Susy and her friends! But the thing that worried me was the gush of blood that wouldn't stop coming from her mouth. When it finally slowed as we put cool cloths to it, we looked for the missing two teeth but they were nowhere to be seen. Susy's mother drove up quickly after my call and took her to the hospital, and when I called at her house that evening Susy was playing with a doll and had her teeth back in place! Her mother said the doctors had sent them to the town dentist after a brief examination and he had found them folded back against the upper palate and swung them forward into place. I saw him several days later and asked if the teeth would likely fall out or start bleeding again?

"No. They'll be all right. It's not unusual to see that. The sockets are quite soft and will reform around the teeth without any problem."

And we never did see Susy spit any teeth out, nor did we see her jump off that small hill for the rest of the summer. How resilient children are! Tigger was right. They *are* made out of Indian rubber.

There were a number of university students living in the series of Quonset huts that were the quarters for the unmarried men who worked at the mill, and although the huts were warm and had a cleaning staff to look after them, they were definitely not the Ritz. If someone sang in the shower at one end of the hut then everyone heard it, to say nothing of the noises that issued forth from the common washrooms. Day or night someone was playing the radio and it always seemed that the only station available was one that ran a 24/7 amateur vocal contest for rejects from other shows. On occasion, if the music came from the room next to yours, a pound on the walls could get the volume turned down a little; not that it did much good since the rooms were divided by only a half-inch sheet of pressed paper wallboard. Each room held two workers and it was possible to make trades and get a friend as a roommate, usually at the price of a carton of cigarettes paid to the original person assigned. On the day that Henry, my new roommate, moved in he had never seen the man whose room next door shared my wall and when the man's radio started blaring Henry had pounded on the wall.

"Turn that damn radio down!" he had yelled.

The neighbour stood six foot four and must have weighed in at over two hundred and fifty pounds; almost immediately his fist came right through the wall and missed Henry's head by only a few inches. We later patched the wall and after that never complained about the music. In fact, we bought a small radio ourselves and played it as well. If you can't beat them, join them. The mill was, among other things, a great educational institution.

There were five of us students that stuck fairly closely together: myself, an Irish Catholic, Henry, Alf and Derrick who were Mennonites and Hoover Wong, a young Buddhist from Hong Kong. Henry and Alf had never learned to swim so they frequently came to the pool for lessons and I got to know them well. They were good softball players and by the beginning of the summer competitions with nearby towns, they had made the first team. Swimming duties kept me away from practices but I was able to get the job of announcer at all the games, which were always played in the early evening. Most of the town turned out to watch these games, for except for the bar in the hotel and a single movie theatre, softball games were the only form of entertainment in town and the nearest city was eighty miles away.

The year was 1952 and television was only a promise, so the townsfolk went to the movie every time the bill changed. They watched baseball, walked and talked and some spent a lot of time at the bar. It was there that you could *always* find George, whose wife had run off with another man and left him with two boys, about seven and nine years old. The townspeople frequently fed the boys because all that George kept at home was corn flakes and milk. The boys never missed a day of swimming and always brought a box of flakes for lunch and ate them dry. Sometimes they would let us share our lunches with them, but usually they were too proud and pretended that their box held the best lunch in the world. They loved their father and didn't want to leave him, and his fellow mill hands were able to keep him sober enough to do his job, but there was no doubt that George was a genuine alcoholic. Some things in life just don't seem to have an answer. Eventually George became ill and had to be hospitalized and the boys were taken by a social agency, but that was in the last summer of my work at the mill.

As Father Bill had recommended, I wrote home every two weeks but never heard back from my parents. But at least the letters home were not returned unopened, so I knew they were keeping abreast of what was going on in my life. Occasionally I'd phone Bill to let him know I hadn't changed my mind about going to the seminary and he must have passed along the information to the Bishop. I got a letter in the middle of August saying that everything was arranged and that I should show up at the seminary before the end of the month. That presented a problem because I was hired as lifeguard up until the end of the summer holidays, and then for a further two days to make sure that all the log booms had been pulled up on the shore for winter storage, and that all the buildings and diving boards were secured.

Losing the children and young people back to their school routine was a sad thought for we had formed strong bonds of friendship over the summer, but the Administration's promise that I could return the next year held out an olive branch of hope. We had a grand closing day at the pool, with pop and hot dogs and even a bonfire right on the beach and all of the hundred children promised they would write, even though I had no idea what the actual address was at the seminary. When the last bus pulled away the animated, happy pool that had been so packed with life suddenly died. One second it was there; full of shouting children and the next it was a cold and lifeless moonscape. The final walk home was so lonely that I couldn't have cared if a bear or two had shown up.

All the students left about the same time, some by bus and some by train. I was the only one going east. The others were heading back to one of the universities in the West. Henry and Alf had been accepted into Medicine and talked jokingly and somewhat fearfully about the hundreds of hours of human dissection that was to be their main subject that year. We cleaned out our rooms and Henry took the small radio since Father Bill had warned me that we were not allowed such 'worldly' devices in the seminary. The more Bill told me about the secluded life the more it bothered me; it was really a step out into the dark and I wished that Henry was going to the seminary and that I had the scalpel and cadaver. We all left with good savings and better memories of the mill, the town and the fine people who lived there and all promised to return the next summer.

Using the train to travel east was a big mistake and after that first summer it was never repeated. The run along the shore of Lake Superior was constantly interrupted by a stop at every small town along the way. Finally in the early evening of the second day it pulled into the city where the seminary was located and I walked out into a torrential downpour. With no idea where the college was, it seemed a good idea to let a cab find the way. The street that leads up to the seminary ends at its entrance, as a road might end at the drawbridge of a castle. The huge property is surrounded by a tall, wrought iron fence with a long driveway that seemed to fade away into the distance. The building itself was a foreboding Gothic structure complete with a tower and a wide set of stone stairs that led to the largest curved double door I had ever seen. The cab driver looked the building up and down.

"Hey, buddy, how long are you in for?"

When I told him the course lasted seven years he called it a life sentence and shook his head in disbelief.

"Come back with me, buddy," he said, "this is no place for a young fella." and for a second I almost climbed back into the cab.

When he had left I rang the bell repeatedly, and stood in the rain for fifteen minutes before the door swung in on creaking hinges and two young men in long soutanes stood there.

"Why did you use the front door?" the taller one asked. "Everyone takes the other road that goes to the back of the seminary where you can unload all your stuff. You're lucky we were walking past and heard the doorbell. Well, come in! Don't stand out there in the rain like a ninny."

And that was my introduction to Jonathan who was to become a close friend in and out of the seminary from that time until the day of his untimely death. They took me to the bursar who welcomed me, told me I was almost a week late, assigned me a room in a wing on the second floor, and asked me for my part of the seminary expenses. I'd saved five hundred dollars over the summer, which was then a large sum, and I gave it to him expecting that some of it would be returned for spending money. None of it ever was. It was an initiation into the value of poverty. He also told me that night prayers were at 9:00 o'clock in the chapel and that I was expected to be dressed in my soutane.

Finding the room was not that easy, for none of the rooms were numbered but the doors were open on most of them and it wasn't difficult to see which ones already had an occupant. I dragged my old suitcase into the first empty one and pulled out a tee shirt, a pair of black pants and the soutane the Bishop had donated. When I put it on I realized it was two sizes too small and had red piping on every seam. What a disaster! To be days late, to have entered a building built for the 18th century, to have lost all my money, and finally to have to dress like a clown for my first introduction to the other seminarians! It was, I hoped, a sign that I didn't belong. A soft knock and the door was opened by one of the Sisters with fresh bed linen and towels. She took one look and laughed.

"You look silly," she said. "Where did you get that costume? You certainly can't wear it. Take it off and I'll see what the former seminarians have left behind."

She was back in a few minutes with a serviceable cassock of the style that the Jesuits wore: no buttons, clasped at the top and the waist and with a soft collar. And it fit perfectly. I wore it proudly for four years; it never seemed to age or look worn and I finally gave it to a new student who had arrived as I did without the proper apparel.

I don't know what I expected to find when the other seminarians appeared. My father had insisted that they all wore dresses and therefore were at least sissies, if not worse, but when I walked out the back door into the recreation area and saw them it was a great relief. They were ordinary young men. Some wore baseball caps, some smoked, everyone seemed to be wearing an old jacket of varying colours and nobody looked all that comfortable about being there. Someone offered me a cigarette and someone else said, "You missed most of the retreat. Lucky you!"

I'd never made a retreat and only had a vague idea of what you did on one and when I began to ask questions about it and the reply was, 'Just wait and see.' A few minutes later a bell rang, cigarettes were extinguished, we went into the basement where the lockers were and then filed upstairs into a large lecture hall and listened for an hour to an elderly priest tell us how to get the most out of the annual retreat. It was warm that Fall. The windows were open and there was the pleasant smell of tobacco lingering on our clothes, and when I shut my eyes I was back in the beloved north woods, sitting along the lakeshore, feeling the gentle touch of life and swapping stories with the other surveyors.

Another bell sounded and we left the lecture hall and walked in single file down both sides of a long hallway and entered the chapel. And it was beautiful! Solid, dark oak pews in three tiers ran along both walls so that everyone faced toward the single central aisle that ran the whole length of the chapel. The altar was all of marble and a miniature of what would be found in a great cathedral. All the lines that formed it were clean with no clutter to take away from the concept of space. Behind the altar, high leaded windows in ascending and descending order, like music scales, looked down on us, and I suddenly thought of the upswept style of the paintings of El Greco. The lighting was subdued, yet bright enough to read from a book of night prayers that was in every pew. As soon as silence had replaced the thump and rustle of young males finding a space, the head deacon led the assembly in a series of short prayers. It was followed by a silent five minute examination of conscience that concluded with a communal Act of Contrition. Since the new seminarians occupied the front rows, we all stared at the marbled floor from our kneeling position. Unexpectedly, the irregular lines of the marble seemed to dance before my eyes and produce memories of earlier times and places and the girls I had known. Imagination can be unnerving at times.

The young man next to me shook me out of this reverie by whispering that 'lights-out' was in half an hour and that one of the priests would make rounds to see that everything was dark. Some stayed in the chapel for a few minutes but most of us left quietly and wandered toward our individual rooms. The rooms were small with a narrow bed, a sink and a small dresser and a window that looked out on the real world. It must have been too much for the teen that roomed next to me, for he cried long into the night and left the next morning. I finally fell into a troubled sleep and endured a series of dreams that had something to do with falling into a dark pit. Again I was lost in the woods and some of the old fears of eternal loneliness returned. At 5:30 next morning I was startled by what at first sounded like a fire bell but which was only the wake-up call. The small Rule book that was on the dresser said that everyone was to be in the chapel for morning prayers and Mass at 6:00 o'clock with breakfast at seven and a lecture beginning at eight. This was a training camp, no doubt about it!

The annual retreat opened the school year and occupied the entire week before university classes began. It was a time of silence broken only by morning and evening prayers, a couple of spiritual lectures, and readings from

The Lives of the Saints at every meal. The only consolation was that after supper we were permitted to talk to one another in the recreation areas for half an hour. A book of meditations had been provided to each student and most of the time was spent in silent prayer. By the end of the first day I understood why the boy had said I was "lucky" to have arrived late. Thinking about all the bad things done or imagined, and wondering about God's expectations for the rest of my life was a draining experience. No radio, no novel, no newspaper, no magazine, no other distraction and no one to talk to was a new and unpleasant circumstance. The older students who had been there for several years seemed to take it in stride, but the younger ones wore long faces and dragged themselves through the day.

The retreat ended the second day and life returned to a more normal pace. The seminary day wasn't much different than a day at most universities, except for the daily prayers and the privation of the usual forms of distraction. We got up early, attended Mass, had breakfast, took a break and then began classes. Classes were broken by lunch and ended at 2:30 in the afternoon and we had a variety of sports activities until 4:30 P.M. Then there was usually a spiritual lecture, supper, a short break and then study until night prayers. Most of Saturday and Sunday was spent in study or recreation but it was all done within the confines of the large acreage of the seminary property. For recreation there were ping pong tables, pool tables, handball courts, a gym, tennis courts, a football field and plenty of open spaces for those who just wanted to walk. A river ran in the ravine behind the school where you could fish if you wanted to, or skip stones or sneak in an occasional swim. Swimming was not actually forbidden but the current was strong enough that only a few of us ever took advantage of the water. In the winter it froze and was used as a second rink, and in the spring break-up we secretly rode the ice flows down the river until we fell off. Boys will be boys.

What had led me to the seminary was not difficult to define. A close friend had died and the reality of the brevity of life and the certainty of death had led to an agonizing search for something solid to accept, something to believe in, something that gave hope. Peace had come through an experiential awareness of religion. The awareness had led to belief, and followed by a number of coincidences, or God's hand, a sense of obligation had developed within me. I was there because I believed He wanted me there; it was no more profound than that. When sailors enter upon a journey they realize that they must do their duty or else the boat will flounder, and I felt that if I ran away I also would flounder and return to the emptiness of fear. But on the first day of classes I became one of the students of Father Anthony in a course in philosophy, and the power of thought began to chase away the sense of compulsion.

Doctor Anthony was a genius; no one doubted that, yet he was a shy and dedicated man who thought through every question of life. He had become a priest not simply because he had come from a solid Catholic family, but because his reason had led him to be convinced of God's existence, and logic had led him to accepting Christ as the Word of God. Although he had won a medal for the highest-grade average in philosophy at a major European university in a ten year review, he had a simple and clear way of communicating his knowledge to any who requested it. We have all met brilliant people who can talk rings around us in their area of expertise, but who don't have the ability to simplify their knowledge so that others can share in it. Tony was different; in class his pace was slow but it moved with a mathematical precision, and the next point was not raised until the previous one was grasped by the class.

In our first philosophy course he chose a short dissertation by Aristotle called *The Principles of Nature* and we spent an entire year understanding it. By the time it was through we understood why universal doubt was a contradiction in terms, how Descartes had missed the obvious, what Time and Motion meant and how any terms of discussion had to be first reduced to their simplest essence. Our minds lit up because they were bathed in the light of his careful thought, and because we were not allowed to accept any idea until we had struggled through every objection that could be raised to its understanding. He knew the work of every living philosopher and the writings of every dead one and could see the strengths and weaknesses of each, but he was himself a dedicated follower of Aristotle, whom he called *The* Philosopher. He taught us both philosophy and English literature for three years and was as *feeling* in literature as he was *logical* in philosophy. He knew how literature worked, but in the great works of the poets, such as Shelly or Keats, when we asked what a particular poem specifically meant he would say in an enthralled voice, "Who cares what it means! It's wonderful stuff!"

What happened in his one-hour class usually took several hours of review and mental struggle to really grasp, so each new class began with a question period on what we had covered previously. Each class was a venture into the exciting world of both thought and feeling; none of his classes were easy for we were required to *think* rather than to just take notes and remember the highlights. Luckily, the classes that followed his were ordinary. They consisted of listening to the learning of other professors in their area of study; some were interesting and occasionally enlightening, and some were downright boring. But it was Tony's classes that brought light into my mind and made the discipline of seminary life palatable. At the beginning of the first year of Theology, after receiving an Honours Degree in Arts, I asked him if I could sit in on any one of his classes whenever I had a spare period.

"That's very flattering, but it's time to move on. There are many things still to learn." he said with a smile. How right he was.

The other subjects in the undergraduate years were psychology, sociology, ethics, French and Latin. Some of the Latin classes were actually taught in that language, which was difficult for me since I had no real ear for languages other than my own native tongue. Once in class the professor asked me a question in Latin and since I didn't understand what his words meant I answered, "Non nescio, magister." (I do not know, sir) which apparently was the correct answer for he seemed satisfied that I was making progress in the subject. The surprising thing about the studies was that we didn't study anything that had to do with religion as such. The Rule required us to privately read scripture for twenty minutes a day, but apart from that, and the three or four times a week we had a short spiritual lecture before supper, nothing was demanded of us. We were encouraged to read the writings of the great spiritual writers, such as those found in *The Lives of the Saints*, but it was difficult for us who had only started in knowing God to be able to relate to their insight into His communion. Instead we read any book that was on the university English curriculum, and therefore had to be made available in our library, and soon became familiar with the great novels of the nineteenth and twentieth century.

When ordinary people think about priests they seem to be at a loss to know what kind of persons priests are, and how they arrived at their vocation. To them priests seem to be like chocolate cake: you put a bunch of ingredients together, mix them up, put them in some kind of an oven for a long time and out pops the priest, chocolate cake all the way through. It might be sweet or sour, have icing or be plain, be puffed up or rather flat, but somehow the final product is not really human. Funny. We don't have that opinion of doctors or lawyers or sailors or engineers or any other specialized career. We accept them for their training and don't pay much attention to how they got the way they are. We believe that their training was long and hard but not difficult to imagine, but with priests it seems that our minds just go blank and we can't imagine their training, almost as if they were eggs that go on developing in secret until they are ready to come out of the shell. But in reality it's not like that at all.

That first year there were about one hundred and fifty young men in the seminary, from all over North America and even some from Europe. They came from all walks of life. Their parents were professional people, or teachers, or factory workers or owners of businesses. We were tall and short, fat and thin, laid back and serious, and we had come for a variety of reasons. Some had come because they had found a role model in their own parish priest and wanted to be like him; others had come to see if they had a vocation, and still others had arrived because they, or their parents, thought it would give meaning to their lives. One of my friends candidly said he had chosen the priesthood because it was the only job he knew of where you could play golf three times a week. We were just ordinary young people taking a look at an unusual occupation. Some stayed the seven years but most left. Our class had thirty students in it and each successive year had fewer and fewer. The usual class size for ordination was about eight but it could be more or even less. But that was long ago. Today, some years see no ordinations at all.

We worked hard at our studies, and we prayed more than most people, but the thing that kept us alive was recreation. You could always find a handball match or a football game, and if it was raining there was always the basketball court in the old gym. The floor of the court was almost regulation size but on the sides there was only ten inches between the court and the walls. Roughing a player on the sidelines usually meant skinned elbows for both. When winter came we flooded the back field, put up the boards and the benches and almost everyone put on their skates. If you hadn't brought a pair with you there was always an endless supply of old ones in the bell tower, the general storage room for the entire building. There were four hockey leagues with two teams in each league, each with a manager who tried to make the best trades possible. The teams were never static but constantly changing so they would be fairly evenly matched. You might lose one game by a large margin and win the next two just because your manager had traded two fair players for one who was a little better.

There was also a school team that played against the other faculty teams at the university, and usually won all their games. Some of the seminarians had turned down professional offers to come to try out for the priestly life. They were from several Junior A teams, and some had already been drafted to a major league farm club when they decided to come to the seminary. And they were *good*. One day in practice the first team was short a goalie and I put on the pads. Most of their shots made it into the net before I even saw them coming, all except the last one. A breakaway forward shot one from the blue line and I watched it travel *slowly* along the ice. A few minutes later I woke up on the ice with everyone standing around. His stick had broken just as he took the shot and the end of the blade had slammed into my chin. Dam! I think I could have stopped that shot if his stick had held together. After that I went back to one of the lesser leagues and gave up goal tending completely. However, I wasn't too bad at my own position and once won the 'Dirtiest Defence Player' award.

The fourth league was made up of novices, boys who had never, or hardly ever, put on skates before, and of all the teams it was the most fun to watch. Goalies were chosen from those who couldn't possibly stand up on skates; they wore heavy winter boots and slid around the goal crease and usually kicked away any puck that came near the net. Others could stand as long as their hockey stick was planted firmly on the ice, but generally lost their balance if they had to check an opposing player. The art of checking was reduced to falling on the other player so the goalie could kick the puck away. There were lots of breakaways but as often as not the player would fall down long before he got near the net. One memorable player could only skate in a straight line and had to slam into the boards before he could change direction. During a Sunday morning game, with all the staff and Sisters standing on the sidelines, he got hold of the puck and started rushing down the ice just as his belt broke and his pants sagged to his knees. But he wasn't to be denied his moment of glory, so with one hand on the stick pushing the puck and the other trying to lift up his sagging trousers he proceeded down the ice toward the opponent's goal, while the audience collapsed in laughter. His aim, unfortunately, was all wrong and stick, puck and slippery trousers missed the net and ploughed into the boards. Over he went head first into the snow bank and ended up with his long-John underwear prominently displayed for all to see. That effectively ended the game. All the players on both teams had collapsed onto the ice holding their sides and for days afterwards, even in chapel, someone would remember the scene and begin to snicker uncontrollably.

Just before Christmas holidays I received a letter from my mother and a generous cheque. Aren't mothers wonderful! The letter said that I was not to come home for Christmas because my father was still in shock, but that she was working on him and probably some reconciliation could be arranged at a later date. The money allowed me to send home some small presents along with a long letter about life in the 'alien zone' and an account of the slipping pants hockey game. From then on life was a little easier, for mother continued to write on a regular basis with news about the family and friends; occasionally she would even mention my former fiancée. One of my classmates invited me home to his place for the holidays and so it became Christmas after all. The day we left for holidays we had a final spiritual lecture, with warnings about how seminarians should act in the outside world. The priest closed his talk this way, "Now, boys, if you want to go to parties while you're home, or date some of the local girls, or go out drinking with your buddies, then go ahead. After all, you are healthy young men." Then he added, "But if you do, just don't come back."

"They work like hell to get you in, then work like hell to get you out." the boy next to me whispered.

After the two-week Christmas break we were back at the books and yearning for the summer holidays, but there was still organized hockey on the rink and pick-up hockey on the frozen river down behind the tennis courts. Down there it was natural ice that was uneven and often cracked open wide enough to capture a skate blade and send the player sprawling without warning. Over the years the river ice had produced some broken bones, but it was worth the risk and much better than sitting around waiting for your chance to get on the regulation rink with your team. If it snowed too hard we'd play basketball in the narrow gym or cards in the basement recreation area. In February the drama committee took over the gym and began to construct the stage for the annual play, and my introduction to the world of 'walking the boards' began.

That year the play was *Twelve O'clock High* and the director cast me in the role of one of the officers. The cast was also the crew and we scrounged up flats, paint, lights and all the tools needed to bring the play to a conclusion. The Sisters, who made our meals and did our laundry, also made our costumes.

They were exceptionally kind and wise and often helped in the rehearsals, offering insightful suggestions. Most of them had suffered through years of student plays and had a wealth of knowledge about theatre productions. The director was a student in first year Theology that everyone called 'Tiny' simply because he stood six foot three and weighed somewhere in the neighbourhood of two hundred and fifty pounds. His weight was a well-kept secret, although the rest of us tried in every devious way to get him to tell it. Tiny was the Friar Tuck type, good-natured, patient, kind, determined and strong. He had a phobia about snakes and when one of his best friends hid a captured garter snake in his locker as a joke. Tiny opened the door, saw the snake, picked up the metal locker and threw it across the room. Then he stamped upstairs breathing vengeance on the perpetrator. But by suppertime all was forgiven and even Tiny was able to laugh at the practical joke...but with an edge to the laughter that warned against any future similar attempt.

The preparation for the play was going well until one of the players decided he'd had enough of seminary life and left suddenly. You could leave or be dismissed at any time so his departure was accepted by the student body as a whole, but it left a gap in the cast of the play. His part as a maintenance sergeant was not large and he only had one brief speaking role. At a given time, about halfway through the play, he was to enter from a door at the back of the stage and announce that the bombers were returning from their night raid over Germany, then he was to take a message for the crews to assemble in the flight hall as soon as possible. None of the other students wanted the part but we finally prevailed on one of my classmates, Big Al, to give it a try.

At rehearsals Al was nervous and often forgot his line or came up with a new one that didn't feed into the script. We assured him that if anything went wrong we would say his line for him if he forgot it, so he agreed to show up on opening night. The stage was raised about three feet off the gym floor and the rear door on the set opened *backwards* against a black backdrop. A set of stairs ran up to a small landing which gave enough room for the player to stand on the landing and wait for his cue before opening the door. When Al walked onto the stage the bright lights and rows of faces were too much for him. He went absolutely blank with stage fright and stood frozen to the spot. We said his lines for him and told him to leave and assemble the men in the flight hall. In his haste to exit the stage he turned and opened the door *inwards* and the whole back flat came down around our ears. There was a momentary gasp from the audience until one of the boys in the front row yelled; "I think the Germans are attacking!" That brought down the house. We straightened out the set and went on with the play after a ten-minute break, but you could hear the people tittering all through the rest of the evening. Al never acted again.

When Easter came all the seminarians were assigned to ceremonies at one of the many churches or institutions in the area. Our group ended up at the monastery of the Sisters of the Precious Blood, an Order of contemplative nuns whose Rule directed them, in small groups, to offer continuous prayer before the Blessed Sacrament exposed in a monstrance on the altar. The doctrine of the bread and wine changing into the real body and blood of Christ at Mass had been easy for me to accept as a new Catholic. If I could change those substances into my own body through the mystery of digestion it seemed reasonable that Christ could perpetuate it without the digestion part. It also seemed clear that God, who hated false worship, would not allow people like St. Paul or St. Francis to continue in this error if they were doing their best to please Him. But the idea of continuous, perpetual adoration night and day as a life's vocation was startling. This was dedication beyond anything I had known, but then, I was pretty new to the spiritual life, and when it comes to God, I suppose, anything is possible. Still I was glad that it wasn't my vocation. Suddenly the privations of seminary life didn't seem so tough after all.

Gradually winter changed into spring and the hockey rink became a great puddle. The ice in the river down below began to break up in large chunks, big enough to support the weight of a man, at least for a few minutes. The ride was exhilarating and almost always ended up with the rider wet at least to his knees. The only one of the senior class to risk this wild and wet ride was Joe Roman, a fine athlete and an adventurous soul. Joe played tight end on the football field and forward on the first hockey team and was one of the easiest guys to talk to in the whole building. He had time even for our first year worries about the duration of the studies leading up to the priesthood. He himself had been there for seven years and his recommendation to us was: "Take it one day at a time and everything will fall into place." He was ordained that June and died two months later when his doctor friend crashed the small plane on take-off.

We found out later that Joe had been working with the doctor trying to reconcile him with his estranged wife, and we wondered if the crash had resulted from the doctor's depression. No one will ever know for sure, and yet we all felt that in some way Joe's life as a priest was not a waste.

Chapter 7
Summertime

Final exams came and went and spring turned into early summer and the three and a half months of freedom finally arrived. Mom had again sent a cheque that allowed me to take a bus to the paper mill where I had worked the previous summer and to have enough spending money to last me until the first pay came. The boys from my old university showed up and we excitedly exchanged stories about our new vocations. They were as interested in the seminary life as I was about their medical studies, and I think all of us had mad dreams of becoming medical missionaries in some far off pagan land. Ah! The wonders of the dreams of Youth! But we were young and as Aunt Liz used to say, 'full of piss and vinegar' and anything was possible.

We started again into the routine of millwork with Henry and I on the same shift and often together. At one point, when all five of us had lined up a free weekend together in June, we borrowed a car and decided to travel to Duluth in Wisconsin, about two hundred miles away. At Pigeon River, the border-crossing station, the immigration officer turned us back because Hoover Wong was Chinese and didn't have a visa, although he was a British citizen. But that wasn't the worst part. When we tried to re-enter from where we had come, the border officer didn't believe that Hoover had just left not half an hour previously. They accused us of trying to sneak an alien in and kept us for several hours while they checked the credentials of each one of us. We ended up spending the weekend in a lakeside motel watching the ocean-going grain boats sail in and out of the harbour. Not very exciting for young adventurers.

One of the older men I worked with in the mill before the swimming area opened up, was Ed, a short, tough ex boxer with a heart of gold, and a practising Catholic. His wife, Betty, was the church organist and a convert to Catholicism just like me. They had three small children, two of whom had been among my swimmers the previous summer. Betty raised the kids, cleaned the church, played at all services and made excuses of the young local priest, who was well on the way to becoming an alcoholic, and who repeatedly wrecked his car at every turn in the road. Not a bad guy to talk to if you got the chance, but he was usually there only on Sundays, and spent the rest of the week at his mother's place in another town.

We were one of the smallest and furthest parishes in the whole dioceses and Father had been moved around by the Bishop until he finally ended up in our tiny community. But a tipsy priest is better than none at all, so the people of the town tolerated him and allowed for his behaviour. The talk was that he was an only child whose mother had raised him to be a priest right from the crib and he had never experienced the real world until after ordination. Apparently the stress of the solitary life was too much for him and he sought solace in the bottle. Alcohol is sometimes called the 'The Priest's Disease'; it's not an easy life being marked off as unique. At the end of the summer every seminarian had to have a form filled out by the local parish priest saying that no scandal had been reported about the young student and that as far as the priest knew, the seminarian had been regular at Mass and had done some charitable works. On my last day that summer the priest asked me to fill it in myself, saying he would confirm anything I wrote up to the point of miracles or visions. At least he had a sense of humour.

Betty was the first person I ever met who had a sense of what is called 'mystic contemplation', the ability to quietly sit and worship God without having to use words. After all these years I still can't do it, and it's a remarkable thing to witness. I'd occasionally drop in to church during the week to help Betty clean and would see her sitting in the pew absolutely motionless. Once I stayed for an hour, saying rosaries, and watching her. She wasn't even aware that anyone was there. Later that day I asked her what prayer she was using and she replied: "None. I was only there for a few minutes anyways." How long she had sat in contemplation before I came was anybody's guess. She really didn't want to talk about it, but one day she confessed that she couldn't use words when she sat in front of the tabernacle but just was aware of God's presence, and felt as if she was full of a bright but silent light. Mysticism is a world all of its own.

Soon enough the end of June approached and the maintenance crews put the floating board-walks back in the water and I opened up the buildings and dragged the water slide into the shallow pool. On the last day of school the kids were back in increasing numbers, all wanting to be the first in the water, even though it was still pretty cold. It was a better summer than the previous one, and it had been a gem. The crowd from last year was ready to move up the scale in swimming badges and the new crop already seemed to have some water skills. To make it even better I was adopted by a small black and white border collie, who arrived on the bus one morning and bounded into my arms at first sight.

Why we hit it off so well I'll never know, but he stayed near me every day at the beach and walked home with me through the woods every afternoon. He belonged to a man in town and apparently would go home every night to be fed, yet he always took the bus to the pool in the morning and ran to greet me as soon as the bus stopped. I didn't know his real name, which was Zipper, until much later but he answered to the name 'Ralph'. He was named by the children, who according to a standing joke among them said that if you asked any dog its name it would answer "Ralph! Ralph!". All summer long he ran from one child to another as they barked his name. He would run through their legs until they tripped onto the sand and then lick their happy faces. When he got tired playing, he would come to the foot of the lifeguard's chair and bark to be lifted up. Then as he sat in my arms he would play 'junior lifeguard', barking at any swimmer who dared to swim outside the log booms. God is good to have given us such friends.

Some of the swimmers were so advanced that they asked me to form a swim team to compete with the other towns nearby. When we formed the team they trained hard and were quite good, but not good enough to win our first meet, which was against our nearest rival, a town some fifteen miles away. At the meet I met their coach, a young man from the United Church seminary in Winnipeg, and it wasn't long before we became close friends. Doug had been raised on a farm in Saskatchewan and loved the outdoor life as much as I did. Soon we were doing overnight canoe trips with some of the children from the swim teams since both of us got one weekend off every three weeks. On weekends there were no lessons anyway and on our weekends off the administration supplied some of their own people who had been lifeguards when they were younger. Our outings were popular and were always well attended. We chose small lakes near the town and on Friday after work the parents would drive the youngsters there and loan us their own canoes. They would pick them up late Saturday, and once or twice we even stayed until early Sunday morning; we would have stayed later but both Doug and I had to be back for Church at eleven o'clock on Sunday morning. He was occasionally giving sermons by then, but I was nowhere near ready to pretend I knew much about religion.

On one outing we had come in two canoes, with Doug in one and I in another and a group of six kids split among us. And after we had set up camp Doug told us he had to return for a friend's stag. In the early evening we took Doug down the lake to his car with the understanding that he would return before midnight and use his flashlight to indicate where he was waiting for us. Everything went well when we returned to the campsite; we cooked supper, sat around a campfire, roasted marshmallows and took turns telling the scariest ghost stories we knew. As midnight drew near the youngsters were excited to pick up Doug and tell him the stories they had heard. We started down the dark lake with the canoes tethered loosely together and with each person shining their own flashlight across the water and up along the shore. Almost immediately we saw a flashing light at the end of the lake and started toward it, though it was about a half mile away. The youngsters flashed back in happy greeting, using any Morse code they remembered, but there was no second response from Doug.

As we paddled down the lake occasionally there would be a series of flashes from the parking lot, but there was never any response when we tried to answer back. Then the children began to become frightened. They saw strange shapes swimming in the water and glowing eyes from the woods beside the lake. It took loud commands and threats to begin to quiet them down, and then the other canoe almost tipped when one of the frightened young canoeists stood up and wanted to swim to shore. Visions of upset canoes in the middle of a deep, dark lake at midnight filled my mind. I grabbed the gunnels of the other canoe and held both together until some semblance of order was restored. Finally, after several minutes and another series of nonsense flashes from the end of the lake, we cautiously paddled *together* to the shore of the parking lot. No one was there, but the answer to the flashing lights soon became obvious. The parking lot was just off a secondary highway and every time a car went by its headlight beams would be broken by the large trees that lined the back of the lot. We built a fire and waited quietly for Doug, who arrived about a half hour later. Doug was the only one talking as we returned to the campsite, and no one offered to tell any more ghost stories.

In July, Terry, one of my senior swimmers from the year before, was killed in a car accident. He was just sixteen and had borrowed his father's car to drive to the next town to pick up three of his friends, who had played on the same hockey team the previous winter. On the outskirts of our town there was a large bridge that crossed the river, which ran in a deep cut down into Lake Superior. Once across the bridge the road took a slight turn, then ran straight as an arrow for almost two miles. It was a favourite place for adventurous mill workers to test the speed of any new car they had purchased. On the return trip the four boys tried too hard to set some kind of a speed record between the two towns and didn't make the curve at the bridge.

Most of the car ended up in the river below, along with the bodies of three of the boys, including Terry, but the young person in the back seat on the driver's side shot out of the car as it slammed into the bridge and ended up in the grassy ditch beside the road. When the ambulance attendants went to pick him up they thought he was a fourth victim, but he had only been knocked out, and was released from the hospital the next day. The police said later that the smashed speedometer read at over one hundred miles an hour. We all attended the funeral a few days later; it was the first time in the history of the new town that we had lost a young student and it had a profound effect on everyone. The police began to give out tickets to anyone even remotely over the limit on that particular stretch of the road and to this day, I am told, the bridge has not been the scene of another accident.

The road that runs along the north shore of Lake Superior slices between the rock hills of the Boreal Shield. It is a pleasant and scenic drive when the sun is shining, and a treacherous devil's paradise when it rains or snows or when the fog rolls in from the lake. It is also a wide path for strolling Bull Moose, and more than one of the mill hands has ended up on the losing end of an argument with the giant denizen of the forest. Peter, one of the accountants whom we knew personally from the baseball diamond, spent two weeks in the hospital after his encounter one night when he was returning to town from the city. He swore to us that it had charged straight at him on the highway when he was doing about fifty miles an hour, and sent his car into the ditch. When he pulled himself out of the totalled wreck he said he saw it walking off into the trees, apparently none the worse for wear. They grow them big in that neck of the woods, and the stories about their bad temper when they're in the rutting season stretch back into native lore.

All too soon the summer was over and the 'good-byes' had to be said to the swimmers, to Henry and the others, and to 'Ralph', who I was going to miss most of all. Then there was the bus ride for eight hundred miles, which is an event to be avoided and by the morning of the second day all the passengers had stopped talking and become quite taciturn. We read, gazed out the windows, looked repeatedly at our watches and longed for the next rest stop to break the monotony of the trip. At about mile six-fifty the bus driver mentioned that a side road that was coming up led to the Martyrs' Shrine in Midland, the place where Father Bill had seen the man's tongue restored. On a whim I left the bus and hitchhiked to the Shrine. It's a beautiful old church made of cut stone and with the whole interior dressed in lacquered birch bark, and in the wings near the altar are hundreds of canes, crutches and other symbols of sudden healing. Were they the remnants of *real* miracles (for those who believe in miracles)? Who can say for sure; the mind is a powerful force, quite capable of overcoming problems that may have been more mental than physical. But the cards attached showed clearly that the original owners of the devices were thankful that the pain had gone away.

From the Shrine to the seminary took another half day, but when I arrived this time I went in the *back* way, found my room on the room list, unpacked and went to see the Bursar. During the summer the Union had managed an hourly raise for us, which allowed me to give the Bursar the $500, the same as the previous year, but keep back the increase, for *necessities* that were sure to come up. To be honest, I wasn't much attached to Lady Poverty and having suffered through one year with no personal funds I really didn't want to make her acquaintance the second year. As usual, the retreat was in full swing but most of it was over. Within a few days we were back at the books and Father Anthony was analysing, with us, Medieval literature and philosophy. He was as good as ever, or maybe even better, as we traced the various ideas that had shaped the world in those times.

The Administration had an odd practice of letting the seminarians walk off the property on Sunday afternoons. Any excuse would do, as long as they wore a white shirt and black shoes, tie, pants, suit coat and fedora. Perhaps the reasoning was that dressed that way we would seem singularly strange to other people and therefore not likely to mix with the outside world. I had most of the outfit but lacked a black suit coat, but one of the Sisters came to the rescue. A discarded one was found, patched, altered, pressed and presented into my grateful hands, and I soon joined the line-up asking for permission to go to the university bookstore, visit an ailing aunt, buy some socks or underwear, or any other excuse that sounded reasonable. Mainly it was a chance to get a coke and a hamburger and sit around *inside* and smoke. We frequented a particular small, out-of-the-way 'greasy spoon' and were usually his only customers on Sunday afternoons. One Sunday we had special services for a local, well known priest who had just died, and therefore we couldn't make the usual 'walk'. The proprietor wanted to close early that day, so like any good businessman, he checked with his clients. His phone call to the Rector ended those lazy, laid back Sunday afternoons.

Every year a series of tasks was apportioned out to the individual seminarians, especially the ones who had been there only one year. There were jobs such as infirmarian, choir leader or bookstore attendant but the most dreaded job was that of the regulatorian, bell-ringer. The person straddled with that job had to be up early so he could ring the wake-up bell at 5:30 in the morning, and had to be the last one up in the evening to ring the 'lights-out' bell at 9:30. It was a task that only a masochist could treasure, and we all breathed a sigh of relief when someone else was appointed. We never knew how the Administration determined who got what job, whether it was an assessment of your mental prowess, your natural ability or just the luck of the draw.

Again fate stepped in to test my vocation, for the newly appointed regulatorian left that year at Christmas and the task became mine. It meant a change in rooms, for the bell ringer had the switch on the wall right outside his door for easy access, and to the uninitiated the switch looked like any other light switch. On more than one occasion a sleepy seminarian on his way to the common bathroom mistook it for a light switch and had us up in the middle of the night. Sometimes, it was rumoured, a bet would be made about the number of students who would dress and go to the chapel if the bell happened to be rung briefly at 2:30 A.M. I was called in several times by the Rector to explain these unusual ringings, but as I wasn't a member of the betting pool I was never able to solve these midnight mysteries.

For Christmas that year I went to my married brother's home in a nearby city, where he had moved shortly after his marriage. The first of the new clan was there; a baby boy named Brad who was the pride and joy not only of his parents, but of his grandparents as well. I think Brad's birth had something to do with my father gradually becoming reconciled to my pursuit of the Catholic priesthood, perhaps now because he had a grandson to replace the wayward son who had moved to the fringes of humanity. Whatever the reason, I exchanged Christmas wishes over the phone with him when he called early Christmas morning. My mother had done a good job of being the peacemaker, for he even asked how my studies were going and whether I had enough money for books and supplies. An uneasy but loving truce was established that day that lasted between us until the time of his death many years later. During the first week of April a letter from mother said that they would be coming through our city later that week and wondered if I could get permission to meet them at the train station. When the Rector heard that they would arrive at midnight he dismissed the request, but he woke me that night at 11:30 and drove me to the station and met my parents. It is hard to say whether my parent or myself were more impressed with the Rector, and it farther softened my father's belief about Catholics.

That same April, 1955. my faith was severely challenged. My beloved Uncle Bill, Father William McWalter S.J., died of a sudden heart attack as he left a theatre with some friends. I was told of his death by another seminarian who was also from my home city. This foolish man belonged to a small, unofficial group among the students called the "illuminati", who thought of themselves as candidates for the next round of heavenly visions to grace the earth. They were seminarians with few social skills, awkward in speech and with no athletic ability at all. It was, of course, a defence mechanism that allowed them to feel confident among a large group of athletic and independent young men. Still, for many years after our encounter I could not meet him without a feeling of anger welling up inside me. He had approached me during morning break and had said with a smile and great enthusiasm, "Good news! Your friend Father McWalters has died and gone to heaven!"

It was as sudden as that. It swept me away so completely I didn't believe him until another friend sent me a telegram later that day. Later on, when the Administration became aware of this strange group's conceit it was disbanded and some of them were dismissed.

Bill's death had occurred on the last day of classes before final exams, and the Rector couldn't understand my desire to attend his funeral, since it fell on the day of the first exam. All I was able to do was to phone Father Will, Bill's close friend, and ask him about the reasons why God might allow such a waste. Bill was a guiding light, not only in my life but in the lives of countless boys who had attended the college and his death made no human sense at all. He told me about his last meeting with Bill, just before he went out to the theatre that previous night.

"After he left the building I asked another fellow priest if he had noticed anything unusual about Bill that evening, and he had agreed with my observation that there was a radiance and special soft charisma about him. I think he was ready. I think he had only waited for God to send you to him in the first place."

The day after the funeral, Father Will phoned and told me that the Cathedral was packed, with many of the students crying openly during the service. These were tough boys from the toughest high school in the city, yet they cried just as I did. A week later Father sent me Bill's ordination cross, which he had worn every day of his priestly life. It still hangs on the wall of my house.

During final exams one of my classmates asked if I wanted to share expenses on a car trip up to Duluth, where I could catch a bus to the mill town and a summer of swimming. His uncle ran a Ford dealership in the west and had contacted him with the suggestion that he pick up a new car from the factory and drive it out for resale. With two other guys and the driver it sounded like a great deal, so when exams were over I shipped my suitcase, and my extra cash, by bus to the mill and together with the others got a ride to the factory and picked up the brand new Ford. We took an easy route on a journey that was to prove to be the most interesting trip of my life. But by the time we had reached Marchette on the south shore of Lake Superior the car had broken down and we had it hauled into a Ford dealership to check out the problem. Their mechanics couldn't find out why it wouldn't run and didn't want to tear the new engine apart to locate the trouble. They called the plant and were told that a carrier would pick up the car and take it back to the factory for analysis. This meant that the driver and his buddy would have to stay with the car until it was repaired at the factory, which could easily be a few days at least. The remaining passenger and myself had jobs waiting for us, so we decided to hitchhike the rest of the way, about six hundred miles. Before leaving, the two of us gave the other two all the spare cash we had and kept back only five dollars each to see us through. How bold youth can be; the two of us set out with little money in our pockets, on a road we hadn't travelled on before and a long way to go before we reached our destinations.

The other seminarian and I soon split up that afternoon as soon as we realized that no one picks up two young, male strangers. Within minutes we were separately on our way, thanks to the generosity of other travellers, and by the time darkness fell I had made it to Ashland, at the base of the Apostle Islands, a distance of over a hundred miles. Then my luck ran out. It started to rain and when I was sufficiently cold, wet and hungry I went into a roadside diner and ordered a plate of French fries and a coffee. The five dollars I had didn't go far and by the end of the meal, which I dragged out as long as I could, I was down to a single nickel. Old poverty had caught me again. Worse still, a couple of State Police came in for a late bite and eventually came over to check my identification. One of them said it was illegal to hitchhike in their State and reminded me of an old law called 'Vagrancy" which applied to anyone caught without a set amount of money on their person. They put me in the back of the cruiser and checked my small duffle bag and all the credentials I had on me, then drove me to the State line and wished me 'good luck' on the rest of my journey. It was still raining, but not so hard and I crawled into a dry culvert and slept for a few hours.

At first light I was back using my thumb on the side of the highway when a driver in a light truck offered me a ride. As we started up the driver asked me if I was the nervous type, and then told me to look in the back of the truck. He was a demolition expert on his way to work on a new highway and the back was filled with boxes of dynamite and fuses. Every time he hit a bump in the road he would say: "Whoops! Sorry." and grin. Thank goodness for my swimming training in holding my breath. By noon we were in Duluth and I walked the whole length of the east side of the city until the streets stopped and the highway north to Pigeon River began. There was a lot of traffic on the road, which was a single lane both ways. About one o'clock a great car stopped. It was a Dodge Desoto, two-door, with a big powerful engine under the hood, and a tipsy driver behind the wheel. He was a mechanic who'd had to work half the morning and had spent the other half with his cronies in the bar. We pulled up behind a long line of cars that were stopped for some reason, and there didn't seem to be any other cars coming the other way. He said, "Sunday drivers!" and pulled out and floored the accelerator. Man! That car could move, and it was a good thing it could. We missed the train at the crossing by inches, and all he said was, "Stupid train!"

Have you ever been in a situation where you begin to accept that you're not going to escape an accident, and hope that the pain won't be too great? I was honestly praying.

"Only a broken leg, please Lord! Nothing worse!" as we sped along at close to a hundred miles an hour.

And we would have wrecked if he hadn't spotted a watering hole that served beer. When we turned in he asked if I was hungry and when I found my voice I accepted his offer of a meal. He bought me a full breakfast and matched me mouthful for mouthful, only his was beer. When I thanked him and got up to leave he said, "Do me a favour. I live a few miles down the road and I'm too drunk to drive. My house is just off the highway. You drive and we'll both get where were going in one piece."

It was a good offer and I wanted to try the car out anyways. He had souped up the engine himself and it wanted to *cruise* at a hundred miles per. It took all the skill I had to keep it at eighty. What a great car! My friend fell asleep and every half hour when I woke him he would peer out the windshield and say, "Nope. We're not there yet.", then drift off back into his alcoholic dreams.

By suppertime I *knew* we had gone too far, and pulled off into a diner on the side of the road and woke him up.

"I know where we are. I just live around the comer from here. Tell you what. Take me home and then you can have the car for the summer. I have another one at home."

Tempting, but the thought of spending the summer, or longer, in some Wisconsin jail for grand theft auto was not a reasonable option. The waitress knew him and said he lived thirty miles back down the road toward Duluth. She got his wallet out of his pocket and found an identification card with his phone number on it, then told me to call his wife to come and pick him up. It was not an easy conversation; the man's wife was convinced I was one of his alcoholic buddies and told us both to stay where we were until we sobered up. She had no intention of running a taxi service for a couple of drunks! The last I saw of him he was trying to buy another beer and sweet-talking the waitress. Another driver took me several miles up the road, and when he let me out the weather had turned warm and I slept most of the night on a table in a picnic area.

Next morning a well-to-do family of two teen-agers and two adults picked me up and wanted to hear all about my journey thus far and were amazed that I hadn't been killed at the railway crossing.

Finally the father asked, "What are you studying at university?" and when I said 'Philosophy' he laughed.

"And what will you do with it after you graduate?"

When they heard that I was studying for the priesthood there was a silence in the car. Then the mother cautiously asked, "Are *all* your studies in Latin?"

I said, "Only one so far." It seemed to break the silence and then they had many questions.

But we talked for a long time and they laughed at my stories about seminary life and shared their sandwiches with me. Nice folks. Kind strangers can be one of the great blessings of life. They were on their way to some vacation spot and let me out when the road turned off toward their destination. The next ride was to be the most memorable, and one of the shortest.

The road beside the west shore of Lake Superior runs along the cliffs in places and the drop off down to the water can be substantial. It is also fairly hilly as you approach the border. After standing at the bottom of a hill for some time an old car appeared and slowed as it came down to where I was standing. The passenger opened the front door and I climbed in only to realize there was no windshield in front of me. Two couples shared the car which was loaded down with camping equipment and all four of them were drunk in various degrees. The woman in the rear seat was crying softly. The driver explained that they had rolled the car a half hour earlier but had managed to get it back on the road and now were looking for a garage to determine the damage. The right front tire was making a loud squealing sound as it rubbed against the bent fender and I mentioned this to the driver.

"Don't worry about it. I've got a spare in the back."

What worried me was not replacing the tire but the possibility of a sudden plunge over the cliff, down into the water a hundred feet below, when the tire let go. Then the cab began to fill with smoke. They had damaged the oil pan when the car had rolled over and the oil had finally drained away allowing the engine to overheat and send clouds of burned oil up from under the hood. Luckily the next hill was too much for the old engine and it seized solidly about halfway up. Once the driver got the car into neutral, we rolled it down a side road into a little park, where as far as I know, they have remained to this day.

It wasn't far to the border and the first Customs Officer just let me walk through but the one on the next border stopped me cold. Who was I? How had I got there? What was I bringing into the country? I had to unpack my small bag and explain every item that was in it. Finally he asked me if I knew anyone who could vouch for the truth of my explanations. The only one I could think of was Peter's sister who lived in the next city, and so I mentioned the names of Julie and her husband, Sarto. It's a small world; they were his uncle and aunt. He stopped the next car going through and when he found out where they were going he *told* them to take me with them. I guess they were afraid of getting tied up at the border if they didn't comply, so they opened the rear door and I climbed in. They never spoke a word all the rest of the trip. By four o'clock I was back in the barracks at the mill, waiting around for the other university students. The real summer had begun.

The first thing I did was to look for 'Ralph' but he was nowhere to be found. He was the one, more than anyone else, with whom I wanted to re-establish our relationship, but all the searching was in vain. Finally I talked with Peter, who lived there full time, and was told that his master and Ralph had moved away. He added that for over a week after I left the previous September the dog had looked everywhere for me and finally had returned home. What sad news! Even today, with all the great dogs that I've had since then, I still miss that little black and white border collie. When you give your heart away it never fully heals when separation occurs. Two years ago I bought a descendant of his and some of the healing is taking place. "Mac" is as bouncy and loving as Ralph was, but he doesn't bark at wayward swimmers.

During the winter the town had become incorporated and all services for the town were done by contract on a salary basis, and that included the summer job as lifeguard. If I took on the swimming program there would be no time-and-a-half and no double-time, nor would I be paid at the basic mill rate and have the protection of the union. I knew I'd miss the kids but the money from the millwork was necessary, so the decision was not too difficult. Because they could use my services as relief lifeguard on my days off there was still some summer work at the pool, but the children were no longer mine. They were glad to see me when I did show up, but they had two senior girls who had qualified as lifeguards and they bonded with them just as they had done with me the two previous years. Oh, the fickleness of the human heart!

Peter was in the habit of going to the city every second week to see his aging parents and the rest of his close knit family, and I frequently accompanied him. Their local parish church was St. Dominic's, for the whole neighbourhood was Italian, and the parish priest was a Salishan Father from Italy who they called "Padre Keena'. Father China was a highly educated man with a doctorate in languages who had spent most of his priestly career teaching at a private boys' school in Rome. The school was one of high profile and mainly catered to the boys from elite Roman families. During the summer he was a personal servant at Castel Gandolfo, the summer residence of Pope Pius XII. He thought very highly of Pius XII, saying he was a scholar and very austere and that he had slept on the floor all during the Second World War, doing penance for not having confronted the Germans more directly. China had come to Canada, and to this small parish, as a missionary, and although he never said so, I think it was to do penance for his own wartime neglect.

We soon became friends and one day he loaned me a book on Padre Pio, the Trappist monk who had the wounds of Christ in his own body. As soon as I read it I wanted to know more about this unusual man and on the next visit asked if he had ever gone to Pio's monastery, which was not far from Rome itself. He hadn't, but he knew many people who had and who came away greatly impressed with Pio's Mass and his confessional insights. One of China's senior students, a young man of no faith, had decided that Pio was a fraud and intended to go to the monastery and ridicule him. China had warned him about such brashness and then had forgotten about the incident. A few days later he noticed the young man crying in the chapel, and thinking that it was some bereavement he had not heard about, went in to comfort him. The student had indeed gone to the monastery, but because of the thousands of people who were already there had not been able to get near Father Pio. After Mass, when Pio went to hear confessions the student waited in line for two hours until his turn came. No sooner did he kneel down in the confessional than Pio got up from his seat and grabbed the young man by the collar, dragged him the length of the church, and threw him down the front steps saying: "I can't *stand* the smell of your sins!"

Father continued his tale. "What a change in the boy! He went to prayers every morning, read spiritual books, began to take his studies seriously and was no longer the brash, arrogant person he had been before. About two weeks later he came to tell me that he was going back to the monastery to apologize, but was terrified that he might get thrown down the steps again, in front of all those people. I told him it would indeed take courage and that I couldn't advise him one way or another. The next Monday he was excitedly waiting for me at my office door when I arrived at school. He had gone back. When his turn came in the confessional he was so frightened he couldn't even speak.

'Now, my son, now you are ready to go to confession.' Pio had said and heard his confession.

The young man said the most amazing thing about the confession was that when he thought he was through, Pio said that he had forgotten several major sins that he had committed previously, and reminded him what exactly they were, and had him confess those as well."

Father China went on to say that after graduation the boy applied to a seminary in Rome and began his own studies for the priesthood. I saw China several times that summer and we often talked about stigmatics and the Church's careful examination of them.

In July we five original university students got together and rented the house of the school principal for six weeks. He and his family ran a summer lodge and were out of town for almost the entire summer. We took turns cooking, but since we were not all on the same shift, whoever cooked had to make enough to leave a meal ready for those who came in at midnight or eight in the morning. In the local food market I discovered a series of foods called 'Meals in a Bag'. Whatever the meat in the bag was, it could be beef or lamb or chicken, there was matching vegetables already in the same bag. All you had to do was to put the bag in a roasting pan and put the pan in the oven. In about an hour the whole delicious meal was ready, and everyone was satisfied. It was our introduction to 'instant' food, or as close as you could get to 'instant' back in 1955. However there was a drawback to my meal preparation; the meals were so much better than the lumpy potatoes and cold ham that the others often fixed, that they tried to vote me in as permanent cook. I had to let the supper burn one night just to help them change their minds.

Near the beginning of August we rented a car and drove home for a weekend, although it had taken some juggling to line up our days off so we could all go at the same time. During July we worked double shifts for other workers, who would then work a double shift for us while we were away, but we did finally managed get the three days off. I went home, the first time in over two years, and was received as the Prodigal Son. Mother and Time had healed the breach between my father and myself, and by the end of my visit it had vanished, never to return. The second day I was home, early in the morning an old girlfriend showed up at on our doorstep; how she knew I was home was a mystery. She had been married about a year and came to show me her new tiny baby, and to quiz me about the celibate life of a seminarian. She held up the pretty baby to show us.

"Look at what you're missing! To say nothing of the loving that makes it happen. How can you possibly live a celibate life? It's unnatural. If you were some little naive virgin that had never dated then maybe I could understand it. But I know you've been around. It's impossible!"

It was the first time I'd been confronted with the question of sex and the celibate life since I entered the seminary, and her rapid but friendly attack left me momentarily speechless. I tried to explain how dedication to an ideal could make it possible, and how cold showers and avoidance of intimate associations could cool the natural desires between the sexes, but she only shook her head and cuddled the baby. She had coffee with me, while mom held the baby, and told us all about her wonderful husband and their new life together, and after an hour, left to return to that life. Up until that morning I had managed my sexual longings *with* cold showers and avoidance, and by not paying any real attention to them when they did arise. In the seminary there was weekly confession and each student had a specific Father Confessor to whom he could discuss such matters. Among the boys there was little or no sex talk, as if instinctively everyone realized that celibacy was a blessing carried in a fragile vase. But now, outside the protective walls of the college and back in an environment where celibacy was a joke, I wasn't quite so confident. I had planned to see Father Will anyway, and that morning seemed like a most opportune time.

Father and I talked for a long time about the sexual urge and how to controlled it. When I asked if it started to go away as you grew older he began to laugh and said that one time when he was in his forties he'd had a particularly tough struggle. He went to see an eighty-five year old Jesuit who lived in the same house and asked him the question I'd just asked.

"Well, when you get to my age the fires burn rather slowly." the old priest said, and Father Will had taken heart. However, the next day the old priest had sought him out sheepishly.

"You had better give me a few more years." he said.

"Stay busy". Will said. "It really helps. Most women will respect your vow but there are some who see a priest as some sort of trophy. This type is usually pretty aggressive, so do your best to stay away from them. Not much more I can tell you. Every one of us gets tempted to a greater or less degree. It's a part of human nature. Take it one day at a time."

Then we went out to lunch and talked about how the local team would likely do when the football season rolled around.

The weekend was soon over and we returned to work at the paper mill. Since I knew most of the shop foremen and had spent some time on a variety of jobs in the plant I began to be shifted around to replace any worker who was on holidays or off sick. I spent a few days on the barker drums, a few on cleanup throughout the mill, a week or so on the bailer where the rough paper was banded and shipped out by rail to a finishing plant, several weeks on the chipper where the four foot skinned logs were reduced to chips the size of a large coin and sent to the giant cooking kettles, and a more continuous job of gathering up the loose paper when it broke on the rollers and had to be placed in the 'hydropulper' for reprocessing. But in the first week of August the odd jobs suddenly ended and our workday went from eight hours a day to twelve, with no days off in between shift changes.

The Fire Marshall had arrived at the plant just after our crew had finished their shift, and he loaded all the men on the new shift into trucks and took them off to fight a forest fire a few miles away. None of the men wanted to go but to refuse could have brought jail time since fire-fighting can be classified as a national emergency. We didn't see them for almost two weeks and when they returned, red-eyed from smoke and lack of sleep, they smelled like something out of a sewer. They had eaten only emergency rations and had slept in their clothes during the whole tour of duty with no chance to shave or even wash. When they first arrived at the mill they didn't even get out of the trucks but just sat there trying to get up enough energy to find their cars in the parking lot and drive home. One of them showed up two days later to relieve me off his regular shift and said that when he first arrived home his wife was so happy to see him that she wanted to take him to bed right away.

"That's the first time in my whole married life that I didn't have the energy for it. I fell asleep as soon as I laid down and she hasn't talked to me since."

At the end of that summer, since there was no pool to close, there was no excuse for missing most of the annual retreat and after goodbyes and promises to write I hit the road to hitchhike again, thinking that if God could keep me safe on the way to the mill, why not on the way back to the seminary. The company allowed the workers to buy new boots at cost once a year and I had purchased a new pair just before the job ended and planned to wear them on recreation throughout the year. They were gorgeous boots: soft, waterproofed leather uppers with thick rubber soles and steel toes and they would have cost a bundle in any sporting goods store. They were my pride and joy. Few things in this world feel as good as a fine pair of boots that fit really well.

About five hours after starting out hitch-hiking I met a fellow knight-of-the-road who was sitting on a fence trying to tape up the sole of his shoe, which was hanging by a thread, and I had this strange compulsion to offer him the new boots. Compulsive feelings are not usually welcomed by anyone since these feelings can't stand up to the light of reason. They usually are based on superstitions of one sort or another, such as the compulsion to answer a chain letter, which everyone realizes is a foolish act, but difficult to turn down nevertheless. The long and short of it was that he got the boots and I went on my way feeling as if I'd been robbed, but within an hour I got a ride from a driver who was looking for company and he took me all the way to the seminary, six hundred miles away. Just another coincidence in a long line of them? Or was God just pleased?

Chapter 8
New Tasks

The seven-day retreat wasn't as bad as the boys had said, or maybe after two years we were all beginning to get the hang of the spiritual life. The routine was well rehearsed by then: up at 5:30, assembly in the chapel by 6:00, morning prayers and meditation followed by Mass until 7:00 and then breakfast, usually taken in silence while one of the seminarians took his turn at reading aloud from some spiritual book. There was a raised pulpit near the centre of the room for just that purpose and each seminarian had to take a turn or two during the year, with hardly anyone paying any attention. Sometimes the reader would be nervous and read too loudly or too softly, or at such a rate that the words all squished together like toothpaste in a tube, and those were the funny moments as the rest of us waited to hear what comment the priest at breakfast would make. Sometimes we were really rewarded by some zinger.

"Who wrote that drivel?" or "Who suggested that book?" or "Are you sure it was your turn to read?"

But usually we just ate in silence and endured the training without paying much attention to the reading. One of the seminarians, Jerry, was from Ireland, where righting was an acceptable recess diversion. He was a feisty little piece of work who was either laughing and telling jokes or challenging someone who had disagreed with his viewpoint to 'back up his argument with his fists', which apparently in Ireland is the court of last resort. I was used to these flashes of Irish temper, having inherited them (and hopefully having outgrown them) from my father and grandfather who used to close off a heated verbal exchange with the words, "Well, it wasn't much of a fight, but better than no fight at all."

After every argument, Jerry would go around to collect those who agreed with him, for his world was divided into two distinct camps: those who were for him, and those who were "agin" him. Since we shared the same belief in St. Patrick and the snakes, I was always on his side.

We sat at the same table in the refectory and one morning Jerry stood up from the table, picked up a full jug of milk, walked to another table and calmly dumped it over the head of one of those who was "agin"' him, then calmly walked out and packed to leave. It was obvious there were too many dissenters among us and he'd had his fill. Years later I ran into Jerry who had retired from a lifetime of teaching and was spending his free time raising money to go to India and buy the young children of prostitutes from their pimps and enrolling these innocents in a Jesuit run training school. He had bought almost seventy children by that time and had a film showing the school and many of the young children, who clung to his legs and called him 'Pampa'. If Jerry had been able to swallow his Irish temper and not washed away his anger with a jug of milk, those children would never have been rescued from a life of poverty, prostitution and drugs. The Holy Ghost moves in mysterious ways.

The routine was still cast in stone: from 7:30 to 8:00 we had morning break, then back to our rooms or the library to study until classes began at 8:30. Classes lasted until noon with a fifteen minute break at mid morning. Lunch was at 12:30 and more classes until 2:00 and then recreation until 4:00, often followed by a spiritual lecture until 5:00. The Rosary was said in unison in the chapel at 5:00, with supper, cooked by the Sisters, at 5:30. Another recreation from 6:00 to 7:00 and then we hit the books or read or wrote home or prepped some essay or project that was due the next day. At 9:00 we met again in the chapel for night prayers and the daily examination of conscience, as we struggled to become "All things to all men" as St. Paul had. As far as I ever found out, the best that the *best* of us did was to become pretty good with a few. The 'lights-out' bell rang (my job for two years) at 9:30 and the day was over. Once a week we went to confession and occasionally we had some entertainment after supper; maybe a movie or a musical session or a lecture from a visiting speaker, but we didn't count on that. The Rule was the Rule and you learned to accept it or you left.

One of the special lectures we got that year was from the Jesuit Director of the Martyrs' Shrine at Midland. He had a slide show of the archaeological dig that he has been overseeing at Fort Saint Marie, on the banks of the Rye River, just below the Shrine, showing the various stages its restoration was going through. Ever since St. Ignatius founded the Jesuits there has been a rule that Jesuit missionaries must keep a continuous written account of what was happening at their mission. These writing are called *The Jesuit Relations*. The

Director had obtained from France the volume of these writings that dealt with the martyrdom of St. Jean de Brebeuf at the hands of the Iroquois, which told that after his fellow priests had recovered Jean's body they decided to abandon the fort and return to France. As was the custom, he said, they dissected the body and boiled the flesh off the bones. The bones were then carefully wrapped and taken back to France with them, but before they left they had dug a grave and poured the contents of the pot into the ground. The writings had given a general description of the grave site, and the archaeologists working with the Director had guessed where exactly the grave might be and had carefully exhumed the earth in that spot. He showed us what they had found about four feet down in the soil: a small lead plate, about three inches by six with the Latin inscription stamped on it reading " Jean de Brebeuf, martyr, 1642". A great example of science and religion working hand-in-hand.

The food the Sisters prepared was generally good and the menu varied to some extent, although the steaks were always rare. They had a special dessert that was made from cake we hadn't finished at some previous meal, with cooked strawberries (there was always a ton of those), covered over by a cream custard topping that sealed the cake and strawberries and allowed them to ferment, if the kitchen was warm enough. They never served it to the priests; maybe they felt we needed a little jolt in our routines. Those who were teetotallers stayed away from it but there was seldom any left at the end of the meal. There was a special surprise one day when our resident janitor added detergent to the soup pot thinking it was salt, since both substances were kept in identical tins. Boy! That cleared the dining hall quickly. Next day, after our strength returned, someone wrote on the recreational blackboard a series of numbers under Hits, Runs and Errors. A few of the boys had even run down into the gully behind the building when they realized that all the 'Johns' were occupied and not likely to be vacated for some time. It seems funny now, but then it was just a pain in...the lower regions.

Studies in the final undergraduate year included Anthony's courses in Modern Philosophy and Literature, plus Metaphysics, Psychology, Latin (Virgil and Pliny) and a course called Theodacy which dealt with the rational proofs for the existence of God. Anthony's courses were the best ever, both in the study of modern poetry and in the field of Kant's Pure Reason, Nietzsche's Nihilism, Mark's Communism and the Existentialism of Sartre. Although he believed that poetry should be enjoyed and not analysed, he had an interesting theory about why it affected people so much. Pure reason, he said, is what pushes us to the limit of thought, and away, as much as possible, from any emotional involvement, for when feelings enter in they quickly cloud the mind's ability to see things in an unprejudiced way. On the other hand, poetry does just the opposite; it brings us to the point where the meaning of words are so loaded with feelings that the poetic statement does not make clear sense and as the mind struggles to attach a meaning to the words a continuous series of possible meanings are suggested. It creates in the reader a sense of mystic wonder, as if to tease the mind into expecting to fully understand feelings. Feelings, he said, are born in us and are present long before thought begins to examine the world around us. Since feelings predate thought, thought cannot ever expect to understand them in any depth, thus poetry should enthral the reader by its very evasiveness. An interesting concept.

There was a team of two custodians who kept the school clean, heated and repaired. One was Abel, who had given us an entree of detergent for supper, and the other was 'T. F.', who wore coveralls and a First World War aviator's leather helmet, complete with ear flaps and as far as anyone knew never wore anything else, summer or winter. T. F. was short and skinny and as hyperactive as anyone could possibly be, and he marched to his own drummer. If a light bulb had to be replaced in a classroom he did it in between six other jobs, regardless of what was going on in the classroom at the time. Both Abel and T. F. were difficult to get to know, for Abel argued with himself almost non stop, sometimes laying down his broom as he swept the halls and stepping from one side of the broom to the other and back again so that the debate was truly two sided, and T. F. never stopped longer than it took to unfold his ladder and climb up to some spot that needed his attention. There was a suspicion that T. F. was actually married to his ladder, but we were never able to substantiate the rumour. During one variety show in the large hall, right in the middle of the program, in came the ladder, and a light bulb was replaced on the stage as we all waited patiently for T. F. to finish and rush off to some place else. Only it wasn't T. F. at all. One of the seminarians had bought an identical helmet and a pair of coveralls at a war surplus store and came in as a part of the variety program. After we recognized who it actually was, it took several minutes for the laughter to calm down enough for the program to continue. I think T. F. must have wondered at our smiles as we passed him in the hall for the next few days.

One of our courses in fourth year dealt with the human search for the existence of God. It started with that essential question attributed to Dietrich Bonhoeffer: 'Is God just an idea in our minds or are we ideas in the mind of God?' and proceeded to examine the teachings of existentialism, atheism and a large host of other beliefs. As the course progressed we realized that if God does exist as a real and distinct person, there is no way that the mind can *demonstrate* this, although it can offer arguments that are reasonable and seem conclusive. The problem is that God is an idea, a spiritual entity, and humans are material beings and all their learning in early life is based on material objects such as 'Mama' and 'Papa' and possessive phrases such as 'my toy.' Human learning doesn't proceed past that stage for many years, and it is only by the time of adolescence that some spiritual concepts become present and we realize that 'loyalty' and 'thought' and 'beauty' are abstractions and not concrete items and although they are real and necessary for life they cannot be demonstrated in themselves but only are to be seen as qualities residing in material persons.

When human language is used to talk about God it is done in anthropomorphic, or allegorical, terms. These are words that allow us to *pretend* we understand. We try to understand God as we try to understand ourselves and others, yet God is spiritual and eternal and immutable, terms that cannot be used in our examination of self or others and terms that we don't really understand. There is a story about St. Thomas Aquinas, who near the end of his life after he had written all his brilliant works, had a vision of God and heard a voice.

"You have written well about Me, Thomas."

Then the curtain of Infinity was lifted a little and Thomas had a fleeting glimpse of God as He is in Himself. Thomas's last words were, "What I have written is just so much straw!"

At a certain point faith must step in and the mind accepts, or rejects, something it cannot demonstrate, based on as good an examination of all the information that it has at its disposal.

Our experience is that nothing that is highly designed could possibly happen by chance. No movie makes itself, nor can the parts of a computer fall together randomly, yet things such as these are made up of a finite number of separate parts, and the universe, which seems to be even more highly designed, seems to have an infinite number of parts. The argument, of course, is that if it takes a clever person to design a finite work, it must take an *infinitely* clever person to design an infinite work. The problem is that we can't conceive of anything infinite, even the universe, since our minds are deeply rooted in a finite world. This is what is meant by the 'leap of faith' when we talk about knowing God, yet such a leap is not a leap in a real sense since leaping puts the leaper in a different place. This leap of faith is not a one-time thing, it is an ebb and flow of the human personality as it deals with the circumstances of daily existence and tries, and hopes, to see a pattern in it. Sometimes the pattern is startlingly obvious, and at other times it seems to vanish almost away. Faith is not something that you can hold in your hand.

These studies were interesting, and they sharpened our minds so that logical errors became more easily discerned when examining the works of historical thought. However they did burden the mind, and to stay on them continuously usually resulted in circular thinking where you arrived back at the point where you had begun. That was why there was very little discussion about our studies when we were out on recreation where the mind could relax and the world could fall back into its ordinary revolutions. We talked about sports and family and vacations and told stories of the strange and wonderful things that had come our way. Although it was against the Rule to have a radio, magazines or daily newspapers, somehow we always knew what teams were playing where and how they were doing in their league. On major events, such as the final in football, the Administration would supply a radio to the recreation hall for the afternoon and we would listen, and bet, on the outcome of the game.

My sister had been dating a young, first year player on the Western team and I was up to my eyebrows in bets against the Eastern team, but the Western players were not doing well. There was great thumping on the back and mocking as the Eastern team surged ahead. Finally as the last quarter started I couldn't stand it any longer and left the hall and went to the chapel to see if God could be persuaded to perform a small, but much needed, miracle, and stayed there for several minutes while the cheering from the hall flooded up through the floor. When I returned there were only five minutes left and the Western team was at mid field without much hope of scoring. The quarterback tried a long, desperation pass that was intercepted by the other team, but their player was tackled so hard the football squirted out of his hand and into the end zone where my sister's young boyfriend stood. It was one of the only catches he made that year, and his contract was not renewed the next year, but it was the one that counted for it led the Western team to a one point victory over their Eastern rivals. Maybe that's what turned me into a true believer.

Toward the end of the school year our bishop paid a visit to the seminary and asked me to try to get a summer job in a French speaking area where I could learn conversational French, since many of the parishes in the diocese were a mixture of French and English. This was to be real challenge since I had no aptitude in languages other than my own. On some of the shorter holidays I'd gone to the homes of boys whose families were perfectly bilingual, and marvelled at the ease in which they switched from one language to another. A close friend was Marcel who was as good at handball as he was at languages, and who tried successfully to help me understand certain theological questions, and *unsuccessfully* to understand either Latin or French. It was amazing to sit around the kitchen table at his parents' farm and listen to what he called "Frenglish", where a story or a joke might start in one language and end in another with everyone but me grasping the full meaning of the conversation. How I envied them their ability, and therefore decided that studying French would be a worthwhile summer adventure that hopefully might bear some linguistic fruit.

When final exams were over and marks were in, my grades were A's and B's in all the subjects except Latin, which was a C+, and was only that because the university examiner had made an error in calculation and assigned 110 to the final exam. It was another answer to a lot of prayers, since I had spent as much time memorizing, and praying to understand, Virgil and Pliny, classical Latin authors, as I had on all the other studies put together. I contacted Father Will about such a summer job and he suggested that I go to St. Ignatius, the Jesuit high school in a French district, as soon as university ended and see if any of the priests there had contacts for summer work. Early in May I set out to hitch-hike to the East coast, and by the tenth of May had a job as a janitor at a Jesuit high school. The high school had a boy's residence attached to it and one of the boys was from Beauharnois, a town on the south side of the St. Lawrence River, where the boy's father worked at a large foundry, and through the father I was able to get a job interview.

The foundry shredded old car bodies and melted the steel in giant open-hearth furnaces, then mixed the liquid with other types of metal and finally produced a number of brittle products that looked like aluminum and were used by steel makers to temper the steel at rolling mills. On the application form at the foundry there was a line that asked for a description of my last job, so I explained how I swept floors, emptied waste baskets and cleaned toilets. They offered me a similar job, but at much better wages, and by the end of May my foundry work had begun. When the men working in the foundry came off their shift, or arrived to get ready to go to work, they entered a building that held lockers, showers, sinks and toilet stalls. It was my job to keep the place clean and well supplied with towels, soap and toilet paper. Not a tough job and the men were very entertaining in the colourful dialect they spoke, but I only worked about two hours every shift, and in between shift-changes had to keep the building locked and secured and guarded, from the inside. I read a lot of books that first month.

When someone started at the foundry he or she received a round metal tag with a starting-date number printed on it, and when a new job was posted on the central bulletin board a worker could hang his tag on the board, and the senior number got the job. One job called 'Yard Work' had been posted for several days with no tags appearing underneath the marker and since the shower building was beginning to become increasingly boring I hung my own tag. Next day I found out why no one else had applied: it was the hardest job in the whole foundry. Eight hours a day piling thirty pound slabs of metal into stacks twenty feet long, four feet wide and five feet tall. The metal was the daily surplus product of the foundry; it had been broken into large pieces on the floor and dumped in the yard by front end loaders, and since different types of metal were produced each type had to be placed in a separate pile. Knowing the density of each sort of product allowed the front office to estimate fairly accurately how much of a certain metal it had in reserve. There were two of us on the Yard Work detail and it would take us a full day of hard work to stack the metal that had been dumped in the yard the night before. When it was to be shipped out, the front end loaders and the trucks would make our lovely pile disappear in a couple of hours.

The work at first was impossibly difficult, with every muscle in my body groaning in disbelief, and when I went home to the boarding house at the end of the shift I was usually too tired to do anything but fall into bed and sleep until the next morning. Luckily, the foundry had an excellent cafe and at lunch time I put away enough food to feed a small army. Gradually my strength built up and the pain stopped, but for the month or so that I was on Yard Work I don't recall ever eating supper at the boarding house. To make up for the missed suppers, the lady who ran the establishment would pack me a large lunch and I would eat it for breakfast on the job. It was a job that quickly robbed the muscles of their energy, as it does in weight-lifting, so every fifteen minutes of work was followed by a five minute rest period and during that time we drank coffee, ate sandwiches and chewed on chocolate bars. Actually, we ate so continuously, supper really wasn't necessary.

In late July a position came open in the foundry itself, shovelling loose coal, or ground-up metal or wood shaving, into large hoppers that sent each type of material up separate conveyor belts to the top floor where the open hearth furnaces roared. The first day on the job the material being shovelled was wood shavings and by mistake I had been given a spade ('beche' in French), which was usually used when working on the piles of shredded metal, so I asked one of the men on the floor how I could get a large mouth shovel, but I couldn't remember the French word for 'shovel'.

"Quel est le mot pour"(What is the word for) and gestured to show the spade was too narrow.

"Ah", he replied, and then in English said, "The word is mergelemerde." and pointed to the foreman.

"He doesn't speak English, so say to him: 'Monsieur, mergelmerde' and show him the spade and he'll understand what you need."

I approached the foreman and held out the spade and repeated the new compound word. When he heard the request he looked shocked for a moment and then smiling asked, in perfect English, "Did that man over there, who is laughing so hard, tell you to say that to me?" Then he handed me the shovel I needed and said: "The French word is 'pelle'. Don't forget it."

It was the only time I ever confused the elisioned word 'mergele' (eat) and 'merde' (poop) for 'pelle'.

Jacques was the foreman for the whole floor of the foundry and everyone except the tappers and the crane operator answered to him. He was the strongest man I ever met and perhaps that was one of the reasons he held the job. His arms were as big around as my thighs and he was strong enough to compete in international arm wrestling events. The men said he had never been beaten. None of the men who worked on the packing floor breaking up the casts with sixteen pound sledge hammers ever challenged him to an arm wrestle, yet these men were very strong and could easily bend my arms over when I used both arms against their single one. He was eminently respected by the men who felt that he was a man's man with the ability to make good decisions that didn't favour any particular person or group. He was a tall man with a barrel chest and a slow walking gait; the only time I ever saw him run was when a pot of liquid metal slipped and splashed some of its contents on the floor. Then he moved with remarkable speed to get all the men to safety.

Anyone could talk to him as long as it had to do with the running of the foundry for he knew every job and had worked on all of them at one time or another, since he had first come to the foundry when he was sixteen years of age. Sometimes he questioned me about my goal, saying that he had never before met a candidate for the priesthood who worked in the labour field. He thought it was a good idea and that all future priests should be trained in that manner.

"Our priests live in another world", he said one day. "They don't understand the pressures of ordinary life. When you go to confession they offer you advice that is impractical except for monks. They need to get down and dirty like you're doing, then maybe they'd be some real help to us."

He must have been impressed with my attitude for on the last day of work that summer the employment manager called me into his office and said that the foreman had recommended that my employment number remain active until I returned the next summer.

Once back at school we found that first year theology was somewhat different than the undergraduate studies had been. We began an introduction to Canon Law (the Catholic rules for the Church), as well as Church History, Ascetics, Sacred Scripture and the theological works of St. Thomas Aquinas and other Church Fathers. The year was mainly one of foundations in all these subjects for our teachers wanted us to avoid the easier path of memorizing a set of dogmas to parrot back upon request. We struggled to understand these subjects, as we had done in philosophy, but in theology the basis of our understanding was not just reasonable analysis, but also included *revelation*, the delivered word of God to mankind, and the insights of others who had fallen in love with Christ, as St. Francis of Assisi had done. It was an opportunity to examine whether the heart or the mind was the final judge in reaching truth, and was much like the argument on whether the electron was a particle or a force. We listened to all the arguments of the great debates on these intuition-versus-reason questions, and came away undecided, with both sides winning.

The university Convocation ceremonies occurred that fall and mother was there to see me get my Degree and told me how proud she was of my accomplishment, which compared to hers was of little consequence. Mother was suffering from cancer that kept flaring up and subsiding and leaving that active woman with little energy. We had known of the cancer and her treatments for some time and all of us had tried to persuade her not to make the trip for the graduation ceremonies, but making a suggestion to a dedicated Scot was like whistling in the wind. She had decided to come and nothing was going to stand in her way. Her visit was heart-warming for there always had been a strong, loving bond between us and we enjoyed our time together that special day. It was a lovely, warm afternoon and the day was one of both sunshine and surprises: she told me that she had overheard my father bragging to a friend that his son was studying theology and going to be a priest. What a change time and prayer can bring! She was glowing, not only with my settled and successful ways, but with the thought of going on to see her new grandson who had been born the previous April. Before she left she said she was glad to have lived and been able to leave a legacy behind. I've always been grateful that her *grandson* turned out so well.

That fall we began a work-program that was to last the whole year. Attached to the building was a long, covered stone cloister that ran out from a rear door on the main floor in a wide three-sided square until it rejoined the building near the front hall. It was gothic in style, with high windows arched at the top and open to the elements, and had no apparent use except as a prayer walk when it was raining. The seminary had received a gift from a wealthy parishioner and the local Bishop had decided to have the walkway closed in and turned into a new library, which was badly needed. But that meant that the under surface of the cloister had to be excavated of three feet of dirt, a floor had to be poured and the whole structure had to be insulated and wired before any work could be commenced on the cloister above. Our task was to shovel the soil out by hand, throw it into a series of wheelbarrows, wheel them out a single door in the base of the cloister and across the back field into the gully at the back of the property. The surveyors and architects came in first, then T. F and Abel jury-rigged a series of naked sixty-watt light bulbs from the ceiling and work began. The cloister door was barely wide enough for the wheelbarrow to pass through, so two of the boys had to stand outside to pull the barrow through while the one pushing it strained at the handles, and as the work progressed the floor continued to drop so that planks and ropes had to be used to bring the wheelbarrow up to the doorway.

It was heavy, dark work and on hot days it was very much like the foundry I'd been in that summer, yet with good hearts and young muscles the work was launched and proceeded at a slow but regular pace. For about two weeks. Then blistered hands and bent backs led to a small revolt, and the Administration was forced to limit the afternoon digging to three days a week on a rotating schedule so that no seminarian missed recreation time too often. When the snows of December hinted at hockey season, the deacon class put up the boards and flooded the back field and ended the bursar's dream of a new library by springtime. None of us missed the digging but spring came early that year and the Bursar bought a shipment of rubber boots in a variety of sizes and had us back on the job in early March. We tore up the back field with our boots and barrows and every worker usually managed to slip down into the mud at least once during a shift, much to the consternation of the hard-working Sisters who had to wash our clotted clothes. But we succeeded and by the middle of April the digging job was over and more than fifty tons of earth had been removed at no cost to the seminary. A fine new library now stands where an empty, wind-blown cloister had once moaned in the night.

Funny and unusual things were always happening, as would be expected among such a large number of young men with tons of energy to burn. One day we found a fox's den in the gully and after we had widened the entrance to the den a young seminarian from the country, nicknamed 'Nature-boy', climbed in head-first wearing leather gloves and brought out two small kits, while the mother fox watched anxiously from a safe distance among the trees. The kits were about two months old with razor sharp teeth that ripped our jackets as we carried them up to the fenced tennis courts behind the seminary. Those among us who really loved animals hoped that we would be able to semi-tame the pups to replace the dogs we had left at home, and for a week we sneaked out all kinds of titbits from our meals for them, but the pups refused to eat and tried every means at their disposal to escape from the enclosure.

From my darkened window at night I could see the mother fox greeting her brood and licking them through the wire mesh that kept them apart, but during the week the pups had yowled so continuously that we finally left the tennis gate slightly ajar one night and they were gone the next morning. Later, Nature Boy also showed us a game called 'squirrel-twirling'. He would chase a squirrel up a tree into its nest, then insert a short stick and turn it rapidly with his hands. The stick wound itself around the squirrels tail and with one quick jerk the squirrel was pulled out of the nest and into his gloved hands. Sometimes he wasn't as fast as the squirrel and ended up with bloody fingers, yet on all the occasions I witnessed he never let the squirrel go before he had examined it to his satisfaction. They grow them tough in the country.

Sometimes the things that happened were sad. I had been appointed infirmarian that year and shared the job with another student. We took turns sitting in the "sick room' every night from seven until nine listening to the physical complaints, some real and many imaginary, that must exist among any enclosed group. We were the liaison persons between the Rector, the local doctor and the seminarians, and we dispensed aspirin, cough medicine, band-aids and sympathy, but sometimes more serious problems presented themselves. On recreation one day, two classmates asked me if I talked to Ted recently, another boy who had entered the seminary the same year as me. I hadn't, but promised to do so that evening. Ted was a bright student and the best ping-pong player in the school and had always stood at the top of the class, or near it, through all three previous years we had been together. But now he was drifting in and out of reality, talking about his failures and his dreams and weeping at the thought of some impending doom. When the Rector was informed he sent Ted and me down to the hospital by taxi and we were interviewed together by a resident psychiatrist, only he kept Ted and sent me back by taxi, shaken by my first encounter with a person standing on the line between neurosis and psychosis.

Ted came up to see us one day the following year, to thank us for hauling him back from the precipice. He was fine, had a good job, was dating a good Catholic girl, and involved as a layperson in his local church. He said that the year before he'd had enough of seminary life but hadn't know how to end it, especially since there was so much to continue to learn in theology and his overtaxed brain had finally rejected his attempt to memorize everything. He had missed the thing that most of us had learned early in the game: that it's best to forget most of yesterday's lessons as soon as possible in order to leave room for the ones being taught today. Just keep good notes so that when you need the information you'll know where to find it. As Christ had said on the Mount, "There's only enough grace for one day at a time. Don't carry yesterday's problems with you into today'. Of course this is a paraphrased version, but anyone wanting the real words can find them in the fifth chapter of St. Matthew's Gospel. It's worth reading.

On a Sunday morning in June a small card had been shoved under my door by the "Holy Ghost' while we were in chapel. The card read 'Ad Tonsuram', which meant that I'd made it to the first level of Holy Orders without being kicked out of the program, or having left of my own volition. We all hoped that everyone in the class would receive the acceptance card, for each one of us freely had previously petitioned the Rector to be considered for the Order. This was a voluntary petition and was made before each one of the seven Orders was received, right up to ordination itself. In a ceremony a few days later all the members of our class knelt before the altar and the Rector clipped a small round circle of hair off the back of each head. We were tonsured, an ancient ceremony to indicate that the person has chosen to become a cleric in the service of God and his fellow man. As time passed there was to be a series of six more small cards from the "Holy Ghost" all delivered on a Sunday morning while we were absent from our rooms, and every spring we worried in case the card would not be there. For some it wasn't, for a variety of reasons. The student's grades might have been too low, in which case the student could repeat the year if he so desired, or the administration might have thought that the feminine strain that is in all men might have been too pronounced in a particular candidate and he was being asked to choose another vocation. Sometimes the seminarian had exhibited some strange behaviour that would suggest that the solitary life of a diocesan priest might be beyond the person's endurance. One case of that showed up with Herbert.

As infirmarian I'd heard talk of Herbert's unusual habit of reviewing loudly in his sleep every class he'd had that day, but I hadn't paid much attention to the rumours, until one night his next door neighbour hauled me out of bed to listen to Herbert's performance. It was loud and quite clear: he was talking on an imaginary phone to his mother and recounting every word that one professor had taught that day. This wasn't a case of summary, but of total recall, for I had sat in the same class that day with him and heard those exact words from the mouth of the teacher! I opened his door quietly to see if he was reading from his notes, but he was fast asleep and talking in a dialogue of "He said', 'I said', 'John said', in perfect pace with the lesson itself. Sometimes he would pause as if listening to the other side of the telephone conversation, then clarify the imaginary misunderstanding of that ghostly partner. Finally, after a half hour of this surprising display of memory, he began to mumble and his dream ended and silence filled the area. His neighbour wanted to tell the Rector, or at least get moved to another room where he could get some sleep at night, but I asked him to wait until I'd had a chance to talk with Herbert privately. Next day Herbert denied any night talks and became angry when I questioned him further, saying that I had no right to pry into his personal life, so I told his neighbour to ask for another room and to tell the Rector why, if he asked. That Easter Herbert's card was not slid under his door.

Summer started later that year, for the course in theology lasted an extra month since it was not a part of the university calendar, and there was another retreat right after final exams. But summer did finally arrive and the work at the foundry was waiting for me. Because my tag had been kept on the active list I was given a job relieving the firemen on the second floor who stoked the scorching fire pits, but first I was issued special clothes. The jacket and pants were made of thick woollen pea-coat material, the gloves had some sort of asbestos covering, the helmet had a swing-up metal screen attached to it and the boots had an extra sole cut from old tractor tires, and all this because the area we stood in while working was hot enough to boil a kettle if left for ten minutes. Each of the three fire-pits had a tall carbon shaft, about three feet in diameter, sticking up out of the centre of the fire, and through the shaft a deadly surge of electricity was fed down into the melting zone. Every twenty minutes we would bank the fires with metal shaving, wood chips, coal and whatever catalyst they required that day, and then poke the mixture down around the electrified shaft using a long steel poker that was set on a swivel at the edge of the pit. To remain there every man had a high powered fan, nearly four feet across, right at his back to keep the intense heat from searing his clothes. It wasn't a particularly hard job but it was as hot as the fires of hell and twenty minutes there were all anyone could stand at one time, then you collapsed on a small balcony that jutted out above the parking lot, and prayed for a cool breeze for the next fifteen minutes.

All the firemen took salt pills to replace the salt lost in the sweat that ran in rivers down every part of the body and sizzled on the floor, but you had to get used to the pills, for the first time I took them I spent all the fifteen minute breaks running to the washroom. And you had to be careful of the wire mesh that was pulled down in front of the face when you were stoking the fire. Most of us had little checkered marks on our fingers from taking off our gloves before we swung the black-hot mesh away from the face. The fuels and electrified shaft melted the metal shavings and they dripped down into a giant pot below, and when the pot was full the tappers used long ark-welding tools to cut a hole in the bottom of the pot and drained the fiery liquid metal into a special vessel controlled by an overhead crane. The crane operator then lifted the liquid metal away from the furnace and moved it across the floor to a hot, sand and carbon-coated iron moulding box. He then poured it slowly into the box, where it was allowed to cool before being broken into large chunks, packed in wooden barrels and shipped to the rolling mills.

When the liquid metal was being moved to the moulding box by the overhead crane, a bell rang continuously, warning the workers of the danger of a liquid spill which could mean death to anyone in its path. The moulding boxes were prepared to receive the liquid metal by first being heated with various fuels and then coated with a thick spray of carbon paste. During the previous winter a crane operator had mistakenly chosen a *cold* box, which stood beside the prepared one, and when he poured the metal it immediately burned its way through the iron box and touched the cold foundry floor. The result was a shower of molten dollops that arced upwards in random fashion and burned a hole in whatever they touched on the way down. Unfortunately one dollop hit the back of a fleeing worker and ended his life. The job was hot, dirty and dangerous but the pay and the working conditions were good and the men seldom complained.

In the first summer at Beauhamois the Cure, or Pastor, of the large church had been very cool toward me, although the two assistant priests were quite friendly. Just before I left I had gone to get the Cure to sign my summer certification form, required by the seminary to indicate that I was still a worthy candidate for the priesthood. He suddenly changed his attitude when he realized that I was Irish ('Irlandais') and not English ('Anglais'), since he had no use for the English who, he said, had used deceit to capture the citadel at Quebec City in the eighteenth century, and then kept the real Canadiens, the Quebecois, in a state of semi-slavery up to the present time. He admired the Irish Free-State parliament who had shown their contempt for the English by remaining neutral during the Second World War. He then took me into the dining room and gave me a big glass of wine and wanted to know all about the

Rule in my seminary, and seemed satisfied that it was a sufficient Rule to train *English*-speaking priests. Then he told me that the next year when I returned I would stay at the parish house rent free for the whole summer, nor would he hear of any objections, saying he would write to my Bishop and tell him that such an arrangement had to be accepted. He told me to bring a soutane and collar with me to wear when I wasn't working at the foundry. So I did the next summer, even though I just wanted to be one of the ordinary foundry workers who had a little more lively faith than most of the others.

The attitude of the people toward their priests was much more formal than I'd ever seen elsewhere. In the 1950's the Quebec people saw the Church as representing their resistance to the English Federal Government, the largely Protestant influence throughout the country and the use of the English language in all federal or international business matters. They smarted under the knowledge that Catholic schools were not funded by the common purse, except in Quebec, where the much less numerous non-Catholic schools were equally government supported. Even in those early days they believed that Quebec belonged entirely to the French, and longed for the day when they would be an independent country. In 1967 when President De Gaulle of France had spoken in Quebec he had closed his speech with the words: "Vive le libre Quebec!" (Long live a free Quebec!), and all the people had cheered; they have repeated the slogan to the present time. Thus, the priests were not seen as common people but as some sort of elite nobility, the rightful leaders of New France, and when met on the streets the habit was to touch your hat in deferential greeting.

On June the twenty-fourth, the Feast of St. Jean Baptiste the Patron Saint of Quebec, the Cure asked me if I wanted to attend the parade with him that day and I accepted. We didn't, however, *watch* the parade, we *were* the parade, or at least we led it. We sat in a chauffeured white Cadillac convertible, followed by parish organizations with large banners and a variety of saintly statues carried by strong, young men, and the Cure waived to the people who cheered as we passed. He represented their struggle for freedom and self-rule and as such, was expected to bear a hostile attitude toward the English. He was in the habit at suppertime to end some tirade against a wrong done to the French by the English with the explicative phrase 'Ah, les jaunes d'Ontario!' and I kept wondering why he was referring to the 'young' (jeunes) people of Ontario. Marcel, my seminary friend who was now a sub deacon, visited us one day and was warmly welcomed by Monsieur le Cure, since Marcel was almost now a true Quebecois, for his family was on the point of moving to Quebec. After supper I privately asked Marcel why the pastor kept referring to the 'young people of Ontario' and he corrected my poor French. The word was 'jaune' (yellow), not 'jeune' (young), although he added, he might be using the slang term 'joual' which meant 'stupid' or 'bourgeois', since he himself never used the term and wasn't sure of its pronunciation. Whatever the meaning, there was no doubt that our Pastor represented the most radical viewpoint of the French toward the English.

At the end of July I was transferred to the packing department and given a sixteen-pound sledge hammer and shown how to break the cold castes which the overhead crane had removed from the mould. When the castes were ready the crane moved them to a set of railroad tracks welded closely together where we attacked them to break them into chunks and put the pieces in wooden barrels. Each barrel was packed with seven hundred and sixty pounds of metal and before being shipped out the barrels were loaded onto a large scale to verify their weight. There were a set number of barrels that each man had to load each shift, and if you knew how to break the metal into the right sized chunks, the job was not difficult. The first thing the men taught me was to let the hammer, not my strength, do the breaking of the casts. The trick was to hit the cast in the exact same place with three or four blows and the metal would part, and then with the large remaining slabs to work from the edge and break off the size of chunks that would just fit in the barrel. If the chunk was too big it had to be tugged out of the barrel and broken again, and if it was too small it took forever to reach the weight needed.

The men were of every size and weight and all were fairly young, and each of them had arms of steel and appetites of horses. All of them were proud of their post in the foundry and not one of them would have traded his job for any other job on the floor. There was camaraderie among them and they joked with one another and baited each other mercilessly, yet each one would have backed any other in a fight. Their language was a colourful French slang, or patois, and sprinkled with swear words taken from their faith; words such as: 'colin' (chalice), 'sacre bleu' (Holy Colour), or 'tabernac' (tabernacle), for as I found out later in psychology, we tend to swear by the thing that is most important to us, which doesn't say much for the current use of the Big F that sprinkles our current English language. The men often poked fun at my misuse of French words and kept telling me that the only way I could possibly become proficient was to get a French girlfriend, for they said that the language of love was the basis of the French tongue. They offered to help with some of their former girlfriends and doubled over in laughter when I turned down their offers.

On the last day of the job I asked Jacques for an extra shift to round out the summer. At first he said it wouldn't be fair to the other men, who were getting one of the highest hourly rate in the foundry and always wanted more time, but toward the end of the shift he came and said he could give me half a shift, but to keep the others quiet I had to pack as many barrels as would be done on a regular shift. Breaking and packing was an art and by this time I had learned it, but I had no idea whether the same number of barrels *could* be packed in half a shift, and that was what made the challenge interesting. None of the others wanted the challenge but every one of them said he could do it easily in *three* hours and that there would even be time for a leisurely lunch break, and probably with those arms each one could have completed the task in that time. But even though I was in good shape there was no way that I could match their output, for on a regular day they spent half the time talking or eating and still managed to reach their daily quota, and I was lucky to take a five minute rest between barrels. All the men went home that night and there was no night shift assigned, but they left eight large castes and twenty empty barrels and asked me to join them for a 'chopin' (quart of beer) when, and if, I finished. I finished, but it almost finished me; even the yard work had never tired me out that much and when it was done all I wanted to do was go back to the rectory and fall into bed, and never get up again.

The Cure and his assistants had been very kind during the summer and I was much indebted to them, but it was time to end my experiment in learning French. Just before leaving I went into a drug store and ordered everything I needed, in French, and even spoke to the sales girl in French, and when it was all done she said, in excellent English, "Will there be anything else?" But it's better to have tried and failed than never to have tried at all.

I put away my French/English dictionary and hitch-hiked to Cap-de-la-Madeleine, a well known shrine East of Quebec City, and there before the altar in the little church offered up my failure to Our Lady; I think she understood, for certainly my bishop never did. Then a train took me back to the seminary where I won the junior shot put competition (those under 175 pounds), so the summer wasn't wasted after all.

In Second Year Theology the studies were mainly on two topics; Scripture and Morals and they were covered in great detail. In First Year Scripture we had studied the Torah, or Pentateuch as it is called in Christian bibles, which covers the first five books of the Bible and which deal with the ancient history of the Hebrew Faith from the beginning of Creation to the entrance of the Chosen People into Canaan, the Holy Land. In Second Year the course covered the rest of the Old Testament, which we had been assigned to read on our own during the previous year so that we would have a general framework on which to examine this marvellous work that had taken over a thousand years to write. Our concentration was mainly on the Kings, such as David, and the Prophets, such as Samuel, but we actually covered in class or on assignment *all* forty-one of the sacred books, Joshua to Macabees II, using *A Catholic Commentary on Sacred Scripture*, published by Nelson, and the largest resource book I had ever used.

The course in Scripture dealt with such topics as the history of the Bible itself, what constituted an *official* text (called a Canon), the languages used in various texts, inspiration, higher criticism, the physical geography and history of Israel, interpretation, archaeological findings, and the great works of non-Catholic specialists. Of course, since the Church had actually put together the first copies of the whole bible around 400 A.D. we learned how the Church had used its living memory, called Tradition, to interpret and understand the sacred writers. Somewhere in second year the writings started to come alive; they were no longer just words of revelation, but a living faith grounded in the lives of those who had produced them and to whom we now began to relate. Four years previously I had entered the seminary under self-imposed duress, for I had felt with St. Paul that it would be '...a terrible thing to fall into the hands of the Living God' if I hadn't attempted the vocation He had indicated. Now I had begun to fall in love with God. It is a strange sounding idea, especially to those who have never experienced it, since it *is* experiential, as is any love and to try to explain it to others boggles the mind.

The course in Moral Theology was on 'Justice', for as we prepared to act as confessors, we had to be able to recognize those cases in which restitution would be demanded for serious breaches of justice, both toward God and toward our fellow pilgrims. Restitution is to give back to the victim what has been unjustly taken from that person, and it could be anything from serious theft to murder among humans, or blasphemy or neglect of God. It was a difficult course, very much like law in its specifics since it involved not only the act, or neglect of the act, but also the knowledge and the intention of the perpetrator. Without full knowledge and full consent the act could not be classed as serious matter for Confession, but it involved the question whether the perpetrator *should* have had the knowledge, as in the case of a drunk driver who killed some other person.

The professor was a stocky man, with a lawyer's mind, who was quite capable of drawing any student into an agreement on some question and then demonstrating how absurd the position was by proving just the opposite. Nor did it matter which side of a question the student took, for we were no match for his clever debate. We learned not only about moral justice but humility as well and during the two years that we had him as the instructor in Morals the only time we ever saw him beaten was one afternoon when he was definitely not up to his usual form. The question on the floor was one involving a nun's confession and he had taken that part for himself, while Tiny, the student director of Plays, was playing the part of the confessor hearing the sister's confession. The 'sister' grew so agitated at the confessor's questions that 'she' demanded a straight answer!

Tiny replied: "Now, now, Sister, we won't get anywhere with impatience." and in the shocked silence that followed the retort, 'Sister' gathered up 'her' books and left the class, followed by muted cheers.

Every other Thursday the theology students were assembled in the lecture hall for a session of 'Polyglot', a word that still strikes fear into the hearts of the men who went through it. All the professors would sit on the stage and the Rector would draw a student's name from a bowl; the student would then take the 'hot seat' on the stage and would draw from another bowl the name of a particular subject. For fifteen minutes that subject's teacher would then ask the student any series of questions on the material that had been covered since the beginning of the term. We all hoped to choose Sacred Scripture because the Rector himself would be the questioner and would usually answer half the question if given the chance, but we feared that our choice would be Moral Theology with the resulting large dose of confusion and embarrassment. Students who did poorly on understanding the question and framing an answer would be under some additional scrutiny in their regular classes to see if the student had sufficient knowledge to deal with theological and human questions when ordained.

Such was the case of my friend, Jonathan, who was immensely talented in art and music, and played the organ at all official functions in the chapel. Jonathan had been the person who answered the front door of the seminary on the night I first arrived, and had called me a "ninny" for standing in the rain, and we had become good friends over the years. He had a great sense of humour and often acted the part of the class clown, but under that facade he was unsure of himself and looked for acceptance from the others. He had a good memory and could recite back what he had learned as long as it didn't require any explanation and analysis, for when it did he frequently went blank and would give strange answers that were totally off topic. His poor showing at Polyglot was probably the reason the 'Holy Ghost' did not slip the Minor Orders card under his door on the next appointment morning. Unlike many of the others, Jonathan did not want to leave the seminary where he had found a place of acceptance and friendship, and where his talents in the fields of the arts were recognized. He was sad to go and we were all sad to see him go, but he and I went on being friends even after he had become a successful art coordinator with a local board of education.

Hockey came and went; the library building was under construction, and the diocese was beginning to build a Catholic college on the far edge of the campus, taking away our regular football field. It was to be a co-ed residential college affiliated with the university and due to open the following September; small at first, it gradually grew until it replaced the seminary in number of students attending. Meanwhile the year was drawing to a close, and we were getting ready for Minor Orders, those steps that were preparatory to ordination in the Catholic priesthood. These Orders were four in number, two to be given in June at the end of the school year, and two the following September as we prepared for the second last year of the seven year training. The first two are called 'Ostarii' (doorkeeper) and 'Lectoris' (reader) and the two in the fall were 'Exorcistae' (exorcist) and 'Acolyte' (server), and of all the Orders the only one I've ever been questioned about is the Order of Exorcist. Can a priest really cast out devils from a person or place? Well, historically speaking, Christ certainly did many times according to the Apostles, and if the people who have seen the movie *The Exorcist* were asked they might be willing to say that it was possible.

Whether the Devil was a reality was one of the first questions I had asked Father McWalter during the days of my instruction in the Catholic faith. It was a scary thought and one we don't think of very often, but then, so is death, and it is a reality, so maybe they go hand in glove. Father Bill had led a wild life before becoming a Catholic, and then had studied and taught within the Jesuit community for fourteen years before he was ordained a priest. On the night before his ordination, while going over the ceremonies for the next day, he was suddenly startled by a human voice.

"Bill, who are you trying to kid! You can never be a priest; look at what you've already done in your life."

Then Bill said, "It was like watching a film of your sins. Every act of drunkenness, conceit, lies, sex and selfishness I'd ever done was there before my eyes! I fled from the room and in panic went to see the spiritual director, an old Jesuit living in the house. When he heard my story he didn't seem surprised and said that he'd often heard of it happening.

"Go back to your room," he said. "Sprinkle some holy water around and tell the Devil to go back to hell."

Bill said that the hardest thing he ever had to do was to climb back up the stairs and enter his room. There was nothing out of the ordinary there, when he got up the courage to enter, but Bill said he hardly slept for the rest of the night.

The diocese had a summer camp for children, just outside the city, and when the director of the program found out that I'd been a lifeguard and taught swimming for several years, he visited me at the seminary one day toward the end of the year and offered me the job of Water Front Director. I'd wanted to return to the foundry in Quebec, but the thought of teaching swimming again made the offer attractive and when the bursar said that the summer work at the camp would cover most of my seminary expenses, I accepted the position. Another plus was that one of my classmates, Vince, had been a camp counsellor there the previous summer and had decided to go back again. He spoke highly of the kids and the rest of the staff, and his stories of the camp revived old memories of those magical moments in my little town on the shores of Lake Superior.

The camp was under the care of a married couple who taught high school physical education classes during the year and ran the camp each summer. Lew and Barbara were a fun loving couple who worked at least twenty hours every day to make sure that the camp was properly organized and that every child had the time of his or her life during the two or three weeks they spent there. There were nature walks, art classes, archery, boxing, campfires, canoe trips, swimming and when it rained, story telling in the converted wartime chapel that they had bought at auction. Unlike my previous waterfront duties there were no formal classes in swimming, but rather a period, or sometimes two, each day in which the children went down to the pool to jump around in the water and attack each other in friendly play. The pool was actually a sectioned off part of a river where it widened out enough to form a small lake, and when Vince and I took the children down to swim, it was to act as lifeguards to fifty children between the ages of six and ten, and although it was great fun for everyone, it was the most exhausting part of our day.

The antics of these concentrated atoms of humanity produced stories that are still told around other campfires at other camps. Every one of those children, and especially the boys, tried their best to run off in all directions as soon as the camp counsellor's back was turned, not to hide or cause concern but simply to examine everything that swam or flew or walked or ran or crawled anywhere on the camp property. They had an insatiable appetite for frogs and spiders and mice and turtles and cardinals and minnows and squirrels and especially, for snakes. When they were gathered around something on the ground we knew they had found a new piece of life, such as a fire salamander or a dock spider or a centipede, and when we heard them thumping around in their cabins after 'taps' we knew that somehow their flashlights had discovered a bat or a small lost bird or, best of all, a garter snake.

In the afternoon, right after swim time, the boys got ready to box and the girls got ready to cheer. We used sixteen ounce gloves which were like pillows on their small fists, and the two rounds in each match lasted only one minute each, with an additional three minutes in between the rounds. They fought by cabin and by size so that each cabin would have some boys in a contest with the other cabins. There were no real winners since we always declared each fight a draw, yet they never seemed to catch on that all fights were rigged, except in one special case. Two of our smallest contestants were swinging at each other when one actually popped the other in the nose and caused a small nosebleed. The victim turned his back on his opponent and seemed to be on the point of taking off his gloves and quitting, when suddenly he swung around in a 180 degree arc and connected with the other boxer, who by this time had let his hands fall to his sides. This type of punch is outlawed in both amateur and professional boxing, and we suddenly knew why. The arced punch knocked the other tiny boxer out cold and ended our boxing matches for the rest of the week. Barbara, as only a woman can do, accused Vince and I of teaching small children how to be violent toward another person, and added that if she had her way, boxing would not only be outlawed in our camp but throughout the entire world.

But the most memorable event that occurred that summer had nothing to do with boxing and everything to do with snakes. Laurie, the camp nurse was a young woman on her first assignment, and so overly professional that every tiny cut got maximum attention and excessive motherly care. Her infirmary cabin was divided into one small bedroom for her and another larger room with two beds for any camper who might fall ill, and the two beds were usually filled with homesick kids who had already learned the art of adult manipulation. One evening two of the boys showed me their new pet garter snake and wondered excitedly about what would happen if they placed the snake in the nurse's cot. Although no permission was actually given for this terrible deed, I suppose that my discouragement of the idea *could* have been more emphatic. Later, when the cabins were finally all quiet and Vince and I were playing cards with Lew and Barbara in the old farmhouse a dreadful scream tore the fabric of the night, and within seconds Laurie appeared in the hall crying and carrying a large, five-celled flashlight. Vince made the mistake of smiling and asking her what was the matter, and got nailed with the flashlight so hard it never worked again.

She sobbed all night on the couch in the living room and called her father at first light to come and end her camp assignment and then went out, suitcase in hand, to sit at the roadside. Barbara, always the perceptive one, said to me with that unfailing intuition against which there is no answer, "Well, you caused it; now you solve it."

The cabin responsible for the event had been rocking with giggles all night, but when they learned that their nurse was leaving they were suddenly contrite. It wasn't difficult to get them to enlist *all* the children in the camp to do an early morning wild flower hunt, and parade, with heads downcast, up to Laurie in single file and present a small fistful of flowers and an apology. The little girls were the clincher, for they cried great drops of tears and said they had nothing to do with the snake, and wouldn't she please stay because they loved her so much. Luckily, her father was late in arriving and when he did show up we treated him to breakfast and tried to explain what had happened. He really didn't think it was a good idea to put snakes in a person's bed. Still, by the time he had finished his breakfast Laurie was back nursing her sick children in the infirmary, but only after Vince and I had done a thorough job of making sure there were no snakes present.

Too soon summer was over and the regulated life once again became our normal routine. Our class, or at least what was left of it, for by this time we were down to less than half our starting number, received the last two Minor Orders during the retreat and began to learn the art of preaching. We wrote sermons rather than gave them, following a basic format beginning with a scriptural text and a 'hook' (something to get the audience's attention) followed by three points in the main body of the work and ending with a summary that encouraged faith and discouraged sin. In class we analysed the good and bad points of delivery and took turns presenting the opening portion of a sermon, and in spare moments went into an empty classroom with one of our friends and attempted a ten-minute 'message'. Each deacon gave at least one Sunday sermon through the year, and some were good and others were dreadful. One deacon, who published the weekly activity sheet on an old printing machine, went blank after the scripture text and stood mute before the assembled school for a few minutes, then tried again with no more luck. After the third repetition of the scripture reading he said:

"It really is a very good sermon. I'll run off a copy on the print machine and post it in the rec hall," and sat down. His eventual parishioners probably loved his short sermons and his sense of humour.

Our attention in Scripture now went to the historical writings of the Apostles and St. Paul and was to remain there for the next two years. The attempt was to see Jesus as an historical person who had taught an 'impossible' doctrine and backed it up with irrefutable signs, which demonstrated that what he taught must be God's own truth. In class the New Testament was studied in Latin in order to capture the nuances of each word penned by the early writers, but our assignments included the study of some texts in Greek and some in Hebrew, as well as those in English and French. We became familiar with the evidence on how and where each part had been written and what the individual viewpoint of each writer likely had been, and we committed to memory many of the quotations attributed to Christ himself. We debated over the meaning of the more obscure passages, and especially over what St. John had intended to communicate in the final revelations of the Apocalypse, and we learned how foolish it would be to attempt to attach any type of chronological order in human years to those final prophecies of John. And we realized that when all the other subjects we had studied in the seven years of training were beginning to dim in old minds, the clarity of the Gospels would remain, for although these startling records were put together, and protected through the centuries by a living Church, the works themselves rang with a truth that could not be destroyed.

The final year as infirmarian was beginning, for George, the chief infirmarian, had moved on into his diaconate year and I now sat in his place in the dispensary, with a younger student assigned to take up the slack. Now it was mainly my turn to contact the seminary doctor on any cases that looked to be above the advanced first aid level and make sure they were transported to his downtown office for professional diagnosis. There was something ironic in this arrangement for the good doctor, who looked after the seminarians without charge, was a gynaecologist and his waiting room was constantly filled with pregnant women. Into this harem of new life the embarrassed future celibate was forced to find a seat and wait for his turn to be seen, and it was this unusual arrangement that probably kept the number of requests for a medical examination down to a minimum.

There was one seminarian, a bit of a hypochondriac, who insisted on seeing the doctor on a fairly regular basis and who evidently finally got on the good doctor's nerves, for his requests to be examined for such unusual diseases as leprosy and hysterical deafness suddenly stopped after one last visit. It took some time to pry the actual happening out of the student but as the rumours flew around he finally confessed that after the examination, while he was leaving through the waiting room packed with expectant mothers, the doctor had suddenly appeared at his office door and asked, "By the way, do you have haemorrhoids?"

The student had blushed and stammered out "No!" which caused the doctor to advance across the room with his hand outstretched.

"Good!" he said, "Let me shake hands with a perfect asshole." To my recollection that student never asked for another appointment and some others who were on the point of visiting the physician suddenly got better.

We found ourselves once again in the presence of the Morals professor, and if he had seemed harsh the year before, he was benevolent then by comparison. The subject was De Sexto, that is, all those actions dealing with the violation of the Sixth or Ninth Commandment; in short, sex. As with any other violation of the precepts handed down to Moses on Mount Sinai, the perpetrator was not guilty unless there was full knowledge of the seriousness of the act and full consent given, or at least had an attitude of 'I won't worry about it now.' It is a complex field and deals with what is probably the most *common* of all seriously wrong actions in which humans engage, for it covers the thoughts and plans of the potential seducer as well as the attempts to complete the act itself. Christ had been clear on this point saying that if a person lusted after another, that person had already committed the sexual sin in his or her heart. And so it was that we prepared to act as priest-confessors, capable of distinguishing between guilty feelings arising from fleeting thoughts, and those in which the person sought and got sexual satisfaction from their own imagination.

The litany of sexual sins is long, beginning with such things as impure thoughts, pornography, masturbation, fondling, oral sex, fornication, and proceeding on to single and double adultery, homosexuality, prostitution, rape, child molestation, bestiality, group sex, bondage, and other devious acts or combination of acts dreamed up by the children of Eve. We saw these wilful acts not as in an increasing order of depravation but as the failings of the human *spirit* when confronted by the sexual urging of the human *body*, but we noticed also that we all tend to start small, dallying with 'interesting' ideas that can be checked, and drifting off into larger violations that deaden the conscience and cause us to convince ourselves that there really is nothing wrong with anything we do sexually. The masturbator, the fornicator, the adulterer, the pornographer, the active homosexual, the rapist and the child molester all claim exemption for their acts, and if they have done these acts often enough, all are convinced they are the result of their own needs. We learned that confession was usually successful when the person was first beginning to struggle with some particular sexual temptation, and less successful when the person had been engaged in the action for some time. And we learned that the pornographer, the rapist and the child molester seldom, if ever, darkened the door of the confessional, as if their actions instinctively led them to deny the need for forgiveness.

Because the students themselves were human and young and therefore inclined to sexual speculation, a tight control was the rule in every Morals class, and God help the student who sniggered at some explanatory remark or answer made by the teacher.

"So, Mr Smith, you find this topic funny? Perhaps you would like to explain to the class the humour you see in this question so the rest of us can join in the mirth!"

Nor would it end there; the student would not be let off the hook so easily, but would stand confounded for several minutes while the instructor examined every facet of wonderment about why the student might have found this serious matter funny. Believe me, laughter was rare in those classes, and well it should have been, for one can imagine what damage would have been done to a penitent who confessed some sexual sin and received laughter as a response from the priest. It was serious stuff and we treated it as such; most people who came to confession were looking for some way of getting away from the sin and the resulting guilt and although they knew their own weakness they were attempting to get up and try again, and our job would be to convince them of God's forgiveness and encourage their continued efforts.

In the midst of these advanced studies on human behaviour came a trial. Over the past six years, through confession, prayer, counselling, athletics and cold showers the memories of my earlier life in the company of young and willing women had faded considerably, and the prospect of taking and keeping the vow of lifelong chastity seemed a likely possibility. Then my old college hockey buddy, Jimmy, phoned in the middle of the night and told the Rector that he had to speak to me on an urgent matter. The seminary staff knew that my mother was very ill, so the Rector woke me and led me to the phone thinking that it was news of her impending death. It took a few minutes for my sleepy mind to realize that a group of the old gang were at a party where the main guest was Mr. Booze and that the topic of conversation was whether any of us had bedded the same girlfriend in times gone by. The specific girl mentioned was one I had only dated casually, and only for a short time, but my denials only brought a round of laughter and rude remarks from the assembled friends. Yet while I talked to them I realized how much I had missed their company and the early bonding that had existed between us, and it was a joy to hear what each was doing and how they were getting on in life. After I hung up the phone there wasn't any sleep for the rest of the night.

The prospect of living a single life, in a city of old friends who were now all married, shook my 'other world' spirituality, and the realization that a final decision concerning a life of celibacy had to be made before the next Fall weighed heavily on my mind. Within a few months we were to receive the Sub

Diaconate and wear the white collar of a priest, and in the Fall the decision for the Diaconate bound the person to perpetual celibacy and the obligation to say the Divine Office, a long set of daily prayers, for the rest of the person's natural life. It was a giant step and it was one in which there was no pressure by any member of the seminary staff for the individual to continue; it had to be a freely made choice, made with full knowledge and full consent and without any outside pressure of any kind. And I, like most of my classmates, wasn't truly sure which way to go. It was a time for deep meditation and constant prayer, especially to Christ, whose life we were trying to emulate, and our favourite saints, in my case, Our Lady Mary, my guardian angel and St. Bernadette of Lourdes.

Over the next few months in conferences with my spiritual advisor the permanency of the priestly calling was examined and discussed, and his eventual suggestion was that I should speak with my bishop and see if I could leave for a year and then, if our doubts had faded, to come back for the final year and ordination. The bishop was far less doubtful for, he said, if during the past seven years the single life had stood the test of all those summers in various worldly jobs and all the rigours of seminary life, then my worries were academic, not practical, since the practical side had already been tested. It was what I wanted to hear and when spring came I had no difficulty in applying for the Sub Diaconate and beginning the daily recitation of the Divine Office. A couple of my classmates, after pondering the future as I had done, decided that their vocation was in the secular world, and left at the end of the school year. We had started out at twenty five and had gained a few along the way, but our number was now down to eight, and it was those eight who took the Sub Diaconate vow that spring.

My folks had moved down east three years earlier, for although the insurance company wanted my father to be the CEO he had refused partly due to mother's illness, and partly because at that time he didn't need any more stress in his life. Still, in order to have him near head office the company had divided up his western area and given him a large section near the company headquarters. My parents and sister had settled in well and Dad had purchased two small cabins on a northern lake, which my brother and he had begun to renovate and enlarge. Joan, my sister, who had graduated from university as a dietician, was working in a city hospital and had become interested in a young water-skier who spent his weekends partying near the new cottage property.

And so it was that summer, after spending a few weeks as a counsellor at camp I was free to join the whole family again, after seven years of separation, and enjoy the family days of summer in a magical setting that was to become so much a part of my future days.

Mother's cancer was by now getting the best of her after many years of treatment and remissions, but she kept up her sense of humour and found great pleasure in my brother's children, who spent most of the summer in the second cabin. She once said to me that if she could spend her last summer in any way she pleased it would be to continue on at the cottage with her children and grandchildren around her. It was a wish that was granted to her, for it was her last summer and she was not to live to see my ordination the following year. But it was a good summer, for her health blossomed at the cottage and it was a joy for all of us to see her soak up the sun on the dock, watch the children cavort in the water, ride in Dad's new boat, eat meals together and play cards after all the children had been put to bed. Sometimes the clock of life does seem to be able to be turned back to earlier, younger days, and the summer of 1959 was such a summer.

In the fall we were assigned to special individual rooms, which contained a standard sized altar with the books and vessels needed to practice the Mass. This became our most consuming task, occupying several hours each day as we imitated the daily Mass schedule, and found time to practice those special ceremonies for marriages and funerals. Classes now concentrated on learning how to perform some of the other sacraments: Baptism, distribution of the Eucharist, the Last Rites and the rubrics that go along with each of them. We had them explained and demonstrated in class with each of us taking turns as both priest and parishioner, and we practised in private until they had become almost second nature, knowing that these were the most intimate sacraments, along with Confession, which brought us into specific contact with the faithful. Other studies included Scripture and Pastoral Counselling, but not much else for we were also spending at least an hour a day in the recitation of the Divine Office, those compulsory prayers said daily for ourselves and the world at large.

Our class received the Diaconate in a private ceremony in the chapel that Fall and then often spent Sundays helping out at local parishes, where we assisted at Mass, distributed Holy Communion and occasionally preached. We were as active as ever in sports and were considered to be the veterans, the ones the younger students would approach to send to the Rector to ask for a movie night, longer recreation or special holidays, not that it ever did much good, but we did try. On one occasion we did get special permission for a film and I, because I had been appointed head deacon that year, was sent down to pick the film up at the rental agency, carrying the majority request for *Shane*, a famous Western, but ending up with another Western entitled *Stars In My Crown*. The renter guaranteed that the film was equally as violent, and would have to do since the reels for *Shane* were already rented out, even though they had been previously booked by us. I took them back to the seminary and that evening set the projector up in the conference room and the show began. Actually, it was not a bad *pacifist* movie but it had little action and no gunplay, and the crowd thinned out after the first reel. I was never again trusted with such a sacred task.

In mid April Dad called to say that mother was dying, and without waiting I joined the family to be with her, and stayed until after the funeral. Just before her death she was lucid several times and spoke to us with love and courage, but the cancer had metastasised and had affected her mind to the point where she often didn't recognize us but thought we were people from her early life. When she died she left a hole in the heart of the family that was never mended. Any love of beauty and of people and of animals that resides in her children came from the warmth of her heart; she was a person without guile and the most sincere soul anyone could imagine. Strangely enough, she was the youngest of four children and all the other three, a brother and two sisters, each lived to reach one hundred years, while her brief but meaningful life saw only slightly more than half of that. Two months later I was ordained in the very church that I had visited ten years previously when looking for the meaning of life, and was able to offer up the Mass for the repose of her worthy soul.

Chapter 9
A Priest's Life

There were four of us ordained back home that June, and after a short holiday all were assigned to various parishes throughout the diocese, all except me, for I was to remain at the Cathedral as one of the curates, to be of service in the central core of the city. It was a busy parish with a large elementary school across the road, multiple daily and Sunday Masses, constant confessional duties, hospital chaplaincy, youth work and the care of a large transient population. Two days after returning from my holidays with the family the rest of the Cathedral staff went on their five day annual retreat, leaving me, as they said, to 'hold the fort', and it turned out to be a real battle. In the middle of the first night I was called out administer the Last Rites to a patient dying on the operating table of the nearby hospital; a scary beginning, with robed figures all around the patient as they sought to save his life while I tried not to be in the way of the anaesthetist and still anoint the dying man's forehead and say the prescribed prayers. In later times it became an easy thing to do, and it is an amazing sacrament, often causing seemingly sudden healing, but that night nothing was easy; the book wouldn't remain open, there was too much oil in the small anointing container, and the doctor said I was in his way. A tough start, but harder things were to come.

The next afternoon a tearful man in his late forties showed up at the rectory door.

"Father! You have to come home with me! My wife is leaving me for the young boarder who lives with us! They're running off together tonight. Please come and talk to her!"

So we got in his car and off we went to the other side of the city, not even our parish, and into his kitchen where a young man was standing sheepishly near the back door. The wife in question was seated at the table and as we talked it became obvious that she was adamant about running away.

"He's no man. Father!" she said pointing at her husband. "He can't satisfy me, but this one can.", pointing to the younger man. He looked scared and embarrassed in my presence, so I turned my attention to him.

"She's not worth your soul, my friend. You have your whole life before you. Go and find yourself a good woman of your own."

To my surprise he answered, "I'm sorry. Father. I'll go and pack right away."

And that was it; the man went to his room, the woman continued to sit at the table, the husband drove me back to the rectory, and I thought,

"Man! This is easy. The Holy Ghost sure knows how to settle matters."

But that night about eight o'clock the woman showed up at the rectory door, all dressed up and with a suitcase in her hand.

"O.K. I'm ready to go. I know you've fallen in love with me!"

Takes your breath away the first time you meet someone who looks fairly normal but who is really psychotic. It took our Polish housekeeper to get her to leave, and afterwards the housekeeper told me to call her anytime.

"When fresh young priests are around there's always some of these weirdos that come out of the woodwork."

As a postscript, about two years later, while I was filling the pamphlet rack at the back of the church, a young man spoke to me.

"Hello, Father. Do you remember me? You had me leave that house I was boarding at. I'm settled now and just wanted to drop by and thank you for getting me out of that awful situation."

It had worked! Most domestic problems were never that easy, nor that successful.

The next afternoon was probably the worse situation of the whole week; they called me from a small hospital in our district where I was to act as chaplain and said that a woman was dying and wanted the Last Rites. As soon as the cab got me to the hospital, I went to the nursing station and asked for the patient and was told she was in room 12, but the room was empty. A passing nurse told me she had been moved to C 16 but she never told me that C 16 was the number of the morgue. A young couple introduced themselves as the daughter and son-in-law of the woman, but even *they* didn't say the mother was already dead, so together we went down to C 16, where the daughter refused to enter. It was a large, cool room with banks of shiny file cabinet drawers set into the far wall, and on a chalkboard the body was assigned to drawer 22. The Church's teaching on the Last Sacrament is that we should anoint in the regular way (forehead, hands and feet) in the presence of *apparent* death, since only obvious decay shows the separation of soul and body, so I pulled open the drawer, but it only came out halfway, apparently to keep the dead weight from bending the steel cabinet. Another thing I learned was that at this hospital the bodies were put in head first.

The lady was wrapped in a paper winding sheet like a mummy and I was able to unwind the shroud from the feet and anoint them but couldn't reach the hands or the forehead. The ritual instructed the priest to act as quickly as possible in cases of these types, but never explained how you were to handle such situations, so I grabbed the anointed feet and slid the body forward along the stationary bed of the drawer so that the upper torso was exposed, but I didn't dare let go of the feet for fear the body would slide onto the floor. You can't anoint the head from the feet-holding position, so the son-in-law had to be persuaded to hold the feet while I unwrapped and anointed the hands and head. It was the first time I had ever been stared at by dead eyes, and it was a little unnerving. When I'd re-wrapped the body I took the feet from the young man in order for us to slide the body back along the bed of the drawer but he suddenly bolted from the room. Then, every time I shoved on the feet the drawer itself began to close, but the body remained extended over the end of the drawer. Luckily, after six or seven slides an orderly showed up or I might have been there until the next patient died. I was glad when the priests' retreat was over.

Jimmy, my friend of the midnight seminary call, phoned me and invited me to his parents' home for supper. Jim and I had always been close to each other's mothers, although both of our fathers were pretty formal and distant since Jim and I had got in trouble together more than once. Jim had been transferred back to the city and was doing very well in his job. He had retired from hockey, except for Saturday pick-up games, and had joined the Scottish Rite Pipe Band and was learning to play the bagpipes. On the way to his parents' house he said he had to stop to talk to a fellow Band member, and invited me in to the house. He left me in the parlour with an old Scottish gentleman who said nothing but stared at me intensely, while Jimmy went into the kitchen to 'talk' to his friend. It was a set-up and I had walked right into it. Jim and his buddy came into the parlour, with great Cheshire-cat grins and sat down in silence watching the old man and me.

Suddenly Jimmy said: "He wants you to take off your shoes."

At first I thought it was a house custom, although everyone else had their shoes on, but I agreed and removed them.

Then Jim said: "He wants you to take off your socks as well."

The old man had not said a word and by this time Jim and his friend were openly laughing.

"He thinks you have cloven feet."

More laughter while the two of these jokers held on to each other in a spasm of mirth, and it suddenly dawned on me that the old gentleman was from that part of Scotland where the Presbyterian belief is that the Pope is Anti-Christ and all priests are sons of the Devil. I took off my socks, wiggled my toes and said: 'Boo!' to the old man, then re-dressed my feet and we left. Weeks later Jimmy later told me that the old Scot still believed that I was wearing some sort of a false foot on each hoof. Prejudice is a strong teacher.

My duties included the chaplaincy at a small hospital run by the Salvation Army, fine people who work very hard at the care of others, and much to my surprise the resident urologist was a friend who had lived just two streets away when we were beginning high school. Dennis was a late and only child of a prominent doctor whose wife had made Dennis her full time concern; he was always studying, always stood at the head of the class, never played Saturday football, never dated and at thirty was still living at home with her, although the father had died by this time. We had coffee together in the hospital cafeteria and exchanged life histories covering the past fifteen years, and he mentioned some mutual friends who he was seeing. But these friends were an unusual crowd for him to be with, for I knew these guys, and they had been a pretty rough bunch, school drop-outs, wild drinkers and fighters and the type who caused a girl to lose her reputation as soon as she was seen with one of them. Certainly not Dennis's social group, but he spoke warmly of them and said they really knew how to party after work was done. It was pretty obvious that he was cutting the apron strings that had held him down as a child. We saw each other occasionally over the next two years, but then he disappeared, and when I questioned the Salvation Army chaplain he said that Dennis's mother had died and shortly after that he had gone to study law, saying that he really didn't want to practice medicine, which had been his mother's vicarious design. Bright man, and probably turned out to be a great forensic lawyer.

The hospital became one of my main weekly duties, and one of my favourite work places, for not only was it satisfying to administer the sacraments to the sick, but the staff was friendly and there wasn't the usual crisis level found in large hospitals, and always there was something new and interesting happening. A new patient sometimes turned out to be an old friend, and one such friend was Tony Kozyra who had run the restaurant in the basement of the college when I was a high school student there. Tony was an institution in himself, beloved by all who got to know him, hard working, honest, generous, a confidant and with an unusual wisdom about the goodness of life. He had run the coffee shop at the college for thirty years and although I hadn't seen him for over ten years he had spoken to me when I was invited to give a talk at the college a few weeks earlier. He had remembered me instantly and had stories of that old gang of mine who had spent so many hours cutting classes and drinking his good coffee. Tony showed up in the hospital just before I left to begin the Master's Degree in Psychology, and he was very ill. We talked over old times and about our future life with Christ, and the day before he died I brought him the sacraments, blessed him and although he was very weak, he raised himself up in the bed and kissed my hand. All the years of training and hardship were worth that one salute from one of the faithful, and the memory of his quiet death will remain with me until my own.

Not all meetings in the hospital were that heart warming. The usual practice for a chaplain was to check the roster for new Catholic admissions and visit them, although I tried to pop into *all* the rooms and ask if I could help in any way. One small room held a patient of about forty-five years of age, who told me directly that he had been raised a Catholic but was now a convinced atheist, but, he added, he didn't have any visitors and would gladly spend some time with me as long as I didn't bring up the topic of religion. So we talked of politics, art, literature, technology and other subjects and seemed to enjoy each other's company for the half hour every week. As I got to know him better I realized that it wasn't only religion that he avoided but any suggestion of where his family was or what had transpired in his personal life. He was well educated and had been an engineer of some kind before the sickness incapacitated him, but even gentle kidding couldn't get him to reveal much about his past life. When I told him that it was customary for a priest to bless a patient before leaving, he became very angry and told me not to bother seeing him again if that was my intention. The next week when I went to his room he was fast asleep, so I didn't bother him, but the week after that he was indignant that I had passed him by.

"I can sleep anytime" he said, "but it's not often that I get to talk with an educated man. If I'm asleep when you come, wake me. I look forward to our conversations."

A week later I called at his room, which was very small and had no window, and found him turned fully on his side toward the wall and apparently sound asleep. I called his name several times and getting no response, touched him *lightly* on the right shoulder. He immediately turned a full one hundred and eighty degrees with his eyes wide open and stared at me with a most horrible grin on his dead face. His piercing eyes made the hair on the back of my neck stand on end. He was cold to the touch and had been dead for at least an hour and yet I felt the strange sensation of being laughed at by his corpse. The duty nurse wouldn't believe me that he was dead, saying that she had given him his lunch less than two hours previously, but when she went into his room she immediately called the emergency staff to try to revive him, but they were unsuccessful. Of all the many cases of the Last Rites that I administered his and only one other, in both cases sudden death of non-practising Catholics, did I ever get the sensation that the sacrament was wasted on them and the devil had claimed them as his own.

Sometimes the anointing of the sick was uneventful, sometimes it was startling and sometimes it offered no visible sign at all. We had an elderly Irish lady in our parish, not far from the Cathedral, who lived in a big old house with her two unmarried daughters and a fifty-year-old son who was rather simple. The son stayed in his room most of the time and played with his collection of stamps and insects, and came down only for meals and to watch his mother receive her monthly anointing. Such repeated Last Rites were not usual, for about once a month her daughters would become convinced she was dying and call the rectory in a panic and ask for a priest's visit. The next day the old lady was always better and one of the daughters would phone to thank us for our prompt attention. She lasted all five years I was at the Cathedral and probably many years after that.

Once I was called out in the evening to the hospital for a man suffering a heart attack. When I arrived he was in the emergency ward writhing around on the examination table while the doctors tried to stabilize him, but the heart monitor showed that he was drifting in and out of auricular fibrillation. I anointed him quickly and the monitor instantly showed a steady, regular heartbeat; he let out a sigh and said, "Hey, thanks. Father." Both doctors turned and stared at me as if I'd just done some marvellous sleight of hand. Two days later they released him.

Another time it was for an eight year old child who had just been run over by a car. She was dying and although she was unconscious it was obvious that she didn't want to leave this life, but after the anointing she suddenly passed quietly away. What grief for the parents, and I was then able to imagine what the mothers of the Innocents killed by the soldiers of King Herod must have felt.

The Salvation Army also ran an unwed mothers' home near the hospital, and I was on call there for any of the girls who wanted to receive the sacraments of confession and Holy Communion, but my calls there were infrequent, maybe once a month. I don't think I was very popular since one of my tasks was to try to help the girls see that adoption of their baby was probably the best answer for both of them, and to get them to start the procedure through a social agency. Most of the girls knew that once they had seen the baby they might want to keep it, and so resisted any definite commitment before the baby was born. Many of the girls were fairly street-wise and angry at the world for allowing the pregnancy to happen, but one thirteen year old was obviously naive and frightened and wanted some information about adoption and what she could do after leaving the hospital. Her story was a sad one, and I believed it, although many of the stories the girls told were of the genre: "It was the first time.' 'I was drunk.' 'He raped me.' "It wasn't my fault.' and so on.

Her father had taken in a new moneyed partner into his failing business, and when the partner had offered to take the girl to a movie the father had agreed. Just before they left, the father had taken the girl aside and sternly said, "He may not want to go to a show, so do whatever he wants."

What he wanted was her virginity, and when he took her back to his apartment she said it happened so quickly she didn't understand what he was doing until it was over. When she went home she tried to tell her father but he said she was imagining things and sent her to bed. Later, when it became obvious that she was pregnant, he believed the partner who said the girl had seduced him and wasn't a virgin to begin with, and had kicked his young daughter out onto the street. A girlfriend took her in and got her to the home where I met her. She did agree to adoption and after the birth we found her a home through Children's Aid, and the girl started back to school in a new area and hopefully to a new and better life. Life can be very cruel at times.

Our parish duties included other things than visiting the sick; we spent hours each week in the confessional and what they had taught us in De Sexto classes *was* true. Sometimes confessions were easy, especially with the children which the good Sisters would march across the street once every two weeks and the little ones would ask questions like, "Is peeing in the snow a mortal sin?', and sometimes hearing confession was hard, as when the penitent seemed to be sorry but wasn't ready to leave the situation in which the sin was reoccurring. Then you could try to dispose the person to start over outside the occasion, but it didn't often seem that it would happen. In such a case, where the priest can't see that the penitent is willing to end a sinful relationship, he can advise but can't absolve. You only get rid of sin when you make the effort to turn back to God, and that's not an easy thing to do. *Saying* is easy; *doing* is hard.

Saying Mass was a joy and we did it at least once a day, and on Sundays sometimes two or three times, depending on whether you were sent to relieve a sick country priest and do his home town Masses and his mission churches as well. Even back in the 60's there weren't enough priests to go around, so almost all country parishes had at least one mission parish attached to them. A mission parish was one without a resident priest, and probably half the parishes in our diocese were of this type, especially in the northern part. If we were not sent out then we stayed at the Cathedral and offered one of the three daily Masses or one of the five on Sunday, and if it was your monthly turn to preach, then you got the seven o'clock Mass and preached at it and at every Mass for the rest of that day. Since it was the Cathedral, the sermon was expected to be quite good, and we worked hard on its preparation, not only for the sake of the parishioners, but also because the bishop usually took one of the later Masses and listened to how you were doing. There was a bit of the 'publish or perish' attitude among the curates, except it was spelled parish, and it meant a parish out in the boondocks somewhere if your sermons started to bore the parishioners.

By the end of the first year, four of the young curates around the city had established a credit line with their local bank and were each able to take out a loan to finance a car. We went as a group to the Volkswagen dealer and got a fleet price of $1800 for the new 1200 cc. Beetle. Great little car, and what a feeling of freedom it gave to each of us. We were able to go somewhere on our day off, somewhere like the country parishes where other young curates lived, or down to the family cottage we had owned when I was in high school. When the family had moved down east Dad had left it in trust to his sister and her family, but they only used it one month a year, which allowed us to use it almost anytime. The little cars were easy on gas and great to drive in the summer time but not so good in the winter, which occupies almost two third of the year in that northern plain. The interior heat came up from the rear engine through the rocker panels only when the engine was hot, so in the winter the driver froze for the first half hour and cooked for the rest of the trip. The windshield iced up so badly that little plastic deflectors had to be mounted over the front vents to spread the heat out enough to clear a patch to see through, and of course for the first half hour it didn't matter anyway. All you could do was scrape away the interior ice until the heat arrived. But they were wheels, and they were our first cars, and we were young, so our complaints were few. We had a saying "Become a priest and remain an adolescent until you are forty.', and that's how we acted with our new Beatles.

After supper and evening Benediction on Friday nights, the young curates would gather in the common room of the old rectory and watch the Friday Night Fights. We cheered Floyd Paterson when he became champion, since we hadn't had a Catholic champion since Rocky Marciano retired, and were saddened when Floyd lost to Ingimar Johannson in their first fight. I felt so badly for him that I wrote and offered him the use of the cottage to get away from people, since it was September and no one would be around the area. He wrote back thanking me for the offer but was already in training for his return match and couldn't accept. Too bad, for he would have enjoyed the area: nice beaches, good sand roads for running, warm days and cool nights and as much privacy as anyone could desire. However, he made the right choice, for the training paid off and he was a much better fighter when he entered the ring the next time. I've always been sorry that I didn't do more boxing myself because I dearly love the sport.

Doreen, Jimmy's sister, phoned me one day and said she was giving a surprise party for her brother, and all the old gang had been invited, then she started to cry. After a few moments she told me that Jimmy had been diagnosed with Hodgkin's disease, a lymph adenoma that was then invariably fatal, sometimes carrying off its victim within a few short months, as was to be the case with Jim. We gathered together that Saturday at his house and only a few of us knew the real reason for the farewell party. Someone shoved a bottle of beer in my hand saying they couldn't recognize me without it, and Jimmy laughed so hard he almost choked. It was a great party and Jim was in high spirits, for his latest treatment had downsized the lymphatic nodes, and he was feeling like his old self. We sang the old songs, told the old jokes, reminisced about places we had been together and girls we had known and found out who had married what girl and what had happened to the other members of the gang who hadn't been able to attend Jim's party.

Among those who had attended the function, Ray and Don had become lawyers, Len worked for the city, Charlie owned a car wash, Doug was an airline pilot. Bill and his twin brother were running a wholesale pharmacy business, and I was a priest. Not bad for a bunch of ne'er-do-wells who had sponged coffee off Tony in the basement restaurant in our last year of high school, and who spent almost half our time in the Dean's office explaining the reason for the latest infraction of the school rules. I visited Jimmy several times over the next few months, as the disease got progressively worse, until one day he told me not to come any more, just as Doc Holiday had done with his friends as he died of tuberculosis. Early in the New Year Doreen phoned me one day.

"Jimmy has gone," she said simply.

I went to the funeral and have had him in my heart and prayers every day since. We were alter egos and hopefully we still are.

Another part of the duties assigned was to act as chaplain to the Junior Youth Group, a small contingent of high school students who lived in the parish. They had been without an active chaplain for some time and were used to running their own activities from the various high schools they attended. The Christmas Break was approaching when the president called one afternoon and asked if they could announce an upcoming dance in the Sunday bulletin and have it mentioned at the end of all the Sunday Masses. Not an unusual request from any of the parish organizations, but the standard procedure was to get the pastor to approve the request, but when he was approached he left the matter to me. The problem was that they were intending to hold the dance in the best hotel in the city and had already booked the event and used up all the money in their account to guarantee the reservation, even before any ticket sales had been announced.

I met with their council and a parent advisor and tried to convince them that it was too much of a financial risk, and asked them to hold the dance in the large gymnasium in our local elementary school instead, at no cost. The whole council, including the parent, voted me down, saying that it was going to be a great success and would earn them considerable profit and really put the Youth Group on the map. On the advice of more mature chaplains I decided to contact the parents of the council members and assure them that we would advertise the event, but not be responsible for any shortfall in expenses. All the parents agreed, until it proved to be a dismal failure with a large unpaid balance due the hotel and the band; then they wanted the Church to cover the shortage, and conveniently forgot our earlier meetings. Eventually they went to the bishop who turned the matter over to the pastor who gave them a small offering and cancelled the Junior Parish Youth group.

We hardly ever saw any high school students at the Sunday Masses since we were a downtown parish with a large transient population, but the one thing I did notice was the large number of young adults who attended quite regularly. This western area has a population of slightly over two million and more than half of these people live and work in the main city, which meant that the small towns and farm districts were constantly sending their young people to the city to find work, or to attend technical or business training schools, and it seemed that these were the people who would profit from a Catholic Youth Organization. The pastor liked the idea that he might rent out the school gym for such a weekly undertaking, and the Sister Principal said we could use the old gymnasium on the third floor of the school as long as we first cleaned it up, since the school had converted some of the unused classrooms into a smaller gymnatorium for the children and no longer used the large gym upstairs. That was the beginning of what became the largest youth group on the western plains.

A few hand-lettered signs were posted in the Cathedral entrance and announcements concerning the Sunday night dance for young Catholic adults was made at all the Masses, and that night about twenty-five young people showed up and climbed the stairs to the old gym. The parish had a portable public address system and we wired up a record player to it and played some old records from the school's collection, and served coffee. The young people danced for about two hours then sat around and discussed what kind of a youth club they wanted to have. Right from the first, these young adults took over the running of the Sunday dances, appointing someone to get some *good* records, another to get coffee and doughnuts for the next week, and began deciding about how to clean up the old place. One of the first things they mentioned was that the dance floor had to be sanded and sealed, since dancing on it in its present shape was like 'sliding across the deck of an old wooden ship.'

The next Sunday nearly fifty people showed up, almost all originally from some small towns outside the city. They were all young working people: office workers, young cops, apprentice mechanics, printers, salesmen and women, and a whole host of non-professional people from any and every job the city offered. Within a month we had a hundred members and an elected executive and started to really put the place in order. We rented a sander and resurfaced the floor, turned one of the classrooms into a canteen complete with coffee, pop, chocolate bars and pastry, charged everyone ten dollars for a yearly membership, bought a good music system, reworked the lighting system and started to branch out into other activities than just Sunday night dancing, such as skating parties, bowling, public speaking courses, debates, Rosary prayers and eventually Communion breakfasts. One of the young men was learning the printing trade and produced a Catholic Youth Organization card that the young people could hand out to their friends, and the ranks of the members continued to grow.

The diocese received a new bishop, the previous one being elevated to Archbishop and moved to a larger diocese. The new bishop was a scholar, and had been the head of a religious order, and was, within the year, elevated to the ranks of the Cardinals. He saw the work that was being done with the young adults and approved of it, since he had come from a teaching background and was youth oriented. He appointed me Archdiocesan Director of the Catholic Youth Organization (CYO) and encouraged other centres to begin similar programs. By this time we had a small musical group, and I had taken enough music lessons to be able to chord on the banjo. With this group we travelled to other centres around the diocese encouraging the young people to start their own local branch of the CYO, and we ourselves continued to grow until there was nearly one thousand youths who belonged, or had belonged, to this central youth organization.

About once a month the elected executive arranged for a Communion Breakfast, at a local hotel, after the 10:30 Mass, with a series of good speakers, including the Cardinal himself, as well as members from an international speakers guild. These breakfasts were well attended, for the speakers were always motivational, and the young people showed their interest by coming up with new ways of responding to the needs of youth. A group home for young men and another for young women was set up especially for those people who felt most adrift in the big city, and needed something to become a stabilizing influence in their lives. These houses were run on an acceptance basis; when a new person was suggested as a candidate for a room in the house, he or she met first with the other members who lived there and *they* decided if the person was agreeable to their outlook on life, would share equally in the costs of upkeep, shopping and cleaning duties, and be an active participator in the CYO.

Usually this process worked well, but sometimes it took an initial adjustment. One new young man had been left alone in the house on a Friday evening and proceeded to get drunk and throw the empty beer bottles through the main windows of the living room, on a night when the temperature was twenty below. When the others arrived home to a freezing welcome he was found passes out on the couch, but they took pity on him and didn't throw him out in the snow. Luckily, he had so much alcohol in his system that he was only slightly hypothermic. The next day the windows got fixed, he paid the bill and life went on. Another person became so withdrawn he refused to get out of his bed for two days, so on the third day we sat around his bed and held a group discussion about the duties and joys of life. After an hour he joined in to the conversation, got up and went back to work. He now owns a thriving tire store in another city.

With over a hundred young people at the Sunday program there was always someone who had a special problem and wanted to discuss it or go to confession, so the executive council built a small office in the other classroom where there would be some privacy. Some of the problems were fairly ordinary, but there were a lot that were serious and often bordered on the suicidal. One young woman came into the office while I was going over the account books and sat down opposite me at the desk. I'd been drinking a coke when she arrived and offered to go and get her one but she wasn't interested. She'd already spent some time on the street, and wanted to discuss her disbelief in God and her anger at life in general. As she talked she took out a small mirror and began to freshen up her makeup. Suddenly she said into the mirror: "You bitch!" and slammed the mirror down on the desk, picked up a shard of broken glass and slashed both her wrists.

"Well!" she said. "What are you going to do about it?" The cuts were not deep but they were bleeding. Using some Kleenex to catch the spill I poured coke over the wounds as a disinfectant.

"Jesus! That hurts!" was her response, but she let us take her to the hospital where she saw a resident psychiatrist.

As soon as she got out of the hospital she came back and eventually became one of the executive members. All it often takes are people who care.

An older Polish priest, Father Jan Warszak, came to the cathedral one day and stopped to talk about his work as a seminary teacher and Youth Chaplain before the Second World War. He was an author, with a Doctorate in theology, and had been teaching at the main seminary in Warsaw when the Germans attacked. Because he'd had so much influence among the young Polish Catholics the Germans feared he would become a leader in the underground resistance and sent him first to the death camp at Mauthausen, then to Dachau for the rest of the war until he was liberated in 1945. His stories of the atrocities were staggering and probably he would never have told them if he hadn't become my mentor and confessor. His wisdom was tested in the fire of martyrdom and he had more insight into the problems of youth and the value of prayer on their behalf than anyone else I'd met. Through his influence my work with the youth expanded and the boundaries of Catholic inclusiveness began to disappear and be replaced by a concern for all young adults of whatever race and creed. Jan died only two years after we had met, for the scars of the death camp had never completely faded away, and the Sisters at the Academy where he was chaplain said he often screamed in his dreams at night. He once told me that in Dachau the practice of cannibalism was not unknown among the prisoners, and that at night when he heard others gnawing on something he covered his head with the blanket. At his grave side his fellow Polish priests poured soil from Poland on the coffin before it was lowered into the ground, and then we all wept for our personal loss of such a Christian warrior.

Although in those days dating among different creeds was discouraged for fear of mixed marriages, the executive council liked the idea that we would hold a special spring dance with prizes for the best acts put on by the young people of the city, and we invited a Protestant Young Peoples' Group, which was run by my old swimming buddy, Doug (now the Reverend Doug), and Ray from the Jewish B'nai Brith organization. Both were exceptionally gifted men in the field of youth work. About fifty of our own group and twenty from each of the other two groups showed up the night of the dance and it was a gala affair.

Doug's group sang spirituals; Ray's members did a series of comic routines and ours put on a silly sit-com about a modern Romeo and Juliet, and every group got a prize. Later Doug, Ray and myself went out for coffee and talked over ways to produce harmony among our prejudiced youths. What we came up with was an idea for an Interfaith Harmony Theatre group, which eventually produced a number of very successful semi-professional stage productions, well attended by all three faiths. We even won a major drama festival one year. Lasting friendships among the young people occurred and even a couple of interfaith marriages. True love knows no barriers.

We also began offering a young adults' weekend retreat in June or late August, using a children's summer camp on the shores of a nearby lake just before their season opened or after it closed. Leaders who were active in the Catholic Action Movement were the usual speakers, and the program had proved to be quite well attended. In the early sixties the country was listening attentively to what was going on concerning desegregation under President John Kennedy. Our young adults were totally against prejudice toward the Blacks, probably because there were so few African Americans in our area, but they were blind toward their own prejudice against the Metis Indians, who came off the reservations at the end of each summer and stayed for the winter in the poorer districts of the large cities. We even had fights when some of the young Metis men tried to attend the Sunday dances at the CYO.

The executive discussed this problem and someone suggested that we get a desegregation speaker for the retreat and have him lead the discussions on Friday and Saturday, then introduce some capable Metis speakers on Sunday so that the local problem of prejudice would be exposed. We knew the young people would condemn Black segregation and we hoped that by the end of the retreat they would recognize and begin to correct their prejudice toward our own minority group. The task of finding the right speaker was left to me and since I didn't know where to look I asked the telephone operator to connect me with someone in Bobby Kennedy's office. She connected me with Rose Kennedy at the Kennedy family home. Mrs. Kennedy listened patiently to my problem and gave me a number for Martin Luther King's office. When I called his office a secretary took my name and number and said she would have one of his assistants call me back the next day. Later I found out that they needed the time to have the FBI check out the Youth Group and myself to make sure we were legitimate. The next day Mr. King's assistant called and wanted possible dates for the retreat, but found out that none that we had could be worked into his itinerary. He suggested John Howard Griffin and I accepted, although at the time I didn't know who he was. John phoned a few days later and we agreed on a suitable weekend.

I phoned the local newspaper and talked to one of the writers who were following the Civil Rights Movement. He supplied me with a copy of John's book, *Black Like Me* and I discussed it with the CYO executive a few days before John landed at the airport. The book was interesting, but not as interesting as John was in person.

John was a sociologist who became interested in the plight of the African Americans in the deep South in the 1950's. In 1959 he began a medical treatment to change his skin colour from white to black so that he could have first-hand knowledge of what it was like to live in the United States as a member of a minority group whose ancestors had been slaves. He prepared legally by informing the FBI what he intended to do, and culturally by conferring frequently with the staff of *Ebony Magazine*, at that time the most widely read American minority publication. Both the FBI and the *Ebony* staff tried to talk him out of the venture fearing that militants on either side would be happy to kill him if they found out what he was doing. But John was a man on a mission, and when the melanin treatments did not darken his skin enough, he used a strong dye to complete the job, one that would not wash off easily. That Fall he road on buses or walked through much of the southern states of Louisiana, Mississippi, Alabama and Georgia as a black man in a white man's world.

Many of the stories he told us were never printed in the book for fear that they would evoke more racial tension among the militant members of both the White and the Black communities, but they are stories that deserved to be told. One day, John said, he was walking along the side of a road that ran through a Louisiana swamp when a pick-up truck came up and rolled to a stop just in front of him.

"Hey! nuncle! You want a lift?"

The term "nuncle" was a common term used by young Whites when addressing an older Black person, and John said the appropriate gesture was simply to walk over to the vehicle and say, "Thank you." and get in. It really didn't matter how far you were going, for to turn down an offered ride was to insult a powerful adversary.

On this occasion John got in to the truck and almost immediately the driver wanted to know about John's sexual successes with Black women. When

John said he was married and didn't cheat on his wife the driver became increasingly angry, saying that John wasn't telling him the truth.

"All you black studs *do* is screw those black bitches day and night! Don't try to tell me any different!"

When John refused to be drawn into the accusation the driver slammed on the brakes, reached across, opened the passenger door and pushed John out on the road with his foot. Then he got out his side, took a shotgun from a boot behind the seat and walked around to where John was lying on the ground.

"You wouldn't be the first Niger I've shot and rolled into the swamp."

John told us that he felt he was dead, and under his breath said "Jesus! Jesus!" The man stood there for some time with the shotgun pointed at John's head, then finally said, "You're not even worth the shell." got back in the truck and drove off.

"I sat there for an hour, weeping and being sick, until a black brother came along in a battered old car and took me home to meet his wife and children. He never even wanted to know what had happened. I guess it was so common it wasn't worth telling. I stayed overnight with this poor family and in the morning I gave the wife a single candy bar for the four children, the only food I had in my bag. She cut it in four pieces and gave one piece to each child."

When the youngest received her share she looked at John.

"No one in the whole world is as lucky as us!" the child said with the biggest grin, John said, he ever saw.

Another story was about the "hate stare" that he usually got when he went to buy something in a store or get a ticket at a bus depot. It was as if the money he gave them was contaminated, or as if he was trying to give them some kind of forgery. The clerk would rip the money out of his hand, examine it, slap down the ticket or produce, scowl and say, "Now move aside!" Yet these same people would seem normal and polite when dealing even with the most obnoxious white customer.

"Black," he said, "just brought out the worst in them."

Our young people couldn't stop asking John questions about the volatility of the situation in the south and couldn't understand why he thought there would be a 'blood bath' there before integration actually was achieved.

"Surely," they said, "the Constitution demands equality for all its citizens, regardless of colour, race or creed. Why can't they see that nothing is to be gained by minority hatred and prejudice?"

Early Sunday morning, just before Mass, the Metis speakers arrived, and the general question from our young people was 'What are *they* doing here!' After Mass the new speakers led discussions on prejudice, and explained what it was like to be a half-breed' in a white society, and it was with great hesitation that our young people even entered into these discussions.

John listened quietly until the discussions were over and then said, "We are all prejudiced. I grew up in a home with a black nanny and black servants and without anyone telling me, I took it for granted that as a white person I was somehow superior. I never thought of myself as prejudiced, until as a young man I lost my eyesight in an accident and my roommate and friend for two years in college talked me into trying out a new medical procedure. It restored my vision and when the bandages came off I wondered who the black student was, until he spoke. He was my roommate and I found myself having difficulty in even speaking to my friend with whom I had shared so many happy months. Then I realized I was prejudiced and always would be, because it came to me in my mother's milk. Now, my first morning prayers is, Please, God, don't let me treat any human being today as less than a full human.' You young people are prejudiced against the Metis, and I can't understand that because I never grew up in a society where they were the *different* people. You can't understand the prejudice against the Blacks because you didn't grow up in their society. It's not that you aren't prejudiced; it's just that your prejudice is directed at a different minority. We all need that morning prayer."

John went home but he had made a difference, at least to some of the young people, for we started a liaison between the CYO and the Indian and Metis Friendship Centre that was also downtown in the city. Many of the young Metis women came to our dances, and occasionally a young 'Brave', but apparently the males didn't seem as welcomed and few of them stayed. One young woman told me privately that she was ashamed of being there, for she had already had an illegitimate child and had given it up for adoption. She felt that somehow she wasn't decent enough to be with the other young people. I gave her the boxer's philosophy that it's not that you're knocked down, or even how many times you're knocked down, as long as you continue to get up and go on fighting, and she accepted it. She became a close friend that Fall and worked happily with the other members of the executive to run programs, such as the Kennedy thirty-mile penitential walk for peace in which seventy of our members participated.

She didn't show up the next spring and it wasn't until the middle of June that she phoned me from a local hospital and asked for a visit. She was in the hospital because she had become pregnant again and was 'spotting' in her second month following conception. The biological father was a young immigrant who said he didn't mind having her as a lover but didn't "...want to be married to an Indian or have a half-breed kid!"

When we talked she asked if suicide was really such a terrible sin, and then asked me to keep a secret. She pulled back the edge of her pillow and showed me all the sleeping pills they had given her for the past week and which she had faked swallowing and kept for a final exit.

"But why?" I asked. "You can always start again. Life is long and you're almost through the toughest part. Give yourself another chance!"

Then she told me that her doctor had said she had to have a bilateral ovariectomy if she hoped to stop the bleeding.

"I'm an Indian and someday I want to go back to my people, but who will marry me if I can't have children!" and she began to cry.

"Let me check it out with your doctor", I said. "Maybe we can get a second opinion." The surgeon certainly didn't like priests, or Indians, and told me to get out of his hospital when I asked for a second opinion.

"They're just a blot on society. They keep popping out kids like they were some kind of a baby factory, and then *we* have to support them! What I'm doing is a good thing!"

Of course it was a bad thing; we don't have the right to play God, so I phoned a friend of mine who was a gynaecologist and told her the whole story. She took it from there. She contacted the College of Surgeons who brought the doctor in for questioning, threatened him with suspension, sent another specialist to see the young woman and on his recommendation released her from the hospital since the 'spotting' was able to be controlled by medication and bed rest. I arranged for an ambulance to take her to her boyfriend's house and she promised that she would return to her own people as soon as she was well. Unfortunately, things don't always go the way you would like them to go. About a month later she phoned the rectory to say 'Goodbye'. Nothing was working out with her boyfriend and she was terribly in love with him. The 'spotting' had not completely stopped and she thought that maybe the baby was already dead in her womb. She had turned on the gas with the oven door open, stuffed towels around the door and windows and was going to drift off into eternity because she was "...tired of fighting." Then she hung up.

I didn't even know where she lived. All I knew was that her boyfriend was called Hans, that he was a young German and that he worked at the university in some department. I had never met him and had no idea of what he looked like, but I immediately phoned the university, told them who I was and that it was emergency and they put me through to Personnel. They took a chance that he was in the maintenance department and had him on the line within a couple of minutes. At first he was very suspicious but when he heard that I knew he was the boyfriend he said, "Don't worry. She's not going to do anything. She threatens suicide all the time. I'm not going to get involved!" and wouldn't give me his home address.

I knew that the ambulance service probably had her address, but I didn't think there was time to go that route, so on impulse I said, "Listen! If that girl dies I'll do everything in my power to get you deported!"

It worked, but it was a chance. For all I knew he was already a landed immigrant or even a citizen. He gave me the house street and number and I phoned the police who broke down the door of apartment filled with gas fumes and took her off to the psychiatric ward of a nearby hospital. The baby was still alive and when she was well I made sure she was going back to her own people, and she told me that she was keeping this baby. Where had the little voice in my head that said: "Threaten deportation." come from? Just another coincidence? I don't think so, and neither did she for just before she left she said, "Now I know that God loves me."

In July of 1963, on the way back from visiting my family, I had stopped off in Milwaukee to watch the Braves play a home game, and next morning went to a nearby convent to say Mass. The Sisters were anxious to know about the Catholic Action Movement and when they learned of the young adults retreat in August they told me to contact Father John Havas S. J. who taught at one of the Jesuit Universities, and who, they said, had a marvellous story to tell. The next week we contacted Father Havas who made room for us on his busy schedule, and came up to run the retreat that year.

John was born in Hungary and became a Jesuit there, but finished off his studies in the States before being sent as a missionary to China, where he taught English and Ethics at the University of Jilin. When China entered the Korean War in 1951 he and a number of his Catholic students were arrested in November and imprisoned for several months as American spies. The next spring, one day at a time, each of the students and John were taken into the courtyard, told to confess, and the student was then shot in his presence, until all the students had been killed. On the final day John was lined up against the wall, told to confess his crimes against the Communist State, and when he couldn't, the soldiers fired blank rounds at him, and then threw him, manacled hand and foot, into solitary confinement in a cell seven feet by four but only five feet high. For the next several months his daily ration of rice was pushed through the opening in the door and dumped on the floor, and often the tin cup of water received the same treatment. Under these conditions his weight dropped to ninety pounds and he developed bleeding wounds on his wrists and ankles from the manacles. He was not allowed out of the tiny cell except for a series of interrogations that happened at odd times during the day or night, or for the occasional session of torture.

His only consolation, he told the young people at the retreat, was to say the Rosary, using pieces of straw from his bedding for Rosary beads. And he would move the small straws back and forth as he meditated on the mysteries of Christ's life, sometimes for the whole day, crouched in a kneeling position since the cell was too low to allow him to stand up. His guards thought he had gone crazy, and John often doubted his own sanity. In December of the second year he began to pray for death for he had become very ill from the starvation diet and the abysmal condition of the tiny cell. Suddenly one day (he found out later it was Christmas Day) a great light flooded his cell, his manacles fell off, the cell door opened of its own accord and a brilliant figure appeared and blessed him. The guard, who had witnessed all this, ran and brought back other soldiers who watched in terror until the apparition vanished, then dragged John out of the cell, loaded him in the back of a truck, drove to the demilitarized zone (DMZ) and threw him across the demarcation line. They didn't ask for a trade, or offer John as a good-will gesture; they just wanted to get rid of him as fast as they could. The Americans didn't know what to do with him since he was still a Hungarian citizen, so the Canadian Forces had him flown to Vancouver where he was nursed back to health.

It was probably John's gratitude for the kindness the nursing Sisters had shown him during his recovery that prompted him to accept the invitation to be the speaker at our Youth Retreat. The young people on the retreat often openly wept as John recounted his life in China, his sufferings in prison, the Visitation, his love for his Chinese students and for the Chinese people in general. And when one of the retreatants asked if he would ever return to China, his reply was, "As soon as they will let me."

Perhaps John imagined the whole thing, but it's not likely, for his was the only case of a prisoner being returned in such a manner. Later, when John's story had been told in the Press, a Private Member's Bill was introduced in Congress, and John was given American citizenship and he returned to teach in the Jesuit university where we had contacted him. After the retreat and John had returned home, I phoned the Milwaukee Sisters and thanked them for their recommendation. He was amazing speaker and had an amazing story. We were glad that he had briefly entered our lives.

Toward the end of the summer our group of Jewish and Christian young people met to decide on a theatre production, and after much discussion it was decided that we would produce Meredith Willson's *Music Man*, and produce it as a professional show. We ordered the librettos from French and Co., held casting sessions for the various roles, rented the Theatre Centre and booked a good orchestra. Then we realized that if it was going to be a professional play we needed a professional director. I'd been doing the evening sign-off prayer for the local TV station for about a year and had met a young director named Don, who had a successful show of his own called *Hymn Sing*, and was himself an ordained minister. He liked the idea of an Interfaith Harmony Theatre and took the position without remuneration and began immediate rehearsals with the cast. Under his direction the play began to take shape, but he needed professional dancers and a group that could carry the barbershop tunes written into the play. Ray, the B'nai Brith organizer, contacted some of the members of the Royal Ballet, and Equity agreed to release several dancers for the project. I contacted the local chapter of the Society for the Preservation of Barber Shop Singing in America and they supplied a group of four harmonisers, and the play, after months of practice and the overcoming of various obstacles, was a great success. Meredith Willson sent a letter of congratulations and we printed it on the inside cover of the program, and National Broadcasting did an interview with the cast and ran it on the evening news. Big stuff for a small start of a small group.

One of the young women in the chorus was Maggie, but everyone called her 'Megs'. We had previously arranged for the social agency to move her out of her home and get her social assistance because her father was clearly paranoid and a danger to her. Her older brother was already in the mental institute and her mother refused to have her husband committed, and Megs was already showing signs of deep depression. We found her a place to stay with a group of Sisters who ran a residence for young unmarried women, and she seemed quite content to be there. However, she still was subject to black moods and so we arranged to have her seen frequently by both her family doctor and a local psychiatrist. To make matters worst, she had fallen in love with a young actor who had held a lead role in the Music Man. Lenny was an actual Thespian, having played with semi professional theatre groups for the past three years; a charming and smooth young man who could talk himself into or out of almost any situation he wanted. During the production of the play Lenny had borrowed my car to pick up materials needed for the rehearsals, and had used it frequently for about a month prior to the staging of the play. A day before he left town two police showed up at the rectory door with a summons for me for a string of over twenty parking tickets he had accumulated.

When they learned who had actually used the car they ran a check on him, found out he already had a rap sheet for passing bad cheques, and also learned that he was married and owed considerable maintenance cost to his wife and child. Megs was heartbroken about the loss and the deceit and often came to talk to me about her feelings for Lenny and how unfair she thought life was. One night, about eleven o'clock, she phoned and wanted to see me, but I still had some work to do, and the rest of the evening breviary prayers to say, so we just talked for half an hour. She asked me to call her at the residence when I finished my work, and I promised to do so, but it really wasn't my intention to disturb the Sisters that late at night, especially since she had already made an appointment to see me early the next day. When I finished my work and the prayers it was twelve thirty, and I went to bed...but couldn't sleep. After an hour the feeling that I should call her was so great that I called the Sister on night duty and asked her to see if Megs was still awake. She returned to the phone and said she was deeply asleep and hadn't responded when the Sister had called her name.

That scared me and I asked to have her woke, but Sister wouldn't do it, until I insisted that she wake Mother Superior for permission. Mother gave me a tongue lashing for waking the residence in the middle of the night but finally marched down to Megs' room with the night duty Sister and found out that she had overdosed on tranquillizers. They tried to make her vomit and then dragged her around between the two of them until the ambulance came. I went directly to the hospital and met the intern just leaving the emergency room.

"I'm sorry, Father. She took too many pills. We lost her."

Somehow that *couldn't* be possible and I asked to see her, and at least be able to give her the Last Rites. When I entered the emergency room a second intern said the most precious words I ever was to hear.

"I think I'm getting a pulse!"

Megs had her stomach pumped and they got most of the tranquillizers out, but she was high for several days. I visited her the next day and after the visit the hospital staff asked me not to come again until she was released, for she was so happy to see me that she started bouncing on the bed, fell out of it and broke her arm. Later Megs spent some time in the mental hospital but after she was released she moved away, married and had a child. She still calls me about once a year to tell me how things are going, and on her last call told me that her son had just graduated with a Master's Degree in computer science.

The priesthood is a wonderful experience; you meet all kinds of people and have to deal with a large number of strange experiences in the course of a single year. Perhaps the most startling *spiritual* experience happened one Sunday when I was to say the nine o'clock Mass. One of my close friends was another curate, Father Ted, who had been born and raised in Holland, but had done all his seminary training with us. He had been ordained a year before me and was also assigned at the Cathedral. Father Ted had said the seven-thirty Mass and as he passed me on the walkway on his way to breakfast he told me that there were only a few consecrated hosts left in the ciborium in the tabernacle. He had filled two ciboria with communion wafers and left them in the sacristy for me to take out and place on the main altar just before the Mass started. Not a problem...except that I forgot to take them out, still sleepy from long counselling the previous evening. For those who are not familiar with the small, flat pieces of bread used in the Mass, it will help to know that the Catholic belief is that these wafers remains just ordinary bread until the priest says the words of consecration over them during the last part of the Mass itself. Then, we believe, they become the actual body of Jesus. This happens at that part of the Mass called the Consecration.

It wasn't until I opened the tabernacle after the Consecration to give out Communion that I realized what a mistake my memory lapse had been. There were perhaps thirty consecrated hosts in the ciborium and a crowd of at least a hundred and fifty waiting for Communion. For one terrified moment I thought that I could get the ciboria left in the sacristy, bring them out and consecrate the hosts in them and solve the problem. But I wasn't sure what the rubric was under such circumstances and I had a suspicion that such act was not permitted, so I did the only thing left to do. I prayed as I had never prayed before! I apologized to Jesus for being so careless, asked Him to multiply the hosts in the nearly empty ciborium and took the ciborium down to the waiting communicants. Toward the end of the long line of communicants I had to break some of the hosts in two, but when it was over there were still a few fragments left in the bottom of the container. Father Ted had come out to help with Communion but seeing that there wasn't a second ciborium on the altar he just knelt at the side and watched me. When the Mass was over he asked me *how* I had done that and I told him that God sometimes has pity on foolish priests. Later, God was to send me a test to see if my faith really was that strong, and I miserably failed the challenge.

Chapter 10
Human Psychology

Unusual things were always happening at the Cathedral: a young parishioner called to ask if taking aspirin was a sin and when asked how many she had taken, she said it was the whole bottle. Her husband rushed her to the hospital as soon as he was informed and she began to sort out her problems with life. Shortly after that we had a case of bipolar illness: one of the marriages that came out of the CYO socials was between our dynamic Vice President and her boyfriend. All seemed idealistic until the baby was born, then on the day she came home from the hospital he disappeared and it wasn't until the Visa bill came in that the family realized that he had bought a motorcycle and taken off for parts unknown. He was finally arrested in Texas two months later after Visa had put a stop on his card and a service station attendant called the State Police when he had tried to buy gas. He was sent back home where to everyone's surprise he was diagnosed as schizophrenic. Apparently the birth of the baby had placed too much responsibility on his shoulders and he fled for the open road.

One evening a bitter ex soldier attended the Sunday night dance and told me his story. He had been stationed in the Middle East and had picked up an intestinal parasite. The treatment the army doctors gave him was so intense that he ended up having a section of his bowel removed and received a medical discharge. He was on constant medication with a special diet and would often get so discouraged that he would go out for 'a night on the town', drink heavily and eat all the foods forbidden on his diet. Then for the next two days he would suffer excruciating cramps. I had no idea how I could be of help to him, but had met a young woman who had recently fled a dysfunctional family and was similarity depressed. On a whim, I left him in the CYO office and brought the young woman in to see him. I didn't know either names and just introduced them people who needed to listen to one another. At the end of the evening I went back to the office and they were gone. A little more than a year later I met them on the street pushing a baby carriage with a beautiful child inside; both of them seemed more settled. Two suffering souls; I hope they found lasting happiness.

But perhaps the strangest was the case of John, a great mountain of a man but with little courage to face life. Years before, I'd worked with John on a summer job in surveying, and he was strange even then. He couldn't follow any instructions, once got himself entangled in a bees' nest and was stung dreadfully, misplaced his glasses constantly and often wandered off line and got lost. But could he ever play the piano! One day our crew went for lunch in a small town hotel that had a piano in the lobby, and John sat down and captivated everyone for an hour. Incredible! The story we heard was that his father was very wealthy and because John was a little unusual he was permitted to do nothing but practice on the piano. He was an only child whose mother doted on him and found the meaning for her life in running his.

He came to the rectory one night to ask for a bus ticket back to the mental institute where he was an inpatient with weekend privileges and we talked for awhile and then I got him the ticket. After that he usually came for the ticket and would talk disjointedly about his life: his father had died, his mother was living in a small apartment in the city and he would force himself to go to see her every two weeks, for according to John, she would spend the visit berating him for having made nothing of his life. Late one night he arrived in tears and stamped around the office.

"I've killed my mother! I've killed my mother!" he cried over and over again.

I tried to call her number but got no answer, so I sent the police to check on the old lady. Indeed she was dead and John was taken into custody. Later the coroner ruled that she had died of a heart attack and John was sent back to the mental institution. A month later a very subdued John came to see me and to insist that he had truly killed his mother. Apparently in the heat of the usual berating he had told her to 'F... off!' and that was too much for her poor old heart. I saw him only once more and that was when I visited Megs at the institute after her overdose session, and he had gone downhill considerably. I don't think he ever forgave himself for that outburst of profanity.

One time the Social Committee arranged for a Saturday supper and show, but the show was an auto show, the first one I'd ever attended. One young woman became so attached to a particular sports car that she made an offer on it to the dealer and showed up several days later as the proud new owner. She asked if I'd like to test drive the car and I couldn't refuse. I should have. I drove out toward the university and the little car performed admirably, at least until she took the driver's seat. I had no way of knowing it but she was bulimic and was on a drug to aid in the weight loss. Within a few moments she had missed an ordinary curve in the road and the car somersaulted down the embankment. Neither of us seemed badly hurt and when we got to a telephone I called a friend who picked us up and had the car towed to a garage. Three days later I ended up in the hospital with a severe concussion and never drove in her car again, but I began to think that I needed more training in order to recognize the symptoms of neurosis and drug use.

The event that shook me to my toes and sent me to the Cardinal asking permission to take a summer course in clinical psychology was one in which I was only indirectly involved. All the young curates at the Cathedral had a caseload of people that came for counselling for marital problems, alcohol abuse, inability to hold down a job, social abandonment and such things, and each client had a particular priest that he or she wished to see. One late evening a middle-aged man that I vaguely knew came to the rectory looking for Father Ted, but Ted was off for the day and wouldn't be back until the next morning. It was a marital problem, compounded by alcohol, and Ted had talked to me about it and said that he thought he was making progress with the couple. The man wanted to tell me the whole story of his life and after half hour of impatient listening I gave him some money to get a meal and a bed in a city shelter just to get rid of him. He went home and blew his head off with a shotgun. The sense of guilt was to remain with me for a long time.

That summer a three week course was being run by the American Psychiatric and Psychological Associations (APA), and it was especially geared for social workers, ministers, priests, teachers and other people directly involved with counselling duties. It was a good practical course, held at a university near Minneapolis, not too far from our city. I explained to the Cardinal my need for further studies and he gave me permission to attend. Toward the end of the course the instructors made the students aware of a number of Master Degree scholarships that were available at various counselling centres throughout the country. With the Cardinal's permission I applied to several of them and received immediate reply back from Dr. John

Whitesel who was running a course for Protestant clergy at the Indiana Medical Centre in Indianapolis, and who wanted a priest on the program. The Bishop of Indianapolis agreed to put me on temporary staff at St. Cleopas's Church, a large central parish in the city, and a letter from my father to the Immigration Branch of the Federal Government saying that he would guarantee my financial security, rounded out the application procedure and I began the course in September. It was originally only supposed to last for one year, but it stretched into two, with an eventual Doctorate offered at the University of Chicago.

Dr. Whitesel's clinical psychology program was based on two concepts: **One**—the counsellor had to be aware of his own neurosis, and **Two**—the patient had to be helped to deal with more than the initial symptoms of his or her problems. Essentially in this program no advice was offered to the patient, nor was there any value judgement attached to the way the patient acted. This made the program very different from what the minister/priest had been trained to do, since sin and goodness did not enter into the picture. The program took for granted that the patient had tried and/or rejected the usual route that religion offered and had not been able to be healed of the problems. It was not a program of salvation or penance, which were effective in the problems of the ordinary walks of life, but one that went deeper and helped the person to face those personal ghosts that had resulted in layers of denials and secondary physical or behavioural symptoms. The program was the result of a number of clinical studies that indicated that the treatment of such patients was equally effective regardless of what type of therapy was used or who the therapist was, as long as the therapist was seen by the patient as being some sort of helpful authority figure.

The Indiana Medical Centre was the premium medical centre for the State. When patients could not be helped in other hospitals they were sent there for final diagnosis and treatment, where specialists in every medical field taught and performed the latest procedures. As clinical students we made rounds and attended lectures with the medical interns, sat in on intake conferences, attended pathology sessions, dressed in the white medical coat and were viewed as members of the hospital staff. We went on duty about eight-thirty every weekday morning and when we were not with the medical students, we visited the patients on whatever ward we were assigned. The ward assignment was usually for a month, as we rotated through surgery, paediatrics, obstetrics and gynaecology, the burn unit and the psychiatric ward. After lunch we wrote up those cases that had showed a need for counselling, and in the afternoon we presented and discussed, in the presence of Dr. Whitesel, what we had observed, and attempted to explain the route that our counselling had taken.

We found out that when a person has a problem and presents it to another, some measure of anxiety is transferred to the second person. If the problem presented echoes closely with an unsettled area in the second person then this second person will have little patience in dealing with it, since the problem is too threatening to face directly, and therefore the listener will advise a masked denial using such terms as: 'Don't sweat it!'; 'Move on in your life!'; 'Take a trip somewhere!' On the other hand, if the hearer is not threatened by the other's problem then the anxiety raised in the second person will be minimal. Then it is just a problem to be considered and the person listening will be able to be empathetic and offer suggestions that might work if they were to occur in his or her *own* case. This may not be very effective but at least, the suggestions will be less threatening: 'Tomorrow will be better; 'Time will heal all wounds.'; 'I'm here if you need me.' In either case the original problem has not been heard at the *speaker's* level. Therefore, the idea is to get the person to ventilate the background and the resulting tangents of the anxiety, and to do so in a manner that doesn't further threaten the person. The counsellor is never looking for a cure, nor for a complete understanding of the cause of the problem, but rather for a sense of peace and self-acceptance within the patient.

The mind is an amazing faculty and will usually surround the person's *key* anxiety with layers of denial, blind alleys and resistance, since the exposure of this hidden anxiety would destroy the mind's protective instincts and likely drive the person from neurosis into psychosis and a break with reality. The counsellor's job is only to remove a layer of the neurosis when it is no longer needed to support the person's sense of self worth. Since the counsellor is dealing with a shifting and manipulative set of denials within the patient, greater insight can often be gained into the world of the patient by recognizing *what is going on* in the counselling session rather than by listening to the words the patient is using. Such words are very often just a smoke screen to deflect the session and to add another layer of defence to the fragile personality. Thus, it is not likely that progress will be made rapidly with patients; rather, it is like the healing of a wound that needs fairly constant cleansing and dressing as health slowly returns. Of course, there are those unusual sudden healings in which the cause of the trauma is suddenly faced and overcome, and which novelists love, but they are rare.

The ministers/priest in the psychology program were essentially *students*; that is, they did not enter into prolonged therapy sessions with patients, but rather were observers of medical teams that diagnosed and treated patients in various stages of stress, both physical and psychological. As we watched doctors, nurses and hospital staff deal with dying patients we learned the process of grief counselling; we listened to psychiatrists during intake interviews with mental patients we learned how to separate anxiety from neurosis and neurosis from psychosis, and as we watched the prison guards in their treatment of prisoners—for the hospital had a surgical ward reserved for convicted criminals—we became aware of how difficult and complex their rehabilitation actually was. We studied different techniques of counselling presented by the various schools of analysis: Freudian, Jungian, Gestalt, Reality, Reflective and others, and held mock sessions among ourselves under the watchful eye of Dr. Whitesel, but the most essential part of the program was the use of the 'hot seat' that went on daily in the afternoon in one form or another.

After lunch we would meet in the conference room and read aloud the write-ups of patient contact from that morning. As each student read his interview notes the others would ask why he had chosen a particular style of interview. For example, it didn't take long for us to realize that we were making personal value judgements when we said, 'The patient was worried this morning.' The others would ask, "How did you know she was worried? Were *you* more comfortable with her being worried rather than depressed? Does depression in others threaten *you*? What environment had you established in the patient by your leading questions?" and so on.

We learned to approach the patient *without* an agenda and to avoid leading questions that would *predispose* the patient to give the answers he or she thought the counsellor wanted to hear, and when we wrote up the interviews we learned to use objective statements.

"The patient said she was worried", or "The patient complained of pain and asked if this was God's punishment because of the way she had treated her sister."

Becoming objective in counselling is not easy, since humans learn to rate things subjectively long before the reasoning power of the mind *tries* to take over and view the world without prejudice.

These daily sessions on the hot seat were usually fairly brief since all the students had to relate their interview notes to the others in sequence, but once a week one of the ten of us would be selected to be the centre of an in-depth analysis for two or three hours, in which anything the person had said, or the way the person had acted over the past weeks was dragged up and questioned. These were devastating sessions and no one walked away from his or her turn without being shaken to the roots of his soul as he wrestled with his newly exposed attitudes, prejudices and denials that had laid so long hidden beneath the facade of social presentation. No one, that is, except one man.

Harry was a middle-aged minister, with a parish in a nearby town, who had a story and a laugh for every occasion. During his daily presentations he defended his counselling methods, saying that he had used such methods for years and always with great success. He was never vehement about his methods being any better than anyone else's, just insisting that they worked for him and that his parishioners were very pleased with his abilities. Somehow he always avoided his turn at the weekly hot seat, deferring to another '...who needed it more.' or being absent on the day he was scheduled to take the centre seat. Finally after months of avoidance, Dr. Whitesel insisted that he take the next Wednesday session and he appeared as requested, only he came armed. He brought with him two large bottles of soft drink, two pipes, a package of pipe tobacco, a pipe tamper, a large chocolate bar and a new pack of pipe cleaners. He took a seat at the middle of the conference table and placed all these objects in front of him on the table. Then for two hours he avoided all personal motivation questions as he drank pop, cleaned the pipe, filled it with tobacco, tamped it down, smoked, ate pieces of the chocolate and told stories of situations in which he had been eminently successful. The next day he left the program.

Being on the hot seat was a very difficult learning process, and at the end of your session you were drained, scared, confused and desired nothing more than to be alone for a few hours. Nothing was sacred, not family, nor vocation, nor sexual preference, nor aspirations, nor background, nor environment nor even your beliefs about life and about God. One of the men actually broke during the program and was admitted to the psychiatric unit in the hospital, but eventually for the rest of us real insight into our lives and motivations brought an end to the ghosts in the closet and produced a tested sense of self worth. I don't think we ever understood totally why we had those hidden anxieties, but at least we had brought these ghosts out into the light and faced them squarely. For myself, the two greatest ghosts were connected to my attitude toward my parents and toward my vocation, and perhaps that was true for all the men, although those who were married had the added confusion of dealing with a wife and children.

The question of sexual feelings, desires and activities were not excluded from the sessions on the hot seat and each of us had difficulty dealing with the real person that lay within us under the cloak of respectability. Perhaps Freud was right in believing that the 'Id' lies at the basis of our actions, covered over by layers of social conditioning, for even those students who seemed to be happily married and satisfied with their own sexual life wavered and became confused when alternate desires were suggested by other members of the group. Al, one of my close friends, told me that he had gone home and locked himself in the bathroom for a three hour to soak in the tub after his session on sexual motives; and Howard got in such argument with *his* wife after his session that she ran away for a day, which worried him and his four children half to death. And *my* hot seat statement that cold showers and avoidance were all that was needed to remain pure was so ludicrous that everyone, including myself, laughed for several minutes.

Dealing with hospital patients was also a learning experience since the variety of ailments and attitudes was so diverse. The young woman who looked so well, yet insisted that she would not live through the surgery, died half way through the operation. The young man with a large, hard lump above his left ear which had a counterpart inside his skull, and who also was sure he would die on the table, came out of the operation totally free of the benign tumour. The woman in her early thirties who had nothing organically wrong yet persisted in making holes in her intestine from some undiagnosed anxiety, died less than two weeks after we saw her. The attempted suicide who had blown off his ear and part of his jaw with a shotgun, was having his new Dacron jaw covered with a flap of tissue which was still partly attached to his chest and kept his head down for weeks in a bowed position. The eighteen-year-old high school student who was absolutely normal except he had the best pair of boobs any of us had ever seen; he was in for a bilateral mastectomy because his basketball buddies kept touching them. But among the most interesting patients were the men from the State Prison who had come under guard for surgery of one kind or other. These patients lay on steel beds that were bolted to the floor and each prisoner had at least one wrist handcuffed to the steel bedpost.

They were a part of my daily rounds on the surgical assignment and were much like any other patient waiting for the doctors to wheel them into the operating room. They were nervous, sometimes really frightened, depending on the surgery that awaited them, and anxious to talk to anyone who would take their mind off the surgeon's knife. Two things became quickly apparent in dealing with them: the reason they were incarcerated wasn't really their fault, and, they were masters at manipulation—for them, anything was worth a try. One patient came back from the operating theatre after his appendix operation and was apparently still unconscious from the anaesthesia, yet he nimbly hopped off the gurney, and with his hospital gown flapping in the wind streaked for the fire exit at the far end of the ward since the nurses hadn't handcuffed him to the rolling bed. The guard and I were standing at the nurses station as he was wheeled passed, and when he began to run the guard quickly upholstered his .44 and put a bullet in his rump. As soon as the gun roared all the other prisoners rolled under their beds on the side where the wrist was chained and stayed there until all the excitement was over. The surgical cart came down from the operating room and as soon as the prisoner was chained hands and feet to the bed the surgeons removed the bullet without even waiting to give a shot of Novocain. As they operated I stood by the head of the bed and asked him if it was worth it.

He replied: "Every chance is worth it."

For the rest of his stay he was secured by one wrist and one ankle and spent most of his time lying on his stomach, yet he never complained. Later I found out that he was a murderer who had been diagnosed as a sociopath. You meet all types.

The toughest ward to be on was paediatrics, for the children cried, the parents suffered and we often felt inadequate. Most nurses were rotated through in short bursts, for those who stayed longer often had breakdowns after a child they had known died. We also learned that those who said that what went on in the ward didn't really bother them were usually the ones who ended up for a stay in our own psychiatric wing. One surgeon told us that persons who insist that nothing will bother them are the very ones that can't be told they have a terminal illness; if told they proceed rapidly into panic or psychosis. One older patient had been with us for over a month waiting for a kidney transplant and when he *insisted* on knowing whether he would get better he was finally told that no kidney was available and that the dialysis machine was being removed because it was urgently needed in the paediatric unit. On hearing this his bravado collapsed completely and he became so violent he had to be restrained. When I went back to see him a few hours later he was no longer aware of his surroundings as the uraemic poisoning took over, and he was deceased shortly after that. Another patient, whom I had given the Last Rites to in the middle of a eight hour heart transplant, met me in the hall a month later complaining that he had ripped his new pants when he tripped running to catch a bus. This was the same man who earlier couldn't walk ten steps without exhaustion setting in. Some stories have happy endings.

The priests I stayed with at St. Cleopas's parish were cheerful and industrious. A large Catholic high school was on the property and at least three of the curates taught there, as well as performing their duties at the rectory and church. We were not far from the Indianapolis Speedway and one day in May I said that I'd probably attend the race when it was run; a foolish statement from someone who had no idea how difficult tickets were to obtain unless you bought one at least a year in advance. The other priests laughed and said that I'd have to watch it on television since the tickets had all been purchased, and even the scalpers had sold their string by that time. Two days later I was making rounds in the surgery ward and spent some time with a lovely older lady who was quite interested in my reasons for coming to Indianapolis. I visited with her all that week and on the day she was released she told me to phone the ticket agent at the raceway and ask for a ticket in her name. She was the wife of 'Tony' Hulman, the owner of the Indianapolis Speedway, and the ticket got me into the main grandstand from where I watched the famous starting pile-up that reduced the field from thirty-three race cars to only seven, and sent A.J. Foyt climbing over the wire fence to avoid the cars crashing together below him. The race was so impressive that as soon as it was over I ordered a ticket for the next year, just in case Mrs. Hulman might not remember me.

Toward the end of the first year in the program I was notified that I had to go down to the main post office and fill out a student's form so I could remain for the second year. On the way back to the hospital the streets were suddenly filled with all kinds of police cars, all heading into the Trailways Bus terminal, and I followed along to see if confession or the Last Rites might be needed. Inside the ticket building an officer was slumped over between two other officers; he had been shot on the abdomen but was still conscious and as I gave him absolution he pointed across the room to where two young men were surrounded by other officers. Three young criminals had assaulted a man in Minnesota, stolen his car and his wallet and were on their way to the sunny south when the car developed mechanical problems and had to be abandoned.

When they attempted to buy bus tickets at the Trailways counter the cashier had seen that the credit card was on the stolen list and had called in the duty officer. They shot him but he got off three shots himself before he collapsed, hitting one young man in the arm and the other in the throat, with the third bullet unaccounted for. After assisting the two wounded youths I looked around for the third and saw a body face down in the parking lot with a policeman standing over it. I went out to give conditional absolution, and as I approached I asked the officer if the thief was dead because I couldn't see any blood on the pavement. The officer never even looked at me but said,

"Let's see!" and kicked the youth hard right in the rib cage, which half rolled him over.

He wasn't wounded at all, but when the shooting started and a bullet zipped over his head he went down spread eagle on the pavement in surrender. Then the officer said, "O.K. son. I'm going to give you a chance you never gave my friend. I'll count to ten and you try to run away. If I miss, you can melt into the crowd."

"Father, don't leave me!" The young man said. So I stood there until he was roughly hauled away to jail. All three wounded survived the ordeal but the officer and the young man shot in the throat had to undergo a series of operations.

My next rotation was to the State Mental Hospital, which was on the outskirts of the city, and where I was to stay for several rotations, a period of over six months. The Chaplaincy had an office there, run by Barbara, the secretary, since Dr. Whitesel seldom came over. She was a very amenable and organized young woman who knew her way around the institution and filled me in on what I should expect a Counsellor-Chaplain, both from the hospital staff and from the patients themselves, but nothing prepared me for my first encounter. We wore a hospital coat with a nametag and had to sign in before actually seeing any of the patients, since every ward was controlled by a ward attendant who checked your identity and then unlocked the door to the ward. On that first morning in the ward I was approached by another attendant who offered to show me around, and warned me about several patients who had tenancies toward violence. After fifteen minutes he excused himself to take care of other duties, but just before he left he asked what time my shift ended, and when he heard it was noon he asked me to mail a letter for him on my way back into the city. Just before noon, while I was talking with one of the resident psychiatrists, my new acquaintance pushed an envelope into my hand and walked away. The first thing the psychiatrist said was, "Better not squeeze that letter. Open it carefully."

It was full of toilet paper on which was written a long, rambling account of the unfairness of the Federal Bureau of Investigation who had incarcerated him without evidence, simply because he was able to hear other people's thoughts. The letter was addressed to the Queen of England. The psychiatrist said that he had a drawer full of the patient's letters, some of which were written on *used* toilet paper.

Another patient was a brilliant university student who had cracked up under the study load, and had been diagnosed as a manic-depressive; he was kept on a maintenance sedation dose and was generally easy to understand. As the manic stage took over he began to talk so rapidly that he couldn't be understood, but when a ward clerk recorded one of his outbursts and then played back the tape at a slower speed, everything was understandable and really quite reasonable. He was interested in dream analysis and had a reoccurring dream of being pursued by a large hawk, which obviously intended to consume him, and as with all flight dreams, his feet were leaden and escape seemed impossible. Just before the bird attacked he would wake up feeling defeated, empty and frightened, and with no understanding of what the symbolism of the hawk represented. Not all my questioning or suggestions got us anywhere until one day his very rich and successful father came to visit. I had never before seen such a hooked nose as that father wore, and the symbolism seemed obvious to me, yet understanding the symbolism doesn't bring a cure. The psychiatrists were already aware of the love-hate ambivalence within the young man, for just before the father's monthly visit the patient would become very nervous, and after he left, the boy would have to be restrained and placed in a padded cell for a day. I never found out if he was eventually released.

The threat of suicide was a constant in the mental hospital and great care was taken to make sure the patients did no harm to themselves, but in spite of our best efforts, some succeeded in welcoming the Grim Reaper. One older man, whom we watched constantly, disappeared one afternoon and the general feeling was that he had somehow escaped the premise, that is until the odour of decay led the cleaning staff to a small area behind a furnace. He had hung himself with a piece of rope made out of strings from a wet mop, but how he had squeezed into the small space behind the furnace and looped the rope around a water pipe no one could explain. Another agitated patient had to be put in a strait jacket, with a full helmet and mouth guard in place, and laced into a special restraining sheet attached to his bed, yet somehow he managed to wiggle out of the laced cover and throw himself head first off the bed onto the floor, where he died of a broken neck.

"When they really make up their mind there's not much we can do," one psychiatrist said.

About every other Saturday we sat in on the dismissal conference for patients who seemed well enough to be released back into society and, with the patient present, everyone who had contact with him or her had to give feedback on what had transpired in their recent interactions. A negative report from a ward clerk or one of the cleaning staff was just as instrumental in denying the release as was the opinion of the psychiatrist. Most patients betrayed themselves under the questioning of the group during those sessions, but some did get released as long as the outside environment to which they were going was conducive to their continued good mental health. In one case we all agreed that the patient was well enough to be released, for no one had given a negative report and he had done exceptionally well during the questioning. While the doctor was actually signing the discharge letter and wasn't even looking at the patient he casually asked the patient what his "voices" were doing at that moment. The man replied that they were cheering, and the doctor tore up the dismissal paper. Often these patients were crazy but very ingenious at the same time.

The medical centre had an excellent swimming pool right on campus and I was able to keep in shape and maintain my Instructor's level with the Red Cross. One day, while talking to Barbara, our secretary, I mentioned that I missed not being able to teach swimming. It turned out she had two children who didn't know how to swim; an eight-year-old daughter and a five-year-old son and almost instantly I was back in the swim. For about six weeks, every Saturday afternoon the children showed up at the pool and we went through a full program of instruction until each had reached a confidence level according to their age. The daughter was the prize pupil for although she had been born deaf and blind in one eye, yet she took to the water like a young trout and delighted in every step of the program. It was very satisfying and the children and I became best of friends. Just before I returned to the Medical Centre for the next rotation, Barbara told me how much she had appreciated all I had done for *her* since I had always treated her as a normal person, even though she was actually an outpatient at the institution, having broken down following her divorce. But I had never guessed that she was a patient there; I always thought she was another member of the hospital staff. She was released the next day, sane as any one of us and able to handle the ordinary stresses of life. After she left, the resident psychiatrist told me that he was convinced that the institution staff, including myself, were every bit as responsible for the healing of patients as were he and his colleagues.

Knowing Barbara and her children had been a welcomed change from life in the rectory and although I'd been to supper several times at their house there were no romantic overtones between Barbara and myself. But about sex and the priesthood...what can be said? No one talked about it among the priests that I knew. Everyone seemed to avoid the topic because, as is pretty obvious, it was a loaded gun and everyone seemed to recognize that. If other priests found themselves in situations similar to mine then they had indeed been offered sex both overtly and covertly. One young woman said she found herself 'flowing' every time she came near me; another played footsy under the table in a restaurant while sitting next to her boy friend; a third parishioner let her dressing gown fall open to revel her nakedness during a parish visit; and even a Sister called me over to her convent under the guise of setting up a CYO and asked if I was interested in sex. The statement 'What do you do for sex, Father?' was not an unusual statement to hear from both gay men and 'liberated' women, but then in counselling it is not unusual for a transference of affection to take place, and this often has sexual overtones attached to it.

The only *scary* offer happened one afternoon while flying back to the medical centre after a short visit with my family. The plane I'd taken had a stop over of three hours in another city. I found myself reading a book in the airport lounge when a middle aged man approached and introduced himself as a former member of the CYO, having noticed the lapel pin I was wearing. We talked for some time and then he offered to take me to a five o'clock Mass in his parish, which he said was only a short distance away. Instead he drove to a large wooded park some distance from the airport and said he wanted to have sex with me. When I declined he said, "I can hurt you, you know!"

He was a big man and probably could have done some damage, so I began to talk about the reality of hell and the eternity of punishment for sin, and he bought it; why I don't know. But he drove me back to the airport in silence and as he let me out of the car he mentioned that I was really lucky. I probably was.

The thing that most diocesan priests seem to miss is the family setting that wife and children offer, since essentially the parish priest lives alone and has few really close friends due to the position he holds in the community. Often these communities are in remote parts of the country where it is difficult to get together with other priests or members of the priest's own family. It is true that priests can hire a female housekeeper, but the relationship is one of employer to employee. Canon Law says that any such housekeeper must be over forty years of age, and a standard joke in the seminary was to ask whether two twenty-year-olds would do if no suitable forty-year-old one could be found. What I and several of my confreres missed most was the presence of children in the house: their laughter, their arguments and their need for a father to comfort and make them secure. In all the dealings I've had with seminarians and priests during my lifetime the question of paedophilia never came up, not even in counselling. We all seemed to sense that somehow children were sacred, even when they were a pain in the neck, and when the storm broke in the late eighties and nineties concerning priests and the sexual abuse of children we found it hard to believe, even after the evidence was confirmed. Such actions carry Christ's severest warning.

"If someone leads a child into sin it were better that a millstone be hung around his neck and he be drowned in the depths of the sea." (Mark 9:42).

For the ancient Hebrew the sea was bottomless, and one would go through the agony of drowning for all eternity. But that wasn't why we never thought of paedophilia; it was because children were unique and innocent and easily excused for their mistakes, and because we felt a love for them that is built right into the adult psyche.

Our Bishop had previously been elevated to the position of Cardinal and was called to Rome to take part in the Second Vatican Council in 1964 under Pope Paul VI. The hope among many of the North American clergy was that the vow of celibacy might somehow be relaxed, even allowing certain priest to marry and carry on their ministry, although this didn't seem probable to most of us. Even back then I thought it was a good idea, since I had grown up in the Protestant faith where clerical marriage was not only permitted but encouraged, and in my relationship with the ministers in the counselling program it began to look even more desirable. I wrote the Cardinal and asked if it was possible that the Church might allow a married clergy, since many of us were, or would be, drawing full salaries as counsellors, chaplains or teachers and could support a family without being a burden to the parish. He kindly answered saying that it didn't look possible at that time although he knew that many of the liberal members of the hierarchy were requesting it, but he added that a program of laicisation, or release from the vow of celibacy was being discussed at that time.

Perhaps the thing that caused me to write to the Cardinal came from several sessions in the second year of the program when it was my turn to be questioned at length by the other student-counsellors. They returned several times to two major suggestions, which I found at first almost impossible to face. One had to do with my relationship with my father, who was so successful in the world and toward whom I began to realize that I felt both love and hate. As a child in whatever game we played he played to win and when he did, and he usually did, he exalted often to the point of mockery. Because as a child I was small and when I complained about losing he would call me a 'sawed off, hammered down, half pint.' and tell me to grow up and be a man. On the other hand he was a good provider, generous with gifts and allowance, and forgiving on the many times I misbehaved, although the forgiveness usually followed a few whacks on the hands from the 'strapping' belt that hung in his closet. He found it difficult to show affection and I don't remember him actually kissing my brother or myself, but perhaps he occasionally did. The question the students raised was whether I had chosen the priesthood so that I wouldn't have to compete with his image in the commercial world. I could be successful in the one area that he never could enter and thus would not have to live in the shadow of the archetypical warrior father figure. Was the suggestion true? Now, I don't think it was, but then it certainly haunted me.

The second suggestion that left me weak the knees was that perhaps I had chosen a life of celibacy simply to make amends for youthful excesses, based on a personal concept that somehow sex was dirty. It was, they suggested, a lived-out permanent penance, accepted for fear of being unable to control the basic urges of the sexual appetite. These suggestions were not in any form of accusations, nor were they particular to me, for they applied also to the few unmarried ministers that were in the program. They were attempts to have each of face those neurotic attitudes that *might* be a part of our personal blindness, so that in dealing with patients we would not be treating our own hang-ups, but trying to assist the others in coming to grips with theirs. Even Al, who seemed so balanced in his marriage, once told me that a beautiful parishioner had come to him for counselling and after several sessions had said,

"Why is it that I have an urge to tear off my clothes when I'm with you in these counselling sessions?"

And Al's inner voice had said to him: "Tell her to do it!"

He shared it so that it could be seen as a normal male response to a young and beautiful woman and not something to be tucked away and pretended to be forgotten.

Early in the second year I was called down to the Unemployment Office in the centre of the city and asked if I was interested in a weekend job. They needed someone to run the swimming program on Saturday and Sunday at Camp Atterbury, a large retraining camp for unemployed young men, about twenty miles outside the city. The fact that I was a Red Cross Water Safety Instructor, had counselling experience and was also a priest who could say Mass for the corpsmen on Sundays, rounded out the job description. They hadn't been able to find anyone else who had those qualifications and they were willing to give me the job so that I could be both a student and a temporary government employee. After checking with the pastor at St. Cleopas's Parish where I resided and sometimes did Sunday duties, and the local Bishop, I was freed to begin the weekend work at the Job Corps camp. The first thing I did was to buy a cheap, used Chevy Corvair in order to drive out Friday evening and return Sunday night. Ralph Nader was right: that car was unsafe at any speed, especially on country roads that had no super elevation, for halfway through a turn the back end would decide to lead, and the car would end up in the ditch. It took some training to keep it under control, but it wasn't too bad as long the speed was kept down, especially on curves.

Camp Atterbury was situated on Federal land that had been set up a prisoner-of-war compound during World War II, and had been remodelled as a military rehabilitation centre after the war. It occupied a large number of acres, some of which were still being used as a staging area for a Reserve Tank

Unit of the Army. The corpsmen's section of the camp had several buildings, which included dormitories for the young men, a large cafeteria, a hospital, a guards' building and small jail, a gymnasium, a boxing ring, and game rooms. Around the buildings there were paved basketball courts, as well as baseball and football fields. Over near the edge of the property there was an enclosed swimming pool complete with change rooms, a secured property room for the swimmers' clothes, a laundry, a chlorination chamber and an office with a sick room attached. The pool had its own heating system, and once during the winter when I forgot to lower the temperature on Saturday night the pool turned into a hot bathtub for the boys the next morning. That morning we opened the panic doors on the side of the pool and the corpsmen alternately rolled in the snow in the adjacent field and then plunged back into the steaming water. They loved the experience but the heat made them lethargic and we got no swimming drills taught that morning.

In the camp there were about two thousand young men between the ages of seventeen and twenty-two, and each of them had been out of school for at least two years and out of work for at least one. The Office of Economic Opportunity was funding the program with the hope that after a nine month stay in the camp each corpsman would have picked up an employable trade, such bus driver, factory worker, caretaker, youth worker, short order cook or similar job. Essentially we were a work-project camp with the facility for each corpsman to try out several occupations to see which one would offer lifelong employment. Almost all of them had a grade eleven high school certificate, although our testing program showed a reading level in most cases of only grade five; consequently the men received some schooling as well as job orientation. The corpsmen came from every State in the Union, including Hawaii and Alaska, with the majority of them coming from the lower economic levels of society. About seventy percent of the corpsmen were African-American, with many of them coming from the Deep South. Their accents were delightful to my ears and we often exchanged good-natured ribbing concerning the way the other talked.

They called me 'Preach' when they found out I was a priest, and a few of them occasionally even came to Sunday Mass which was held in an Interfaith Chapel right on the base. Mostly, I got to know them through the drown-proofing program, which was compulsory for every corpsman. The Administration didn't expect me to make expert swimmers out of them, although some actually did become certified Red Cross Life Guards through one of our programs. What was expected was that any corpsman who fell into water would be able to keep himself afloat until help arrived. Drown-proofing consists of breath control by taking a breath on the surface to see if the person could float, and if he couldn't then still holding his breath, letting the body sink to eye level for thirty second, then moving the arms and legs to push the head out of the water for another breath. The seven-year-old daughter of the head lifeguard had been able to demonstrate the ease with which this could be done and had stayed in the pool, with her hands and feet *tied*, for five hours without a break and without any negative effects. It was essentially a method of overcoming the panic that often accompanies a sudden emersion in deep water, and as the students learned to relax most of them found it quite easy to remain safe and comfortable in deep water for the ten minutes required to pass the drown-proofing compulsory test.

There were two other weekend lifeguards who usually came on Saturday and Sunday mornings. Both Rick and Don were students at the University of Indiana at Bloomington, in Recreation Leadership and both were in their final undergraduate year. Rick was the more serious of the two, but Don had no end of stories that were both fascinating and doubtful. He arrived one morning to tell Rick and myself that he had just blown his hot water tank apart with a twelve-guage shotgun. Don and his wife lived in a small house in a country wooded area near the Kentucky border, and that morning his wife had told him the hot water tank in the bathroom was knocking something terrible and wanted him to fix it. When he got down on his knees to check under the tank a six-foot rattlesnake warned him to keep his distance. He said he got so excited that he had got the gun and blasted the snake without considering what effect his action would have on the hot water tank. He said his wife was so mad at him he wished he'd been bitten instead of blasting the tank.

Whenever we had a new set of corpsmen to learn drown-proofing we spent the opening fifteen minutes rescuing them from the bottom of the deep end of the pool. The entrance to the pool from the change rooms was at the deep end, and invariably some of the new cadets would immediately jump or push one another into the water and have to be rescued. After a rescue as they spluttered out the inhaled water on the pool deck they would complain loudly that they had never seen *clear* water that was more than two feet deep and ask why we hadn't warned them. We had, of course; it was just that they were too excited and playful to pay any attention to our opening remarks when they first entered the building. At first we used the standard form of spinning the immersed 'victim' around, grabbing him under the arms and swimming him to the side of the pool, but eventually we found it more practical to just get behind these 'victims' and push upward on their rears toward the pool's edge. It was quicker and they swallowed less water, but sometimes in free swim time we actually had to use the standard rescue method because they had ended up in deep water in the middle of the pool. All three of us agreed that we made more rescues that year than we had ever made in all our combined, previous years as lifeguards.

The corpsmen were mainly street-wise tough kids and some of them had been sent to us by the Courts. Because there were so many of them we had to have a way of controlling them and keeping the peace. The first step was left to the dorm leaders, who were each in charge of about a dozen corpsmen. In order to be a dorm leader you had to be over six foot tall and two hundred and twenty pounds, and it helped if you had some boxing experience or a black belt in karate. We had campus police who could step in and haul the more aggressive ones off to the lockup, but we tended to use them more for show than for actual control. The actual enforcement was done by a select group of really tough corpsmen who could physically manhandle any cadet who the police or dorm leaders couldn't control. These men wore a special uniform, had their own dorm and got special privileges, such as going to the front of the chow line, and getting to go into Indianapolis every second weekend, as long as they kept the others in line. They 'persuaded' the others to behave, sometimes to the point of sending them to the camp hospital, and our threat of calling in the 'Diplomats' usually brought an end to any ruckus by a corpsman. If even the Diplomats failed there always was solitary confinement, and the toughest corpsman wilted under a three-day sentence. However, most of the boys were pleasant and responded well to fair and welcoming attention.

Everyone except the Diplomats wore the same semi-military uniform and it had to be kept neat and properly worn. Corpsmen that Security warned were 'out of uniform' would get demerit points and could lose their 'off-campus' time, which was usually a couple of days per month. Actually the camp was well run and we had few real incidents, although occasionally one would happen. One of my swimmers was absent for two weeks and when he showed up he had over sixty stitches in his scalp, which he received from not giving his loose change to a bully, who had used a piece of iron bunk bed to persuade him to be less stingy. The boys ate well for the camp set a good table and you could always go back for seconds and thirds; the average weight gain over the nine months was about twenty pounds, mainly because of the milk they drank. They loved fresh milk and would often drink a whole jug at every sitting. The Army had a fancy recruiting booth right outside the cafeteria and the standing joke was that the Government was fattening them up so they would be heavy enough to join the Army. I once heard that over thirty percent of the graduates actually did join up at the end of their nine months at the camp.

The swimming pool was its own building and stood at the end of the Atterbury property, with private land adjoining it. The closest field had the remains of old farmhouse on the top of a small hill, and the belief among the corpsmen was that it had belonged to a farmer who had murdered his wife, and that on certain nights she could be seen walking around the old house, dressed in a nightgown. One Sunday evening as I was locking up the pool and getting ready to head back to Indianapolis, I noticed that a small crowd had gathered outside underneath the field light that illuminated the entrance to the building. One of the young men was very agitated, and claimed that he had actually seen the ghost about hour earlier. He had run back to his dorm and told his friends that the story about the murdered woman was true, and some of them had come out to see for themselves. But when they got to the front of the pool their courage had evaporated, and they stood there daring one another to cross the field and walk up to the ruins of the old farmhouse. As a psychology student I felt that their actions were worth studying, especially those of the one who claimed to have seen the ghost, so I said I would lead the way to see if the sighting was actual, or only the work of the evening shadows.

We started off across the field but by the time I had reached the bottom of the hill only the 'witness' remained with me, the others having stopped in small bunches as they reached the level of their fright-endurance, somewhere between us and the swimming pool. Suddenly he shouted, "There she is!" and stood transfixed, pointing up the hill towards the ruins of the house.

It was getting dark and I could see nothing, but he was so adamant that the hairs on the back of my neck started to stand up. I told him I couldn't see anything and began to walk up the hill, saying that when he saw me reach her he should tell me and I'd try to catch her. He shouted, "No! No!" and begged me to come back.

There was no doubt in my mind that he actually did see her, and when a low moan uttered from the gloom, he took off on a ten second hundred yard dash, picking up all the stragglers on his way back to the safety of the field light at the pool. Then I heard laughter and went over to a small ditch where two other corpsmen were killing themselves laughing at the memory of the herd charging back across the field. When they stopped laughing they said that earlier they had hidden in the ditch to smoke some weed and had used the moaning to scare off the original witness who they had seen timidly approaching the old ruins earlier that evening. The interesting thing was that when the three of us joined the others back under the field light we couldn't convince any of them that it was all a joke, nor would they believe that the ghostly apparition had not actually been there, since some of those who hadn't even made it to the bottom of the hill claimed that they too had seen her figure. The imagination is a powerful force.

Most of the corpsmen seemed to believe in ghosts, witches, werewolves and vampires and often told tales about someone they knew, or had heard about, who had seen a zombie or a witch casting a spell or a monster lurking in a dark corner. The first time I attended the camp movie theatre with them the film was about a young couple who ended up in old castle which naturally had several vampire coffins in the underground vault. As the movie started the young man was making pleasant conversation with the young woman, but the corpsmen were too impatient with the niceties of romance and kept shouting out: "F—her! F—her!" It became impossible to follow the conversation being presented on the screen because of the loud laughter and catcalls, but suddenly there was a total hush over the whole theatre as the first vampire slid along the darkening corridor toward the young couple. Some of the boys actually got down on the floor behind the seats, and a few of them ran out of the theatre as more of the vampires appeared. Whatever we strongly believe does become a reality for us, and for them the living dead were real.

Once, someone in Administration thought it would be a good idea to bring several bus loads of girls from their Job Corps camp near Chicago to our camp for a Saturday night dance.

We only tried it once. Two hundred girls arrived by bus one Saturday afternoon and were given the use of several unused dormitories in another section of the camp. They used our cafeteria but the boys were all kept in their dorms until the girls had returned to their quarters; in fact, the two groups never saw one another except at a distance until the evening dance was set up. Then two hundred of our corpsmen, who had been chosen by lottery, were bussed to a large tank hanger that had been prepared for the occasion, and the dance began. Every camp worker that could be spared was on duty at the hanger to prevent fights and open sexual encounters, and for the most part we were fairly successful. The dance ended at midnight and the girls, guarded by their female chaperons, were loaded back in their buses and taken back to their dormitories. Not that it stopped there. The boys ran the half-mile to the girls' quarters and arrived just minutes after the last girl was safely locked inside. We beat them there in our camp vehicles and formed a human chain around most of the buildings, but the boys were not to be denied, and the girls didn't help either, leaning out of the windows, lifting up their pullover jerseys and calling out: "Here I am, baby! Here I am!"

We spent most of the night hauling corpsmen off the roof of the dorms and trying to convince the girls to turn off their lights and go to sleep. One athletic corpsman actually hung upside down off the edge of the roof and got a kiss from one of the girls at her window before a one hundred and eighty pound female chaperon hauled the girl inside and thumped the corpsman with a professional right cross that sent him tumbling to the ground. It was a night to remember.

When I arrived at the camp on Friday afternoons the pool was already closed, but after eating supper with the corpsmen in the cafeteria the pool was opened for a two hour free-swim period, closing for the night about eight o'clock. Usually I took some homework and a novel with me to occupy the evening after I'd cleaned the pool and washed and dried the towels. About ten thirty I'd go to bed in the sick room that was attached to the pool's office. I'd open up the pool about nine o'clock the next morning after breakfast, when the other lifeguards arrived, and we would run our programs for the rest of the day, with the two university students leaving about two-thirty. Then the boys could swim freely for the rest of the afternoon or practice their drown-proofing skills. We had an aluminum canoe with flotation chambers at each end which we used to demonstrate how to use their new skill if they ever upset while out in a boat. One afternoon I watched from the guard's tower while about a dozen of them tried to get in the canoe in the deep end of the pool and were finally able to sink the canoe in spite of its flotation chambers. Then suddenly they let it go while one end was higher than the other and it acted like a torpedo, rushing across the water and right through one of the large underwater lights that illuminated the pool. It shorted out all the lights in the building and could have shorted out the corpsmen as well. They thought that it was the funniest thing they had ever done, and there certainly was a suggestion that it had been aimed on purpose. Whatever the reason, I locked up the canoe and never allowed it to be used again on the weekends since those underwater lights could only be replaced after the pool had been half emptied. It took a full day for maintenance to repair the light and refill the pool.

Chapter 11
Romance

As well our work at the Medical Centre we attended some classes at Butler University, which was the institution that certified our training and accepted our Master's thesis. It was our privilege one day to hear a lecture by Doctor Eric Fromm, a Jewish psychiatrist who had endured the hardships of Auschwitz Concentration Camp for several years during the Nazi occupation of Western Europe. From his personal experiences in that death camp he had developed a clinical method of treating patients who had serious emotional or mental problems. The treatment was called Logo Therapy and is to be found in his book entitled *Man's Search for Meaning*. The day after his lecture we had the opportunity at the Medical Centre of watching him apply his method to a severely depressed older patient. The treatment was done before an audience of medical students, doctors and psychiatrists, in the main pathology theatre. The patient was wheeled in and presented to the assembled staff but showed no signs of acknowledging her surroundings, the staff or Doctor Fromm. She sat listlessly, hands clasped together in her lap and with her head bowed as the doctor began a one sided conversation telling her to ignore the audience and the surroundings and think only of things that had happened in her life.

In a quiet voice he told her a little of his sufferings in the death camp and his faith in God and how he had finally realized that people have very little control over the environment in which life, or fate, places them. No one designs the life into which he or she is born nor can they totally control the way they spend their adult years. He said that we are far more conditioned by our environment than we ever want to admit and that the very best we ever can do is to try to make a good effort in whatever environment we find ourselves. This, he said, is the only worthwhile test of humanity, not what advances we have made in science or technology, nor how successful we have been in business, but whether we have done a good job, not even excellent one, in relating to those we know and the work we do. Then he began to question her about her life and she responded. She had been an ordinary housewife, bearing and raising four children; her husband had died as had one child, and the others now had their own lives and problems and finally had stopped coming to see her. She felt as if she was a failure, never having amounted to anything in the world, and that when she died no one would miss her.

He asked her to go back over the stages of her life and as she did he pointed out that her choices had been ordinary ones, in tune with her environment, and that at each stage she had done a good job. In the ordinary sense of the word she had been a good wife, a good mother, a good worker and a good friend. She had not asked for life but once it was given she had done all that could be reasonably expected of her, and was, in short, a successful human being. During this doctor/patient session it was obvious that she had forgotten that we were there but we could see her brightening as the dialogue proceeded; her hands relaxed and she used them as she explained the highs and lows of her life, and she smiled at the doctor as they discussed her life. Just before the long session ended she asked if he would come and see her the next day and he said he would but he added that now that she understood she was a successful human being she should reach out to others as she had done before her depression began. Success is to be found in our efforts, not in our accomplishments, he added. We gave her a standing ovation and she smiled at us as the orderly wheeled her away. After she left we thanked him for the demonstration and someone asked if the therapist had to feel successful himself in order for the therapy to work, and Dr. Fromm began to weep.

"I am not successful", he said. " I did not do the ordinary things of life well. Instead I prostituted myself, acting as the personal Freudian analyst to a German Sergeant in the death camp just to stay alive. The really heroic and successful humans died in the camp. Now I am making amends. No, you don't have to feel successful to show others that they are. Now, thank God, I have been given some time to regain my humanity."

Dr. Whitesel must have been pleased with my counselling progress for he asked me to write for a doctoral program in Psychology at the University of Chicago, and with his support I was given a scholarship and set up with a part time job as a night-time guard in a high security apartment near the university.

In the interview for the job I was told that I'd be issued a magnum .44 revolver and be expected to take target practice at the Chicago police range every two weeks. Apparently they were serious about protecting the patrons in the apartment for when I was getting my gun permit I asked the officer if I'd be trained to shoot someone in the leg or arm and his reply was that if I ever had to draw the weapon I was to shoot for the heart and leave the consequences to them.

The Cardinal wrote saying that the diocese could no longer support my absence, but that if I could raise the funding myself, then I had his permission to proceed. He had a Ph.D. standing himself and had belonged to a teaching Order before being appointed Bishop, and therefore was interested in advanced education.

Then my life turned around. Even after all these years it is difficult to make sense out of what happened next. One early spring day an airline stewardess showed up at the Medical Centre asking for me. She was a former member of the CYO, whom I knew slightly. Her older sister had sent her to me three years previously for some counselling over a family problem. She was only nineteen then and slightly chubby, but she had grown up, slimmed down and become quite beautiful. It was good to see her and she had news of many things that were going on in the home diocese. I spent the afternoon with her and took her out to supper to a good Polish restaurant I knew, and had her back to the airport in time for her flight at midnight. Two days later I received a letter from her that was more than friendly, and which I discussed with the group during examination session. 'Was I falling in love? Was this an answer to my vocational indecision or just a test?' I wrote back a few days later, being friendly but non-committal and within two weeks she showed up again, since one of her airline routes was to Chicago, and the flight to Indianapolis was free for her. We went out again, and she went home again, but she kissed me before she boarded the plane and that hadn't happened in a long time. This was trouble and my feelings were laced with confusion and indecision. I even made a two-day retreat at a monastery in Kentucky, but when I returned more of her letters were waiting for me and they were serious love letters. Prayer is good but in some situations it has to fight against an equally powerful desire, and it doesn't always bend the free will of the person in the best direction. On her third visit she stayed the weekend.

Perhaps nothing would have come from our meetings if 'George', another priest at St. Cleopas's parish, hadn't called me one Friday afternoon and asked if he could come out and talk to me at the swimming pool that evening. A strange request, and my immediate thought was that somehow my meetings with the stewardess had become public knowledge and the Bishop was sending him out to ask me to leave the diocese. George was about twenty-eight, very athletic and good looking, and was doing work with a youth group similar to my own CYO organization. When he arrived it was dark, and as he entered the pool office he seemed quite nervous. He started to talk about my training in counselling and about a personal problem he had himself, and wondered if I could be of assistance to him. Then his story came tumbling out. One of the young women that was on his Youth Executive had invited him over to her family home for supper several times, and her parents were quite taken with his charm and obvious intelligence. Her father had said that if he ever decided to leave the priesthood there would be good job waiting for him in the family firm, for they were always looking for bright young men. He went on to say that the daughter was beautiful and had confessed that she was in love with him, and now he thought that he had also fallen in love with her. He had hardly finished talking when I started to laugh, and he reacted angrily, saying that my reaction was not what he had expected. Then we talked and I told him about my similar indecision, and before he left, after we had shared for a long time, we had agreed to abandon our vocations and start on a new path.

I'm sure it was a bad decision, but God's greatest gift to mankind is His gift of free will. No sane person has to argue to the existence of free will because it is such an obvious internal awareness, but free will supposes the presence of a Supreme Power. How can we be free and God be All-Powerful and All Knowing? That's the mystery, but unless free will exists along with God then nothing in life makes sense. Not Law, nor Government, nor love, nor loyalty, nor right nor wrong, for without God we are just bits of chemicals that accidentally brush up against other bits of chemicals by chance. That idea is enough to drive anyone insane, but then, there wouldn't be anything real about sanity or insanity either. What George and I did was to act out of weakness and I don't believe that it was what God wanted from either of us. Six months after we left and were both married a fire started in St. Cleopas's Church and both arms of the main crucifix were burned off. The symbolism was not difficult to understand. Someone sent me a clipping of the newspaper account, and likely sent one to George as well.

Our marriages were outside the Church and mine at least was doomed from the start. Both my wife and I had fallen in love with an *ideal* and neither of us was able to live up to that ideal. To her I was the mature, wise, romantic figure who could take her problems away, and to me she was the essence of youth and spring, a nymph sent to comfort my loneliness and give me the children for whom I longed. By the time the honeymoon was over, essentially so was the marriage, although we cohabited for about three years. Disappointment is a bitter pill and the aftertaste lasts for a long time, but there is no use in crying over spilled milk. I had given up the Ph.D. program just before the marriage and we moved back north, and for a year I attended the College of Education while working part time in a clothing store and as the night manager at a dry cleaning establishment. That spring the University Placement Office ran an ad for summer sales persons with a large book company and I went to their training program. The program was an eye-opener! We memorized everything we were to say during the forty-five minute sales pitch, went out with a seasoned salesman and watched him in action, and finally got to try our own hand in the field. The product was a set of books that contained everything that a teacher would need to prepare lessons, and although the price was high, the Book Company had a generous interest-free monthly payment plan that appealed to many buyers. There was a lot of money to be made, and the second summer I worked at it I won the Best Sales Award and made enough to buy a new sports car.

After the year at university I was hired to teach in an academic high school in the west end of the city. The subjects were English, Drama and Counselling, and in Counselling several of the students displayed the same anxieties and neurosis that had been present in the mental institution; it was like old home week except that their symptoms were more sudden in their onset and usually disappeared quickly once they came and got them out in the open. One young man whose girlfriend had just dumped him, raged and raged in my office until Administration called in the police for fear he would do some damage to himself or the girlfriend. Before the police took him from my office they first unloaded the cartridges from their guns, for he was a big senior student and might have wrestled one of the weapons away from them. He quit school after they released him but came back to see me occasionally and eventually started his own rock band and forgot all about his lost love. I went to see him perform one Friday night about a year later and his band was good, and so was his new girlfriend.

The Drama class wanted to see a real Broadway play and since there was nothing to keep me at home I arranged a bus trip for about fifty of the students and off we went to New York City. The School Board gave us Friday off, so our buses left after school on Thursday in order to catch a Friday night performance of a current Broadway hit. We booked into the old Edison Hotel, which had seen better days, but was just off Forty-Second Street and close to the live theatre where Dustin Hoffman had the lead in *Jimmy Shine*. Four other teachers came along as chaperons and after we arrived in New York and the students had been fed we returned to the hotel and spent the remainder of the night chasing the boys out of the girls' rooms and vice versa. We were glad to see the sun come up because the students finally went to bed and slept until the late afternoon.

That evening we went to the theatre. We had good seats and all our girls fell in love with the youth Dustan he bounced across the stage. He was good, and afterwards some of the students wanted to meet him, so the manager directed us out of the theatre and around to the stage door. He came out with another player and stopped to talk with his new fans and after a few minutes remarked that we had a strange accent. When he learned we were from up north he said: "What can I do to cement New York-Toronto relationships?" and without hesitation one of our girls told him he could kiss her. So he kissed her on the cheek and laughed when she said, "I will never wash again!"

We saw him the next day in Tiffany's, with one of the showgirls who must have been six inches taller than him, but I wouldn't let the girls ask for his autograph; he looked like he wanted to be alone with his tall friend. When you are successful, a thing like size drops out of the picture. From there we went to the Bowery, splitting the students into two groups, each window shopping down one side of the street, until we met at the far end, only to find we were missing one of our youngest girls. We found her in a bar, drinking with two of the patrons, who moved off rapidly when they found out she was only fourteen. What a scene she made! She was her own boss; she could do whatever she wanted; her parents let her do her own thing, and so on. Luckily all the students' parents had signed a waiver saying they would allow us to send their child home by air, at their expense, if the student became intractable. A call home was followed by a call to her uncle, who lived in Queens, and who came to the Bowery and took her off our hands. I hope he had more success with her than we did.

Saturday night we split up to go to different restaurants around the hotel and one group wanted to try a famous New York steak house, so I accompanied them. On the way down on the elevator from the tenth floor, a young pro got on and squeezed up against me.

"Hey, big boy. How about a little action?" and I started to laugh because the noisy students behind me had suddenly become as quiet as church mice.

She said: "Are you laughing at me?" and seemed shocked when I pointed to the ten students behind us and said,

"I'm laughing because these are *all* my kids."

"All your kids! Man I don't want anything to do with you. You're too fertile!"

When the elevator stopped and she was out of hearing range the questions and the laughter started.

"Sir? Why didn't you take her up on it? Did she really think we were your children? Do you often get offers like that, sir?"

And of course, when we got back to the hotel, and later the school, everyone knew that I'd been propositioned, and every male student that was there said it was a good thing she hadn't asked *him*.

The School Board was on a Intelligence Testing push at that time and every student had to be tested and assessed for post-secondary education and job streaming. It was a time consuming work and probably was of no actual value except in one case. We had a grade eleven girl who on the general assessment test was rated in the ninety-ninth percentile, and since we were counselling all the students her scores came to my desk. In the interview she said she wasn't surprised that her scores were that high and agreed to take a more sophisticated assessment test the next day. Her scores went off that scale as well, so her I.Q. range was at least above 180, the limit of that test. Her teachers told me she was their prize pupil who could answer questions that even sometimes stumped them. I contacted her parents and asked if they had considered sending her to the university as a special student, and they gave permission to approach the University Board and ask for a review of the case. The university agreed to let her take two Arts courses the next September, with consideration of picking up another two at Christmas if her marks were good in the first two, but when I approached her with the offer she declined, saying she wasn't emotionally ready and still had a lot of high school growing-up to do. She really was a bright girl.

In another school where I worked one of the teachers was gay, although few of the students or teachers were aware of this. On weekends he dressed in drag and had an act at a Queen Bee bar downtown and from what some of the others told me he was the most beautiful 'girl' there. One of our more liberated lady teachers took her straight husband to see the drag acts and arranged for our friend to come to their table after the act and pretend to fall for the husband, who was covered in confusion when the drag queen sat on his lap and ran 'her' fingers through his hair. The following Monday we learned that the husband was so attracted to 'her' that he suggested to the wife that they attend the show the next weekend and was heartbroken when he learned the 'she' was really a 'he'.

On the I.Q. rating tests some students scored so low that it was obvious that they had purposely answered many of the questions falsely. A couple of higher quality tests separated those who were malingers from those who were seriously depressed, and from the second group I started a series of group counselling sessions which seemed to lessen their anxiety and provide them with a more positive outlook on the future. One bright but depressed senior student, who had a retarded younger brother at home, came to realize that it was not her life's work to care for him, an idea that both her parents had fostered in her from her early years. She broke free of the family and went on to graduate from university as a Physical Therapist and found work in a hospital where she could use her learned skills without feeling that the patients' disorder was somehow her fault. Another student, who was overweight, told the group that she felt she was living 'behind a wall of fat' and was surprised and helped to find that other members of the group felt the same way about themselves. Another boy had to be committed after we found out that the reason he kept his hand on the wall as he walked down the hallway was that it was the only way he could feel he was in touch with reality. He felt that if he removed his hand from the wall he would disappear. When I visited his home to suggest the commitment it was obvious that the mother was far worse than the boy, but eventually we were able to get the father to commit the son. What happened to the mother I left to the Social Service Agency.

And the most unusual case I ever encountered also came out of the group setting. One of the Grade 12 students admitted privately that he was considering suicide because he thought he was losing his mind. He had never studied music in his life but found he could play most instruments after a short practice, and was able to write the musical scores that he used in the band he had started. The thing that frightened him was that his mind was filled with the notes of orchestrations of scores he had no recollection of ever hearing. His parents finally agreed to come in for interview and were so adamant in their denial that anything was wrong with their child it was obvious that they were hiding something. The boy grew worse and finally the mother agreed to come back for a second interview, and in a tearful session admitted that her only child was adopted. She and her husband had at one time been the managers of a highly regarded playhouse that catered to professional orchestras, which toured North America, and over the years had made friends with many of the artists who came on a regular basis. A famous maestro and a brilliant cellist, both happily married to other partners, had an affair while on tour with neither of them wanting the child of love that resulted, and had agreed to a private adoption to the childless couple that ran the playhouse on the condition that the baby's new parents find work in some unconnected field. Because the couple had so badly wanted a child for so long they agreed and kept all mention of music out of the young child's life.

He had to be told, and that weekend they sat down with the eighteen-year-old boy and told him of his natural history. For awhile he avoided my office but just before the end of the school year he showed up one day: everything now made sense to him; some day he would trace his birth parents down; he was no longer depressed but rather excited about his future in the world of music and his immediate goal was to get through his exams and go on to college. Jung's concept of residual genetic memory had seemed a mere academic theory until this time, but now seems quite reasonable.

One of the teachers rode in one day on a Second War motorcycle, still wearing its battle dress pea-green coating, and a forgotten longing began to take hold. He was willing to sell it and move on to a more modern set of duel wheels if we could come to agreement on the price. That Friday we met at his mother's house to iron out the final details of the transaction and the only question Frank had was why I wanted such a vintage machine. But as a child I had watched them come down the street from the Army barracks near our home during the war and I remembered what impression they had made on my young imagination. Frank also had war memories and brought out an old scrapbook full of snapshots of a young U-boat Commander in the German Navy, his father. After the war Frank and his mother had spent some time in a displaced persons camp and then immigrated to join relatives who ran a food service in a small local city. Frank hardly remembered his father, for his mother had been barely thirty when they left Germany and within a few years had married her employer, after war records indicated that the birth father had died in a bombing raid on his submarine.

The next summer Frank went on his first holiday to Germany and contacted the International Red Cross to see if any of his birth father's relatives had survived the war. He was told there was a chance that his father's younger brother was living in a large apartment complex in a city not too far out of the way of Frank's travel plans. After he came back home at the summer's close he told me that he had arrived at the complex, which had a large number of stone tables on a patio in front of the apartment, and had asked a group of young people on the patio if they knew Herr Schroeder. They pointed out a man reading a newspaper not far away and said they thought he was the one.

Frank said: "When I stood beside the man I had overpower sense that he was not my uncle but my father, and when he looked up I told him who I thought he was. When the incredible introduction was over we sat and talked for a long time, filling in what had taken place in our lives since we had separated years before. He had scuttled his sub at war's end and taken the identity of his brother who had died in a bombing raid. Later we went up to his apartment and I met his new wife, small son and grown daughter and spent the rest of my holiday with them."

Both Frank's birth father and his mother, when she found out, thought it was best to leave sleeping dogs lie and never contacted one another, but the next year Frank returned to Germany and as far as I know he is still there.

Teaching night school brought me in contact with adults who were trying to upgrade their educational standings to move on to a better job. An exception to this trend was a twenty-eight year old *successful* mechanic and body repairman named Rene. Rene's father owned a garage and body shop and Rene had learned both trades working with his dad from the time he was able to hold a wrench. After school one night we talked cars for a while in the school office and then he came out to see my sports car, a yellow Jaguar XKE, and fell in love with it just as I had. We worked out a deal where he would tune it, and fix any fender damage it picked up, in exchange for the use of the car on certain weekends. My wife and I had agreed to a separation and she had moved out, which left me free to attend auto and motorcycle shows and watch Rene work his magic in the garage where he worked. Rene felt that his only shortcoming was his lack of formal education and with a little prompting he went to university and over the next three years earned a Bachelor's Degree in Arts. In the intervening years we talked of travelling the world to broaden our practical awareness of how other people lived, and it was Rene who came up with the idea of building a sailboat and seeing the world by sea, although neither of us had any training in boat building or navigation. Eventually he did build his own boat and sailed around the Pacific with his girlfriend for several years, but by that time I had returned to university, and that's another story.

Jonathan, my artistic friend from seminary days, showed up at a teacher's conference one Spring day and we took time out to catch up on the absent years. He had done well in teaching and was the Arts Coordinator for a school board and was responsible for setting up and overseeing all the visual arts programs in the elementary schools in his district. He accepted an invitation to meet my sister and her family at our cottage that summer and demonstrated what a talented artist and teacher he was by enthralling her two small children with endless projects using paper and glue, flour and water, sand and plaster and, of course, paint. Jonathan had never in his life made an overnight camping trip, and when in the evening Joan and I recounted some of our experiences he begged to be taken on one. The overnight canoe trip was a great success and he returned determined to become a latter-day frontier's man. As soon he went home he contacted a fellow teacher, who was a regular camper, and set up a weekend excursion into the wilds of Algonquin Park, first visiting a high-priced outfitters store and buying almost everything in sight. Unfortunately, in the early morning at their first campsite Jonathan heard a noise outside the tent and when he stuck his head out he saw a black bear eating most of their supplies. When the bear began to amble over to see if there was any extra sugar, Jonathan set a new record for getting the canoe into the water and keeping out of harm's way. His fellow camper chased the bear away but Jonathan remained fixed in the canoe and only left it when they reached the area where their car was parked. He left all his new gear at our place and never asked to go camping again.

He visited at Christmas time and seemed unsettled and drank too much, but there was no clear indication of what was troubling him and he avoided any discussion about his own problems. When the school year ended he showed up on my doorstep again, just stopping off to say goodbye on his way to a vacation in France. He seemed to be in good spirits and talked about his intended trip and his fear of flying but he was determined to sample the French culture, since he had come from a French background and was perfectly bilingual. He asked a lot of questions about the airport and how you were boarded and agreed to let me see him off on the plane. Just before the attendant let the passengers on the plane he disappeared for a few moments and came back with an airline insurance policy that can be purchased at a vending machine. He told me that if his worst fears were realized and the plane crashed in the ocean he wanted me to take the money as the beneficiary and have some Masses said for the repose of his soul. He finally got on the plane and flew off safely. Two days later the airport phoned me and asked me to come down take him off their hands.

They brought him out of the First Aid area in a wheelchair with his luggage following behind, and he looked like a man who had visited the damned and come away without hope. Back at the apartment he walked unaided into my unit and immediately fell into a deep and troubled sleep in the bedroom. Twelve hours later he was able to recount the events that had brought him to the edge of insanity. Jonathan had a haunting awareness that he was attracted to males but had never faced the prospect of actually being gay for fear that his family and friends would totally reject him. It was these very relationships that formed the central core of his being and defined him a person. The confusion over his sexual identity had been hidden inside for many years, slowly eating away at his sense of self worth until he could stand it no longer. The reason he had bought the airline life insurance policy was not because he was afraid the plane might crash, but because he intended to go swimming just as the tide was going out, once he had registered as a tourist at a prominent beachfront hotel in southern France. His death would then be just a tragic accident and his years of self-doubt and self-disgust would be over and his family and friends would never know his terrifying secret. Whether he would actually have gone through with his plan we will never know for he never got the chance to carry it out.

Jonathan always dressed well and traditionally wore a suit or sport coat. He had a long billfold that was kept in the inside pocket of his jacket, in which he had stored his passport, credit cards, personal identity papers, the airline return ticket and his cash. When he came to the Customs area at Heathrow Airport he set the billfold down on the counter while he was opening his suitcase for the officer to examine. When the officer asked for his passport Jonathan reached down to retrieve the billfold but it was not there; it was disappearing into the crowd in the hand of a woman who had just been cleared through Customs. He shouted after her and when she didn't stop he charged through the Custom's line in full pursuit only to be tackled by Airport Security before he reached her. They had not seen the robbery and concluded that he was trying to enter the country illegally, especially since he had nothing to indicate that he was both a tourist and a professional person. After a couple of hours of questioning by police, who were used to illegal entry attempts, he was reduced to a nervous wreck and had to be sedated by one of the doctors on call at the airport. The next day they were able to check his disjointed story that his uncle was an important official in the Federal Government, whom they duly contacted back home. The uncle wired a return ticket and arranged for a nurse to accompany him back to the airport where I picked him up. It had been his longest journey into night.

He stayed with me for two weeks during which time he contacted his family doctor who made an appointment for him to see a psychiatrist in his home area. I phoned the psychiatrist and gave the background for the temporary breakdown and after several sessions Jonathan was ready to return to work when the school year began. He phoned me several times in the Fall to give a first hand report on the progress he was making under the doctor's care, including the news that he had met a girl and was entering into a new and pleasing relationship. We got together once at his home in October and made plans to visit during the Christmas holidays, but in early November his heartbroken mother called to tell me that he had been killed in a car accident on the way to work at a new country school in his district. Apparently he was unfamiliar with the country road near the new school and had tried to cross a set of railroad tracks as a freight train was approaching, and didn't make it. The coroner had pronounced him dead at the scene of the wreck. He was only thirty-three.

At the funeral I was introduced to his new girlfriend and accompanied her to the funeral Mass and the internment and afterwards sat with her at the funeral luncheon held in the Church hall. Jonathan and his family were well known in the district and the hall was packed with people, but his mother had arranged for the young lady and myself to be seated near them. Several people gave eulogies, including one by his older brother and when he had finished we overheard Jonathan's mother insisting that the father get up and say a few words of final farewell. He was objecting because most of the participants were English speaking while he spoke with a heavy French accent and might not be understood, but the mother would not accept the excuse and he was forced to go up on the stage and make his speech. Then something supernatural happened. The father stood on the stage gripping the edges of the podium and at first seemed at a loss for words; then he suddenly straightened up and in a clear English voice said, "I want to thank you all for coming. You should not grieve over this death for life has been good and *I* am at rest with my Lord." My skin prickled and the young woman next to me gasped: "That's Jonathan's voice!" and indeed it was.

The father returned to the table visibly shaken and I heard him say to his wife:

"I don't remember saying anything."

Many times since then I have felt Jonathan's presence near me when life has become difficult, and I am sure that our friendship did not end with death.

Chapter 12
Underwater

Jonathan's death remained a haunting experience, and it soon became necessary to find something to take my mind off the loss of this friend. The motorcycle needed a new part and on the way to the dealer there was a small shop with a sign in its window that read: 'Why not learn to scuba?' This might be just the thing; something new and yet connected with the swimming skills that were already in place. Without knowing it I was stepping into an underwater world that would hold my attention for over thirty years, and lead to the sport's highest underwater rating, the formation of an independent scuba company called Halcyon Divers, and to the establishment of one of the largest scuba clubs in North America.

That first morning there was no one in the store except the diver behind the counter, so there was plenty of time to ask questions and to begin to consider entering this new and frightening sport. It was a frightening undertaking because of a deep-water phobia that had existed since early childhood. One of the earliest movies I remember seeing, and certainly the one most vividly remembered, was *The Red Witch*, where to my horror a giant octopus had oozed up the side of the ship and mangled several of the sailors. What an ugly monster it was, capable of paralysing its victims by its size and shape alone, and when in the following summer the family vacationed at an ocean resort on the West Coast its memory almost cost the life of my aunt and myself. She had rented a small pontoon paddleboat and taken me out a short distance from the shore, and as we paddled over the small waves a long piece of kelp floated across one of the pontoons. To my young eyes it was a tentacle of the monster from the movie and in my haste to escape, the small boat was upended. Luckily we were not far from shore and my aunt was able to swim there in spite of the dead man's hold I had around her neck. Over the years the fear had grown dimmer, so dim it never even came up in the counselling discussions, yet my first dive into Caribbean waters found me carrying a home made spear just in case the monster showed up again. More than once it did.

The scuba course occupied one night a week for eight weeks, was held in a local city pool and covered all the essential information and water drills necessary to survive in this new environment. It also included a measure of training in what to do if the equipment failed underwater, which in those days was not *just* a possibility, since the early equipment allowed very little room for error. The scuba tanks were not set up to register the amount of air left in the tank while diving and only when the diver realized that he was actually *sucking* air rather than breathing it did he know it was time to head for the surface. As well as the tank and regulator the main safety device today is an underwater floatation device called a buoyancy compensator which allows the diver to balance the downward pull from the diver's total weight to the upward lift desired at any depth. In those early days our only flotation device was a small Second World War air force 'horse-collar' that we bought for five dollars at the Army-Navy Surplus stores; it provided lift while the diver was on the surface but once he reached twenty feet of depth it only added to the downward drag. On the bottom it could be inflated more than on the surface because of the pressure of the air in the lungs, but the only way to do it was to remove the regulator from the mouth, press the four inch inflator valve inward by pushing on it with clenched teeth, and blowing into the hose at the same time, a difficult manoeuvre. But there really was no sense in doing this for on the way up it was virtually impossible to dump the expanding air out of the device because of the small valve, and at about thirty feet the horse collar exploded leaving the diver to make the rest of the ascent under his own power. It didn't take long for us to stop running to the Army-Navy store for replacements.

Today a course can be taught in the classroom and pool in a short time since most of the essential training is done in the water of a quarry, lake or ocean, but in the early seventies the usual procedure was to take a long time in the pool and then do a single open water certification dive. There were twelve of us in the class and the instructors decided to do the one open-water dive in a quarry north of the city. We met there on Saturday morning, donned the old rubber wetsuit after applying cornstarch to the inside of the suit so it would slip on, adjusted our tanks, regulators, masks and fins and jumped into twenty-five feet of murky water in groups of two. The instructor led us out to a marker and took us down one at a time to the bottom where the first diver was to wait until the other student was also brought down. In our couplet I was the first to be left on the bottom while the instructor went to the surface to fetch the next student. But they never arrived and eventually I ran out of air and surfaced only to find all the instructors in a frantic preparation for beginning the standard search patterns for a body recovery. It turned out that the second student had not been able to clear his ears and had to be taken back into shore before the instructor could continue our drills. When the instructor returned from shore I had stirred up so much bottom silt he couldn't find me and had eventually gone for help. They never even bothered with the rest of my drills; they were so happy I hadn't drowned they graduated me on the spot. And two weeks later the next dive was on a 'ghost' ship down seventy feet in midnight water.

The Waome was a small passenger and mail boat that plied those waters in the early days of the twentieth century before the advent of modern roads. Most cottagers took the train to the cottage country than sailed up the lake to their summer home on one of the fleet of passenger boats that stopped at a number of deep water docks along the way. The *Waome* was the smallest of these wooden steamboats, measuring only about sixty-five feet in length, and in 1932 on the last day of the season it sank in seventy feet of water, rolled over by a sudden powerful gale. It carried down with it two passengers whose bodies were recovered a few weeks later and whose spirits, many say, have never been able to find their way out of the wreck. After thirty years of diving on it there still is the distinct feeling that you are being watched as soon as the ship begins to reveal itself to the probing of the underwater flashlight. It sits absolutely upright, with all its cargo doors open and invites the diver into its depths, with the suggestion that it may be a one -way trip. A few years ago some of our divers took a professional underwater photographer, who had logged over a thousand Caribbean dives, down the buoy line until the ship showed itself in the divers' lights. He put one foot on the deck of this ancient monument and aborted the dive instantly. Less than two minutes later he was back on the deck of the scuba boat.

"You guys are absolutely crazy! That thing is a death trap! You can't even see your hand in front of your face down in that black, cold water."

This was the boat we dove on for our first real dive after certification.

In those early days the captain of the scuba boat would begin to drag an anchor on a long rope once we were in the general vicinity of the wreck. If we were lucky it would hook on some part of the *Waome* and a diver would go down the rope and tie off a descent line for the others. If we were not lucky, and this happened several times, we would drag all afternoon without locating its position and head home disgruntled without ever having entered the water. Sometimes an instructor would try a free descent or go down the anchor line as it lay on the bottom, but never with any success and with some danger, since this haunting wreck rested on the edge of underwater cliff that ran down to over two hundred and fifty feet, far too deep for out primitive equipment.

On our first dive, once the line was secured to the wreck, we pulled ourselves down wearing only enough weight to break the surface buoyancy, otherwise we would have weighed so much on the bottom we'd have had to crawl over the ship rather than swim around it. Roger was a big man and needed extra surface weight in order to begin the descent. After five minutes on the boat the cold water caused him to become hypothermic and confused and he signalled that he wanted to ascent. Two of us tried to swim up with him but no matter how hard we finned he was immovable; eventually we dragged him to the anchor line and went hand-over-hand lifting him up a few feet at a time to the surface. A diver can pull himself up a buoy line carrying over a hundred pounds of weight, but can't move from the bottom if he is wearing twenty pounds, unless he is wearing a good buoyancy lift device. That was our first wreck dive and we didn't really get to see much of the ship but we all agreed there was something really spooky about the dive, and Roger said he had felt a cold shadow pass over him almost soon he set fin on its deck. Perhaps it was just the onset of hypothermia. Perhaps not.

The next day we tried to locate the wreck again but were unsuccessful. Some of those disappointed divers wanted to party and talk over their adventures so I offered my house, which was in a small town outside of the city. My wife and I had previously tried the house-stage as suggested in marriage counselling but by this time she had left and we were well into the process of getting a divorce, so the house was available. The divers went home first to get rid of their gear and showed up about four in the afternoon with loads of fresh corn they had stolen from some local farmer's field. The problem was, it was cattle corn but they ate it anyway. Later I found out that one of them had been rushed to the hospital next day where an intern had poked his abdomen until he 'passed air'; we joked that if he had that much gas inside him on the dive he would never have needed help in ascending.

Years later when diving in Tobermory with Roger we ran into another incident. We had finished three boat dives that day but at four o'clock Roger wanted to make one more dive before calling it quits. There was a broken up wreck in about twenty feet of water that could be reached from the shore and since he had never dove on it we made plans to meet there as soon we had our scuba tanks refilled. When Roger showed up he brought another man with him, a boyhood friend from the east coast who told us that he had lots of diving experience. He had not brought a rubber hood to cover his head, which is necessary on cold water dives, but since the water was warm and we were not going to dive too deep we started out. At about two hundred feet from the shore an underwater cliff showed up that ran down to seventy feet and Roger's friend indicated he wanted to go down, and up, just to say that he had reached the bottom, so we followed him, going through a thermocline of very cold water on the way down.

On the bottom he made signals that he was cold and wanted to ascend and we turned around to go up the cliff when he suddenly spit his regulator out and tried to swim up without filling his buoyancy compensator. We both jumped to help him, tried to give him one of our extra regulators, dropped his weight belt and began to haul him straight up to the surface. At forty feet Roger went down to retrieve the dumped weight belt and I was left to complete the ascent. When a person is drowning he actually coughs and blows millions of tiny bubbles out of his mouth and immediately sucks them back in as he struggles for air. For the rest of the way up he did this repeatedly and when we reached the surface he seemed already drowned. With his compensator now filled he lay on his back, bleeding from both ears and was given in-water artificial respiration. By the time he had been towed to shore he was conscious but needed help to remove his diving gear; then he left all his gear, walked up the shore to where his truck was parked, got dressed and drove off. We saw him at supper in the restaurant two hours later and he was having difficulty carrying on any conversation. Near the end of the meal he suddenly put his fork down.

"How did I get here? Weren't we just on the bottom of the lake?" he asked.

And to this day he has no recollection from the time he was cold on the bottom to the time of the meal in the restaurant. The mind can blank out horrible experiences.

In September I moved to a new school where the job description was one of full time counselling, and met some remarkable students. The first task after moving there was to get win the confidence of these students, so I spent as much time as possible out of the office and in the general gathering places the students frequented around the school, where we talked cars, or music or dating or rumbles or weird happenings. It was probably here that I began to use my stories with students, an undertaking that has remained to this day. The outreach worked and it was not long before the students were coming to the office to talk over problems, suggesting ways the school could improve its spirit and complaining about some of the teachers who refused to see them as real people.

These were city kids who had never been introduced to country life, so on Saturdays I'd often take a group of them out to my sister's horse farm to see the animals, and especially the puppies from the dogs she was breeding. They loved those outings and helped around the farm, mucking out the barn, building dog pens and learning to ride the horses. That winter one of these groups was isolated by a sudden historic storm that closed all roads and turned the cars into indistinguishable features in a sea of snowdrifts. We were there for three days until rescued by a snowmobile brigade that took the students out to the cleared highway and home to their worried parents, but even that period of isolation in the old farmhouse the students loved, and talked about it at school for weeks afterwards.

There was a quiet student in his final year of high school who I knew vaguely; one afternoon two of his close friends came into the office and asked me to go with them to a local pub where their friend sat nursing a beer and feeling very depressed. It was an introduction to a common practice among senior students of sneaking out at lunchtime to down a couple of quick beers before going back to complete the rest of the day's classes, but this was one of the first times that this student had ever joined his buddies and his feeling of depression had worried them so much they eventually came for help. He and I sat there for much of the afternoon discussing his feelings of frustration and indecision about his future studies; he wanted to be a doctor but his marks were not high enough and his parents wanted him to go into the family business. He was an excellent wrestler and had competed in city competitions and by the end of the afternoon had made a decision to go into Physical Education at the university and see where that led him. He also decided to take up scuba diving and when he was certified we often dove together and he was very good.

I don't think I ever met a more determined person than this young man; whenever he took on any task he applied himself wholeheartedly to its accomplishment in spite of any drawbacks it might present. When he graduated in Physical Education he applied once more to the medical school and was again rejected, but obtained a teaching assistantship and did a Master's Degree in anatomy, working in related medical fields in the summer months. Each major problem and rejection brought him back to see me and it was always as if we were again back in the pub in the last month of his senior year, and at the end of each meeting he was more determined than ever to pursue his goals. That year he received a scholarship to do a Doctoral program in anatomy with a specialization in respirology, and again applied to medicine. This time he was accepted. He graduated in general medicine and went on to specialize in breathing disorders. Today he is married, has a lovely wife, also a graduate in his field, three beautiful daughters, and, oh yes, his own clinic. Determination can move mountains and his faith and effort, in spite of setbacks that would have crippled lesser people, has made him example to those who aim for the stars even when they seem unattainable.

Perhaps it was the fact that my own life was so difficult at the time I met him that caused the empathy between us. My wife had filed the divorce papers, the house had been sold, Jonathan had recently died, my dog had to be farmed out since the apartment didn't allow animals, the sports car was sold, I was drinking too much and getting into trouble, and I wasn't happy with the way the counselling program was going at the school. Finally I made a decision to go back to school and that year, while still teaching, took extension courses in science at the university and also taught a summer course in counselling for teachers. At the end of the summer one of the young teachers invited me to join a ski club which she belonged to with her friends, as soon as the snow began to fall, and by Christmas time it had proved to be such an exciting sport that I was hooked for life. Many of the students at school already knew how to ski and when it was announced that two other schools in the Board were travelling to Switzerland on the March Break and had space for ten more students, our students set up a committee to raise funds and talked me into applying as a chaperon.

It was a package deal run by a carrier airline that did nothing else but recreational flights on a low budget basis and funded partly by the Swiss government. We landed in Geneva and were bussed to Zermatt, one of the most prestigious ski resorts in the world where we stayed, all sixty of us, in a large student hostel set off some distance from the town. Up at seven and on our way to the slopes after a quick continental breakfast, we were the first ones on the cable train when it began its daily run up the side of the mountain at eight o'clock. The air was cold but as soon as the sun crested the mountaintops the whole world was bathed in warm sunlight that reflected off the miles of snow-covered trails that led downwards like narrow legs on a gigantic spider. At noon we would all meet at the mountaintop chalet for lunch and sunbathing time, then back on the slopes again until the shadows began to announce that another day in paradise was coming to a close. The only drawback to the holiday was the poor supper that was provided by the hostel where we stayed, often consisting of boiled noodles and nothing else, so it was common for the students and chaperons to frequent the restaurants in the town where the cuisine was outstanding.

The students had a ten o'clock curfew with 'lights-out' at midnight, for all our muscles, in spite of the denials and bravado of youth, needed the chance to renew themselves after a hard day on the long ski trails. One evening our small group of chaperons returned to the hostel just after curfew time and found that a brigade of Swiss soldiers with fixed bayonets ringed the hostel and prevented our access into the building. Eventually the hostel manager came out and demanded that everyone pack their gear and leave the building immediately, naturally without any refund on the money paid, and only became reasonable when we threatened to call our Embassy and lodge a formal complaint. When the smoke from the hotheads cleared it turned out that two of the boys had sneaked booze into the building, got a little drunk and knocked a door off its hinges. It was all the excuse the manager needed to get even for the remarks the students had made about his poor culinary skills at preparing supper.

Next day we missed the early mountain train, called in a local carpenter and had the door repaired, put the two trouble-making students into another hostel, agreed that we would eat supper in town for the next two days as long as he would improve the fare for the final two days, and were forced into one final agreement. We had to pay each Swiss soldier ten dollars for the two hours duty they had put in surrounding the 'hostile' hostel the night before, since they were a local Reserve Unit on 'Stand-By' for any such civil disturbance. It was adding insult to injury but there was nothing we could do if we wanted to hit those beautiful ski slopes for the remainder of the holiday. And although all the travellers complained about the unfairness of the manager's actions we all dug deep into our resources and settled the bill.

The next day we realized it was worth it, for we raced to the top lift on Zermatt and skied seven kilometres down a precipitous mountain face into Italy, a never-to-be-forgotten experience. It took until noon and the small Italian village where we stopped for lunch had never heard of pizza, which was all the students wanted to eat; they settled for spinach lasagna. The way back up was by gondola and at mid point up the mountain face there was a landing with a restaurant where we stopped for a drink before proceeding up a second breathtaking ride in a crowded swaying cable car hundreds of feet above the mountain floor. At the top we did a head count and realized that one of our prettiest and youngest skiers was not with us. After waiting until the next two gondolas arrived without our missing student I headed back down to the mid point landing, leaving the others waiting at the top. She was there, backed into a corner by two Italian 'Romeos' who obviously were doing their very best to talk her into going back down into Italy with them. She was still bravely smiling but her bottom lip was trembling as they tried in broken English to convince her that they meant no harm. It was over quickly. I took out a pad and wrote down the numbers 14, her age, and when they looked incredulous followed with the word 'policia' and they departed with obvious apologies. For the rest of the day this gregarious, socially skilled flirtatious girl was as quiet as a heartbeat and stuck to us like glue.

By the last day the lower slopes were disappearing and occasionally a mountain flower would poke its head out of the wet earth among the trees that lined the trails. It was a day for sunbathing near the top of the mountain and taking short runs on 'corn' snow wearing only T-shirts, but by two o'clock even the short runs were exhausting in the hot sun that owned the entire cloudless sky. After waxing our skis we headed down single file to the tree line where it was cooler and the snow was crisper and where some speed could be achieved. Part way down there was a small cliff, perhaps fifteen feet high, with trails leading down it both to the right and to the left, and each skier made his or her own decision which path to take, for the trails eventually joined back together some distance from the base of the cliff. When we reached the junction we gathered to remove our skis, for the snow had turned to soup and we were going to have to walk to the halfway station on the cable train line.

The last skier was one of the women teachers who had come along as a chaperon, and who actually was a pretty good skier, but who in this instance could not make her mind up which trail to take and sailed off the top of the cliff into the fresh mountain air. The students were impressed, until they realized she was airborne *unintentionally* but they watched as she perfected a downward arc leaving her skis stuck point first in the remaining snow at the base of the cliff while she herself was propelled forward, out of her bindings, flat down among the large mountain rocks that the melting snow had revealed. We rushed forward imagining broken bones at least and perhaps something worse, but although she had knocked herself out cold, miraculously she had missed every rock and left a snow angel imprint among them. The sharp rocks outlined her body, jutting up on both sides of her head and along her outstretched arms and legs. If a trained stunt man had practised repeatedly he couldn't have made a more perfect landing. We half carried her to the train where she repeatedly passed out on the way down, but there was such a crush of people wedged into the small train that we were able to keep her upright and no one seemed to notice. At the local hospital they said she had a mild concussion and advised no skiing for a few days, but that really didn't matter for the next day the whole lot of us headed home.

That spring Rene tried to convince me to leave everything and head west to the Pacific Coast where we would buy or build a boat to circumnavigate our ordinary lives. He had just graduated from university and the wanderlust was upon him; unfortunately my horizons by that time pointed back to university and the continued study of animal science, with a dream of lay missionary work in the high Andes. He raised the necessary funds to begin the search by selling a number of cars he had bought and repaired, put all his worldly possessions into a rented U-haul, drove to the west coast, found a job in a body shop, bought a piece of steep land and began to build a ski chalet. Within two years he had completed and sold the chalet and headed down the coast looking for a sailboat to fulfil his dreams, but every one he saw was either too expensive or not sea worthy. He got down to Santa Ana in California and was just about to give up the search and head back home when the impossible happened. Riding on a city bus he noticed that a young woman was smiling at him, which wasn't unusual for he was ruggedly handsome, but he was startled when she moved over and sat beside him.

"Aren't you Rene? Don't you remember me? We went to the same high school together."

It was old classmate who had married a fellow student and moved down to California with him. She insisted that Rene come for supper and meet her husband and because he had no time line to prevent it, he agreed. The husband was an innovating, friendly character who had moved to California to begin a small boat building business and was producing fibreglass forty-foot double-ended single-masted ocean going sailboats for the Pacific market. By the end of the meal the two men had enjoyed each other's company so much that the owner offered Rene a job and Rene had agreed to stay for a month at least.

The small factory used the mould the owner had designed to make each fibreglass hull, then he would call in carpenters to complete the interior, and it was this carpentry work that slowed down production, for each piece had to be individually produced and fitted into the interior of the boat before the next hull could be pulled from the mould. Rene suggested that they fire the carpenters and hire a few extra workers to assemble the interiors on a modified mass production assembly line since he could make 'dies' for every piece of wood, plastic or metal that went into the interior of the boat. They would have one group of workers producing and installing the interior while another group made the next hull in the mould. He reasoned that because each fibreglass hull was exactly the same as the previous one, having come from the same mould, then every piece of interior work would also be exactly the same as the same part in the last completed boat.

Rene stayed for almost a year and they doubled the output of the factory. The owner offered to make him a full partner but all Rene wanted was a hull and permission to set up a work station in the yard and work on *his* boat on his free time. Within six months Rene had finished the sailboat and he and his girlfriend, Leyette, had almost completed a series of classes on sailing and navigation offered at a nearby marina. The new boat was barely launched when the factory owner received notice that it was against the law to give work to a person who didn't have a Social Security card and the two new sailors had to slip away in the night and sail into Mexican waters. Their immediate plan was to sail part way down the Baja peninsula for a week to work out any bugs that might be in the boat and to learn how to handle it in the open ocean, then to turn around and head up the coast to Washington where they would stock up on supplies needed for a trip to Hawaii. They had only started down the Baja when they were boarded by the Mexican Coast Guard who confiscated several 'suspicious' articles such as their propane stove and Rene's new pair of binoculars, but thankfully, said Rene, they never found his 30-30 rifle or they would probably have lost the boat and ended up in a Mexican jail. Two days later he was doubly thankful, for he had to use the weapon to keep at bay a tough-looking group of men in a smaller powerboat that came out from shore and circled for twenty minutes before leaving.

After that they made sure they were out of sight of land until they made it back into American waters. At night they would take down the sails, put out a sea anchor and drift slowly until dawn and the beginning of a new day on the surface of the water planet, except for one night when another worry presented itself. It had been a calm, clear night when they went to sleep but sometime in the middle of the night a light 'rain' began to fall across the cabin intermittently. It was such a strange sound coming on a calm sea that Rene finally got up, took a marine flashlight and went out on deck to check the sea anchor, but what he saw in the beam of the light was a large single eye staring at him not ten feet away. During the night they had slowly drifted into a pack of resting whales until their small sailboat was entirely surrounded by these ponderous mammals.

The 'rain' they had heard was the occasional spray from the blowhole of their nearest marine neighbour. It was a dangerous spot for them to be in, for one thump of a tail across the boat would have at least cracked the hull, and if one of the whales decided to dive under them the boat could easily have capsized when the whale's back tilted the weighted keel upwards. After watching their surrounding neighbours for a few minutes it became obvious to Rene that they would not *drift* out of the pack since the boat and the whales were now resting as a single unit. At first light the whales would likely begin to 'sound' and that was too dangerous a situation to leave to chance. With prayer and breath holding they started the small marine diesel and inched forward as the gentle giants slowly moved apart and released them. Once free of the pack they kept the engine running and moved off slowly in a northerly direction for the rest of the night. Another night to remember.

By the time they got back to Seattle they were seasoned sailors with navigation skills adequate for their voyage to Hawaii. While Leyette got in the necessary stores Rene went to the marine library and took out twenty-five of the world's great literary masterpieces to while away the long hours of the windward passage. They made it safely, weathering several small storms along the way, and stayed in the Hawaiian Islands until forced to leave. He said he learned several things from talking with others who had also brought their boats to those magical islands from distant shores. The most important one was that once at sea you did not approach any other sailboat unless it was absolute necessity, for on the approach you were likely to get shot or get boarded and thrown overboard, depending on what type of people crewed the other boat. Stories of drug runners boarding the boats of innocent victims who were then thrown into the sea with a length of chain wound around them, was the talk of the sailors at all the marinas. These pirated boats would be used for drug runs, then sunk as soon as the powerful speedboats had come out from the West Coast and unloaded the high priced cargo.

Chapter 13
Life Changes Again

While Rene was sailing the briny deep my generous but distant father had grown ill and died of emphysema, having been a smoker all his life. Nevertheless it had caught us all off guard for he had been healthy up until a few weeks before the end. It was a large funeral for a man who was well known and respected and was missed by many, including his children, for he had been a solid rock in the vicissitudes of their lives. After the funeral I took an apartment with Danny, a long time friend, and began spending all my spare time taking extension courses in science, with the hope of completing a science degree and perhaps getting into vet medicine. My ski partner had by now given up on establishing a meaningful relationship and was getting ready to spend a year in Europe. This young lady had seen a large painting that Jonathan had made for me shortly before his death, and being much impressed by the boldness of his brush strokes had asked if she could borrow it to grace a wall in her apartment until she left for England. I took it over and hung it on a secure screw in the wall, confident that it would remain in place as it had always done in my apartment. Next day she phoned and said it had fallen off the wall in the middle of the night, and joked that I wasn't much of a picture-hanger. When I said I would re-hang it she replied that I needn't bother, for her father would do the job properly that afternoon. He did excellent job, replacing the string that had held it previously with proper gauge wire and wrapping the wire several times around a new larger screw that was set into a plug in the wall. But she phoned me in the middle of the night demanding that I come over immediately and take it away; it had jumped off the wall again. Once at home it has remained secure wherever I've been and I've never used more than a small nail to keep it on the wall. Jonathan always was a little possessive.

The following year I went back to university, this time in Science and rented a house with a group of Catholic students who were from such far away places as India and Algeria. Living in a house off campus was a good arrangement for we were not a party crowd, but rather people on their way to a specific goal and we spent most of our time studying; in fact, we didn't even have a television in the house. Because we were busy we took turns, week about, in preparing meals and keeping the house tidy. One of the members became interested in the Charismatics, an ecumenical movement based on a strong belief in the presence of the Holy Spirit, and he finally talked us into attending a meeting with him, all except Ben. Ben was a third year student in veterinarian medicine and was sceptical about what went on at these meeting and especially about a part of the meeting called 'being slain in the Holy Spirit' in which a person who was touched by one of the believers suddenly become rigid and fainted. He was finally talked into attending a meeting, and guess who got 'slain'? Ben then became a true believer in this movement and is still involved, as are his wife and grown children. I had never seen this 'slaying' before and when Ben went down I was one of the most surprised persons there. It's really quite a remarkable thing to witness, for there is no preface to it; the leader simply walks down the line of those attending and places his hand on the forehead of each person, saying the ritual blessing, 'God be with you' and receiving the answer, 'And also with you'. Those who are 'slain' don't say anything; they just collapse. Some *wanted* to collapse but just ended up standing there with the others. The 'Force' apparently had a mind of its own and it was anybody's guess who would succumb.

Father had left a substantial inheritance to each of his children, and it seemed like a good idea to invest it in something practical. Our student group was going to remain at university for at least another full year and maybe longer, and when a large old house not too far from the university went on the market I went around to see it with the prospect of making an offer. It certainly was large enough for all our needs but what clinched the deal was that the owners, two older unmarried sisters who had a wonderful outlook on life, had built a new house on the property next door and were to be our neighbours, and as it turned out, our house mothers. Grace and Emma had inherited the house when the other ten children had grown up and moved away and the parents had passed on. For years the house had been a gathering place for the family and one of the conditions of the sale was that the family could go on using the back yard as a large vegetable garden and could care for and harvest the grapes from the double row of vines that ran down one side of the property.

Moving in was like being adopted into a warm and outgoing family, and just what we all needed. The two sisters often brought whole suppers over to feed us, as well as their home-made wine which was delicious. It was a very good year, made better by having my Great Pyrenees dog back with me, off my sister's farm where he had stayed while I lived in the apartment.

That summer I worked in a factory, drove cab and did a lot of repair work around the old house, but half way through the summer a sense of uneasiness began to make itself felt. My ski partner had returned from England and occasionally drove down see how Casey, the dog, and I were doing, but there was no commitment between us, and the thought of eventually going into the mission field was still in my mind. The divorce had come through and a dispensation from my vows, so I was free to marry but not inclined that way. I was still scuba diving regularly and had bought an old van and fixed it up so it was a home on wheels on the weekends, or at least on those weekends that I wasn't working. Casey and I would load our food and gear into the old van and off we would go, with me driving and Casey alternately sleeping on the bed and hanging his head out the passenger side window.

The idea of making a week's retreat at a monastery some distance away resulted from a book I'd been reading, so we two took off one Friday afternoon and headed out the back roads on the way to the future. The idea was to board Casey at a kennel near the monastery for the week, then pick him up at the end of the retreat and head back home. If the retreat at the Trappist's centre turned out the way I was beginning to suspect, it could mean that in spite of my being a former priest and married man the Abbot would be understanding and take me in as a novice, as soon as my temporal life had been set in order. Secretly I was afraid that there really wasn't much chance of this happening, but then, hope springs eternal in the human heart. If it did occur the move would mean some sacrifice, the biggest which would be finding a good permanent home for Casey and severing the bond that had grown between us.

By the end of the first day of driving Casey may have suspected what was in my mind for when we camped in a lonely part of the Boreal forest he was no sooner out of the van than he took off for parts unknown. At first I didn't notice, for he usually hung around, especially at suppertime, but by the time the meal was cooked over a small bonfire he hadn't shown up. Alone in the middle of a forest, well off a seldom used road, the chance of finding him in the dark, or the next morning after he had wandered miles away, seemed bleak at best.

Still, the attempt had to be made and after building up the fire as a point of reference I began to call his name and circle through the trees going up to the point where the fire was barely visible. Finally I gave up and headed back to the van, and on the way he was silently and suddenly at my side, but there was a disquieting sense about him if he was trying to tell me something. It had occurred once before when we stayed in a northern cabin and he had whined all night. In the morning wolf tracks were everywhere in the soft soil around the cottage, but here the woods were quiet and deep without any sense of a predator presence.

We started off to the east early the next morning but something wasn't right. The farther we drove the more uncomfortable I felt, while Casey alternately wandered in the back of the van and whined as he stuck his nose out of the window, often on my side of the vehicle. By eleven o'clock that morning the forward motion of the van seemed as slow as if pushing through a field of mud and we stopped and turned around. Almost immediately Casey got up on the bed and fell asleep and I myself felt as if a heavy weight had been lifted off my chest. We started back toward home without any definite plan and by four in the afternoon had arrived at my sister's farm feeling refreshed and peaceful. And waiting there was my ski buddy, Linda. Apparently she had found her way there, which was surprising for I wasn't aware that she even knew how to get to the farm, yet she came forward, hugged me, then hit me.

"Don't ever leave me again!" she said, and I said I wouldn't.

We were married in the Church the next Spring and Grace and Emma gathered up a crew of chefs and put on a wedding party in their old house that couldn't have been matched by the finest caterers anywhere.

As a married man, hoping for children, it was time to leave the university and get a full time job but this time it was not as easy as when I'd first entered the teaching profession. Then, the School Boards were in desperate need of teachers and often bid against one another, but time had filled the need and jobs were hard to find. One interview turned me down because it was a Catholic Board and they had a policy not to hire teachers who had left the priesthood; another Board could not make up its mind whether a large high school actually needed another teacher or not, but finally a large private school called me in for an interview and asked if I'd be willing to run their senior Guidance program and teach a full compliment of classes; and so I began a twelve year association with the staff and students of a prestigious private school. Most of the teachers were from other countries and were teaching on letters of permission, yet they seemed to be well versed in their areas and the students got as good an education as they would have received in any other academic high school that valued the students' progress. The pay wasn't as good as that given in the public schools but there were other perks that offset it, such as being able to convince the parents to fund almost any trip a teacher dreamed up for the students.

It was a long day at school, for the teachers met the buses at eight when they arrived and saw them off at five when they left, and in between those times the teachers were with the students full time, except for a break at recess and another after lunch. Following the afternoon classes there were compulsory sports for all the students and for all the teachers as coaches, and from the first day on the job I ran the swimming program and later the scuba certification courses. The students were enthusiastic and friendly and since it was costing their parents a considerable amount of money to send them to the school, they worked harder at their studies than most other students did. If homework wasn't done or a test was poorly answered, a call to the parents usually corrected the wayward youth and progress continued. If that didn't work then the student was assigned a special detention: a parent had to drive the student in by nine o'clock on Saturday morning for a catch-up and pick him or her up at noon. It was an effective remedial program for it was obvious that none of the parents enjoyed slicing up their own Saturday.

By the end of the first week of school the teachers had introduced themselves to all the new staff and had begun to show them the expectations that were tied to private education. A teacher named Gary had a flare for scuba diving and it wasn't long before we were off to the various quarries and lakes around the area. Each of us had done several of them but without overlapping and that meant that each was able to take the other to a dive site he had not tried before. We were enthusiastic about learning more about scuba and by the end of the first year we had taken advanced courses wherever they had been offered and risen to the level of Assistant Instructor. The next step was to prepare for the weeklong Instructor's Course and to select the scuba agency that seemed to have the most promising future, since there were five or six of them that offered such a course. One agency that seemed to have the most promising future was an organization officially named the Professional

Association of Diving Instructors, P.A.D.I. for short, and as it turned out they were offering a course in Florida during our March Break holiday. Gary had already made plans for that holiday, but with Linda's encouragement I flew off to attempt the next level of expertise.

This intensive course was held in Jacksonville, Florida, beginning on Saturday and lasting until the following Saturday, with hardly any time in between to eat or sleep. When it started there was about twenty of us; when it finished there was scarcely half that number that lasted through to the end and passed all the required tests. The agency's standard was quite simple: you either passed everything or you came back for the full course the next time it was offered at no extra charge, except for plane fare, board and room and time away from work. It really was a do-or-die program, with some of the instructors out of the Navy's Underwater Demolition School, who seemed bent on showing the civilians what wimps they really were. We began the first morning at nine o'clock with a 100 question test on underwater physics and by ten-thirty were downtown, swimming unending lengths around the outside parameter of a standard sized city swimming pool. That got rid of five of the candidates and others followed as the week progressed.

One young man from New York City broke down in tears when he couldn't come up with his mask on and cleared after free diving to retrieve it in twenty feet of water in a local lake, but the saddest case was that of athletic young woman who had done well in the course until the very last day when she had developed a slight head cold. She elected to take an antihistamine to open up her middle ear and sinuses so she could descend to the bottom of a shallow lake and complete the required drills. Those drills were lengthy and by the time she had completed them the drug had worn off and her tissues had swelled causing, what is called, a 'reverse block'. The high-pressure air in the middle ear was trapped and as she tried to ascend the air expanded causing so much pain that she had to go back down. Eventually we were able to get her close to shore in about ten feet of water and on the advise of a doctor who feared she was becoming hypothermic, we dragged her kicking and screaming out of the lake and sent her off to the hospital for a two day stay. But she was a fighter and there wasn't much doubt in anyone's mind that she would eventually come back and take the course again.

Signing up for scuba began almost immediately upon my return, with each student paying a nominal fee for the course and the school paying for the pool time. We started off small for there wasn't much money to buy used tanks and regulators but we ended up with six of each, so while one group worked on their snorkelling skills in the pool the other group donned the tanks and went underwater breathing out of their regulators. That first time underwater when you feel the air rushing into your mouth on demand is a never-to-be-forgotten experience and the students loved it. Some came to the pool the first day just to see what it would be like, but all went away excited and hooked on the new experience. After six weeks of pool and classroom training they were ready for the open water. Administration gave us a school bus and time off to get the students fitted for their gear at a local scuba diving rental shop and on the long weekend in late May we piled everybody and their equipment into a yellow school bus, which Gary drove. I followed in my truck similarly loaded with our gear, dive flags, safety lines and a ton of foodstuff and we all headed north to the Lake District. That first day with our first class it snowed.

We had billeted the ten boys in a series of small cabins not far from the family cottage and Gary had stayed with them while I went to the cottage to prepare the boats and set up the dive site. When the boys had settled into their cabins I returned with the truck, put all their dive gear in it and drove back to the cottage while they followed in the bus. Because the cottage road twisted and turned they had to leave the large bus some distance from the lake and walk the rest of the way. It had started out as a nice day, and even while we dressed in our scuba gear on the dock the sun was out and it was fairly warm, but just as they finished putting on their wet suits and tanks the sun decided to cover itself with storm clouds and down came the snow. Someone took a picture, which still hangs on my finished basement wall, showing Gary and myself trying to 'encourage' the students to take that first plunge into the ice-cold waters of the bay.

Eventually everyone entered, lost their breath from the sudden immersion in the spring lake, then gradually warmed up as the water that had seeped into the wetsuit picked up body heat and acted as a thermal layer. They loved it, and they scared us half to death as they immediately tried to swim off in all directions in order to find the deepest spot in the bay and play underwater tag with one another. As instructors we learned as we went along, and the first thing we learned was to convince them that if they swam off without our control they would automatically wash out of the program. Luckily, after an hour in the water and everyone's lips had begun to turn blue, the sun came out and chased the winter away. We undressed in the boathouse, hung up the suits to dry and retreated into the heated cottage for hot chocolate and a debriefing session. Then while they walked back to the bus I loaded all the scuba tanks into the truck and drove fifteen miles to a dive shop so they could be refilled with compressed air. By the time I returned it was suppertime, which pretty well ended our first day of Open Water training. Gary and I were ready for bed but we could hear them talking in their cabins well on into the night. They were euphoric.

After a full day of diving on Saturday we took them to a Drive-In theatre and parked the bus sideways in the last row. The students took their sleeping bags and climbed up on the roof of the bus and watched the shows from there; at least they did that for the first show, but by then the cool night air forced them back into the heated bus where they promptly fell asleep. Gary and I watched the second show, of four, for it was a dusk-to-dawn opening of the Drive-In, but by that time even our eyes were heavy and we headed back into the cabin area with a bus load of sleeping wards. The toughest part was to pry them out of the warm bus and into the cold night air so they could go to bed. We never checked, but I think they all went to bed in their clothes for when we knocked on their doors in the morning they were all dressed and ready for another adventure. They did exceptionally well and by the end of Sunday all ten of them had passed the Open Water section of the course and had received their C-card that informed the world that they were now *certified* scuba divers. Once they told their stories to their school mates every senior student, and even some junior ones, were begging to sign up for the next course. We were off to a great start.

It was obvious that we had a ready market from which to draw new divers, but we were limited in our ability to train any more than ten students at a time, which meant that our income, and hence the possibility of buying more equipment, was severely limited. We decided to branch out and run adult courses at local pools and charge the going rate, which was double what we were charging the students at school. There was a ready market for lessons and soon we were teaching two or three nights a week and beginning to draw in responsible young adults who wanted not only the Open Water certification, but more advanced courses as well. Within two years there was a dozen young men and women who had progressed past the Advanced Diver level and received their Dive Master certification. Our equipment multiplied and improved and the school courses could now handle up to twenty-four students at a time since the new Dive Master group was more than willing to come up to the cottage for a weekend of diving and assist in the training of the students. In all, Gary and I remained at that school for ten years and probably introduced about two hundred young students to the excitement of the underwater world.

There were many wonderful and funny things that happened on those annual May weekends with the students, but the one that stands out in the minds of all those who helped in the training was one of the last ones. It was a big class of both boys and girls ranging in age from thirteen to nineteen and we filled all the cabins at a small lake resort. They had been a particularly strong group in the classroom and the pool sessions and we expected no less from them in the Open Water section of the course. On the first two days of diving they were superb and we were getting ready to take them to the Drive-In theatre on Saturday night when a delegate of the students asked if they could go into the local town and split up into a number of smaller groups, each doing their own thing. One bunch wanted to go to the indoor theatre, another wanted to play pool, a third wanted to pig-out at the local pizza parlour, and so on. We agreed and drove them in expecting to pick them up at eleven when the theatre emptied but by ten o'clock they showed up at the local dive shop where we were talking over old times with some friends.

We drove them back and prepared a bonfire and wiener roast on the shore of the lake but they soon claimed they were tired from the diving and wanted to go to bed early. At midnight I did a check of the cabins and everyone was in bed and all lights were out. At one-thirty the last Dive Master returned from a dance and I asked him to do a cabin check to make sure they were asleep; he returned to report that they were as quiet as the night air, with no light to be seen anywhere. At two o'clock a Highway Patrolman pounded on the door of my cabin and said he was investigating a complaint that a bunch of teenagers had been seen drinking in the local graveyard and upsetting some of the grave marker. He wanted to check that they were not our group. Naturally our cabins, every one of them, were empty. The oldest boy had collected money and bought booze for them all just after we drove them into town and each student had hidden part of the loot on their person when they boarded the bus for the trip back to the resort.

They were nowhere to be seen at the graveyard when the officer drove me there and as soon as we returned to the resort he was called away on an accident report. I called Gary who was staying at the cottage and he said he'd come right down, and while waiting for him I went into every cabin, turned on the lights and was greeted from the beds with a chorus of 'sleepy' voices.

"Hi sir. What's up?" was the general acknowledgement.

Pulling back the covers revealed that all the students were fully dressed and giggling, except for a few, including the youngest students there, who as soon as they realized they were caught promptly hung their heads over the bed and barfed on the floor. Gary wanted to call their parents, immediately load them all back on the bus and fail the whole lot of them, but the officer had mentioned a charge of 'Desecration of a Graveyard' and wanted to see them in the morning; so we couldn't leave. At seven they were all up, many still hung over, loaded into the bus and driven to the graveyard where they had to repair the damage they had done and clean up the entire site on pain of being disqualified in the scuba course. The ironic thing was that many of the local people on their way back from Church stopped to congratulate us on what '...fine and civic minded young students' our school was producing. The local police Sergeant let them off with a berating and we let them finish the rest of the scuba course, but the school eventually suspended every one of them for a week, and threatened to cancel scuba if anything like that ever happened again. It never did.

In the meantime, Linda and I had been hoping to start our own family but no new life was being formed out of our prayers and our love. We were sitting in the kitchen one Saturday and she was feeling unfulfilled, a state that is apparently foreign to the male who finds his fulfilment in his work and his games, when quite clearly I saw a small red haired boy and a smaller blond girl playing in the adjoining room. It was only for a split second but the image remained fixed in my mind and I told Linda that we would be parents before too long and described what I had just seen. It wasn't the first time the future had briefly revealed itself, for it had happened on one of those early days when I'd first entered a Church while I was still searching for religion, and again just after becoming engaged, as well a few other times. As far I know, these images had nothing to do with any wish-fulfilment for they came suddenly, lasted a very brief time and had no follow-up, as a series of dreams might present. They couldn't be forced or expected or controlled in any way, and apparently had been present for generations in my father's side of the family.

His ability to see the future from 'reading' tea leaves in a cup was so exceptional that he had become a family legend and his predictions had finally frightened my mother to the point that she said she would leave him unless he gave up the practice.

Within the year Stephen arrived and like St. Augustine's son, I called him Deo Datum for he truly was a gift from God. Slightly over a year later Elizabeth arrived, my princess who still can melt my heart and change my ' No!', to 'Well, OK.' when she looks at me with her lovely eyes. Sometimes there are no words that can be used to tell the depth of feeling involved in a relationship and we are reduced down to using that most inadequate word 'love' simply because there is nothing better available. Steve and Beth have been, and continue to be, our greatest treasures, and there are few memories over the last twenty-five plus years that don't involve them in one way or another. Life is God's gift to humanity and it isn't until children enter the family that we begin to realize just how great a gift it really is. Humans are meant to grow and to reach out into the world and there is nothing as effective in producing this as the entrance of children into the home. It is what Christ meant when He said, "...for of such of these is the kingdom of heaven." (Mark 10:14)

The new life children bring is *infectious* and in our case it started with Linda and me and spread first to her parents and then to my family and all our friends, and has reached the point where we are welcoming strangers into our family as they bring home their friends to share with us. Linda tried staying at home, first with Steve and later with both of them, but she was ambitious to further her own career and we soon hired a series of baby-sitters who cared for the children during the weekdays. One was even an 'au pere' who came over from France and stayed for a year before marrying one of Linda's fellow teachers and settled down here to raise her own family. For us, the weekends were no trouble at all, for Linda's parents arrived most Saturdays, and if they couldn't come there was always Grace and Emma from next door. And of course, Linda herself wanted to be with the children as much she could, which actually left me free to do the Open Water scuba courses on most summer weekends. Linda had tried only once to spend a weekend with the scuba group at the cottage, and that was before the children were born, and it had turned out to be such a disaster that she never offered again. She had a low tolerance for a bunch of macho men who loved to push the danger barrier in the daytime and spend the evening bragging, drinking and telling dirty stories to one another.

The group of dedicated scuba divers continued to grow and by the third year Gary and I had bought two large pontoons and built a 24 by 12 foot diving barge, powered by an old fifty horsepower outboard engine, and named the Manatee. Once we had found and marked the *Waome*, the sunken lake boat, which was only about five miles away, we had so many experienced divers who wanted to help out on the open water training that we had to limit the number that could attend on any given weekend. A typical training weekend saw the beginning adult divers, who had found their own accommodations, getting a shallow water introduction on Friday night, a nine o'clock morning dive and a one o'clock afternoon dive on Saturday and two final dives on Sunday. Our assistants, all twenty of them, stayed at the cottage, sleeping on the floor in their sleeping bags on both Friday and Saturday night, and diving on the *Waome* in between the times they worked with the new divers. The best dive of the weekend was on Saturday as soon as the students were finished their training. The safety divers would load their gear on the Manatee and off we would go with the barge often almost underwater from the weight of the divers and their equipment. The rule was that you couldn't drink for six hours before diving and six minutes after diving, which meant that the bottom of the lake for the five-mile return trip ended up being littered with empty bottles of peppermint schnapps. Since the journeys went on for over ten years, the glisten on the bottom of the lake must be substantial.

Every so often as you go through life you meet some unforgettable character who becomes an alter ego, another self, and such was Max. Born in Germany during the Second World War he grew up in a devastated country and by the time he was sixteen was out on his own, working at odd jobs until he finally signed on a fishing trawler and spent the next ten years at sea. Max has an endless series of stories, most of them infectiously funny, so funny that often his audience is in such gales of laughter during the story that they don't even hear the final outcome. One of his stories concerns the time he was a commercial fisherman and his trawler sank off Iceland. Max, who is powerfully built, was able to keep the unconscious captain afloat until he could get him into the sea-going dingy. When they were picked up later by another trawler, Max had been able to keep the captain supported so that he didn't slide down and drown in the water in the bottom of the dingy. They ported at the main harbour in Iceland, where the captain lived, and within a day Max was the hero of the whole island. He told us that so many people bought him drinks and so many unmarried women invited him home, that he finally signed on with another trawler just to save himself from a life of debauchery.

Nothing was too much for Max. Almost as soon as he was certified he wanted to go wreck diving on the *Waome* and within a few months he had talked a pilot friend to fly him and Gary down to the Caribbean for some ocean diving. When they returned they were so full of diving stories that they convinced many of the regular divers, including myself, that life was not liveable until we had tasted fresh, liquid sea salt. One of the divers interested in the holiday was a young man who was the victim of multiple sclerosis. We had trained Tom only after his doctor had said that the excitement of diving would do him more good than harm, but he had also warned us that we must make sure that he was under the care of a strong buddy diver every time he entered the water. We went to Tobago for a week and by the time it was over Tom was as stuck on diving as any of us. Diving on unspoiled West Indian reefs is an experience that rivals involvement in any of the world's great art forms; it is introduction into the greatest beauty the world, or its inhabitants, are capable of producing. You forget to breathe as the explosion of colour from the coral, eels and small fish flashes around on every side in a symphony of grandeur. Max, Gary and I took turns diving with Tom and it was so difficult to stay beside him rather than watch the underwater life forms that we had to go to the use of a hand line between us just to make sure that we didn't abandon him.

We were desperate to go shark diving but our native guide had great respect for 'dat big fish' and put off our pleadings until the very last day; it had taken a week of prompting him with drinks before he finally consented. That night the eight of us sat around and discussed the next day's dive; since we were looking for one of the famous 'sleeping sharks' we drew lots to see who would be first to have a picture taken with their arms around the body of the shark. Unfortunately I was fifth, which local custom insisted was the one who usually got bitten, but next day we were all ready with fresh film in the underwater camera. Just as the boat was being pushed from the shore the owner of the resort asked us to take along a young French couple who had just arrived and wanted an exciting dive. We refused, until the owner threatened to impound the boat unless we complied, so after checking their qualifications the dive went on as planned.

At over a hundred feet we came across our smooth, black beauty, all eight feet of him, resting on the bottom close to a coral head, and we took our positions for the camera shots. But the camera only got clicked once. The monster seemed to be watching our every move from the one great eye directed toward us, and his chilling glance proved to be too much for the young French wife who immediately spit out her regulator and clawed for the surface in a sudden paroxysm of terror. Luckily, her husband caught her ankle as she bolted past him and holding her firmly did a shared-air rescue all the way to the surface. Seeing what was happening the native guide aborted the dive, but not before that great fish roused itself and swam directly *through* our stunned group as we headed upwards. The camera recorded only one picture, a blurred image of a large nose and a row of teeth, made by our photographer who was wildly back-finning to get out of harm's way. The wife later claimed her regulator had jammed, but we tested it and it worked admirably for us. Whatever the cause, they did not ask to accompany us on any of our next dives.

We had pushed the safety limits and done twenty-four dives in seven days, and although we had stayed within the decompression limits of the navy dive tables, we had absorbed too much nitrogen. Everything was fine until the homebound aeroplane reached its cruising altitude and the lessened air pressure let the residual nitrogen squeeze out and form tiny bubbles just under the skin. The free liquor on the holiday flight didn't help either, especially since we were in a euphoric mood to begin with, and by the time we arrived home all of us were scratching. Max's doctor thought he had a case of sand chiggers and kept him medicated and off work for several days, but the rest of us merely entertained our friends for a week showing them how we could make the bubbles just under the skin squeak if we rubbed them. Later dive tables became much more accurate and current tables recommend no diving at all on the day before leaving if the divers plan to return home by plane. We had left the resort at noon but still had managed to squeeze in a morning dive before we packed up our gear. Come to think of it, we probably got off easy.

When they heard we were ocean divers, the students at school begged us to set up a trip for them, and the next March Break we took a dozen students to the Cayman Islands. Our resort was in a remote area, where large, ocean-going ships had dropped anchor and discharged waste so frequently that their pollution had killed off all the small, colourful life associated with the reef. Still, we were anxious to make a check-out dive to familiarize the students to the more buoyant ocean water, and planned a dive as soon as all the students had settled into their rooms. The owner said that there was an underwater grotto of large boulders some one hundred metres off the beach and slightly to the west where we could see moray eels and large sea bass, and off we went with fresh tanks and our underwater cameras. After swimming for fifteen minutes and seeing nothing except the flat rocks of the dead reef, I motioned to the others to stay on the bottom while I ascended to the surface to get a bearing on our position.

We had gone too far to the east and I pointed out the correction to Gary and the students, some forty feet below me in the crystal clear water. They responded by beginning to take pictures of me looking down from the surface, which seemed rather strange, until I turned around and met my first large barracuda and suddenly understood their interest in my situation. He was as big as me and had a set of teeth that made mine chatter, yet he kept perfectly still, ten feet away, with only his small pectoral fins moving. It was a situation out of a Stephen King novel and my rate of breathing doubled as we hung together just below the surface. If I descended so did he; if I rose up toward the surface, he was my constant companion. Finally I became sure he was going to strike and drew my chrome-plated knife from the scabbard on my leg in a mad hope of defending myself. He liked the way the knife flashed in the sunlight and came closer for a better look, while I motioned to the rest of our party to come to my aid. In desperation I dropped the knife hoping that he might follow its flashing path down and give me a chance to escape, and as I watched the knife descend I saw that my buddy Gary and the students were swimming off to find the grotto, disappointed, no doubt, that the fish hadn't bothered to consumed me. My new aquatic 'friend' hadn't followed the knife down and I guessed it was because he felt he didn't need it to consume me.

A quick glance at my air gauge showed that there wasn't much left and that I had to make a choice between drowning or being eaten, so I began to fin slowly toward the beach expecting at any moment to feel the jaws of death on some part of my quivering body. Once I looked sideways, just to check where he was, but I only looked once. He was right beside me, not two feet away, and measuring my speed with his own. After a millennium I reached the beach, and fell limply on the sand like some dead Portuguese Man-of-War, and when I ventured back in the shallow water there was no sign of him. The resort owner wanted to know why I had come back early, and when he heard my tale he laughed.

"You have just been introduced to *Snaggletooth*, our resident beggar barracuda. If you go diving tomorrow morning I'll have his feeder give you a demonstration."

Which he did while we took pictures and marvelled at the speed of that great fish as it caught the pieces of bait-fish the feeder hurriedly dropped. I knew then that I'd have been a tossed sea-salad if the 'coda' had been really hungry the day before.

We moved to another city that summer in order to be closer to work, renting a small house near the south end of the city, and one sunny afternoon in August Gary, Max and myself began talking over plans to do more than just teach scuba. What was needed was a scuba club that could offer its members continuous upgrading in underwater skills, and at the same time plan a series of summer fun dives for the growing number of students we were producing. That afternoon 'Halcyon Divers Incorporated' was born, with the three of us as its founding officers, and it continued to be one of the largest scuba clubs in North America for the next twenty years. One thing was lacking, however, and that was the need for additional scuba instructors, since I was the only one certified in that area. It meant that I had to achieve *instructor* status in a number of related fields, such Red Cross Scuba Bronze, Underwater Search and Recovery, Advanced First Aid and C.P.R., and eventually P.A.D.I. Master Instructor and Course Director status, in order to be able to certify as Instructors those of our members who were already Assistant Instructors. Those courses took a couple of years and a final trip to the west coast to take a demanding course in how to train scuba instructors, but all the effort was worth it and Halcyon Divers was soon able to run its own courses and add to our membership new instructors including Max and Gary.

We were holding so many Open Water training sessions at the cottage that finally Linda said I was not spending enough quality time with Stephen and insisted that I take him with me on the next session. Knowing that this was likely to happen I'd made arrangements with the teen age daughter of one of the new instructors, to come along with her father and look after Steve, who was only five at the time. W.T. and his daughter were to go directly to the open cottage while I brought up eight stand-by scuba tanks and the other gear necessary for the weekend. My utility vehicle was loaded to the top, although I'd made a bed in the back seat in case Steve wanted to sleep on the way up, and we had just reached the major highway going north when the computer in the engine failed and we drifted silently to the side of that busy highway. It was eight o'clock at night and no one paid any attention to my signals for help.

This was before the days of cell phones and there were no houses anywhere in sight, only a few factories, all of which seemed to be closed. I couldn't leave my sleepy son alone in the SUV so I placed him over my shoulder, climbed the six foot high highway fence and lowered him down to the grass on the opposite side, and climbed over after him. Then I carried him a half mile until we found a partially lighted factory with an open rear door, and went inside. The custodian on duty nearly fainted when we came up behind him as he was cleaning the floor, but he allowed me to use a phone and call a tow truck. Then back to the fence, over it again, and waited in the SUV with my sleeping son until the tow truck arrived. The driver hauled the disabled vehicle to a garage that was still open but they didn't have the computer part needed to fix it. From the garage I phoned a taxi that took Stephen and I to the airport, the only place that would rent vehicles that late at night. All they had was a *small* car and when we loaded all the tanks and gear into it back at the garage, there was barely enough space to squeeze in. Stephen curled up on my lap all the way to the cottage and was tucked into bed at two thirty in the morning without ever waking. Whatever profits came from that course were eaten up by the repairs and the small car rental, but it was a weekend that made me realize just how precious he was to me, for the entire ordeal had turned his presence with me into a special bonding rather than a trial. Childless men never experience that wonderment.

Steve liked the weekend with the divers and convinced his mother that it was both fun and safe, and so it wasn't long before Beth was allowed to go along as well. But she missed her friends and her mother, and although she was the darling of the divers she soon tired of their rough jokes and bragging behaviour. She came with us only a few times after that original exposure but Steve became a fixture on our weekend trips, and by the time he was six he was diving around the dock on a pony bottle that had been adapted to fit on his back. While in elementary school he became certified as a Junior Open Water Diver and even went along with the students to the Caribbean when we went to Bonaire in the Netherlands Antilles. He earned his Dive Master qualification while he was in high school and became a regular diver with the other members of the Halcyon club. We have had some great dives together including the time the older divers introduced him to vodka 'bangers' around a campfire while I was off doing a night dive with some students working toward their Advanced Diver rating. The next morning, in spite of his hangover, he kept to the rule: If you drink with the boys you have to dive with the men. It turned out that the dive on the *Marie Rose* was just about the coldest dive we made that summer.

The general practice of the certification dives at the cottage was to finish by two-thirty on Sunday afternoon and have award ceremony as soon as the new divers had dressed and packed up their gear. Then after the instructors and safety divers had encouraged them to come out to our next fun dive we all waved goodbye and sent them on their way, while we went to dive the *Waome* one last time before the weekend closed. We usually got back to the cottage by five o'clock and then closed up the boats, packed up and left. I was the last to leave, having to make sure that the cottage was spotless, since my sister and I both used it and the rule was, 'the last one out leaves it clean'.

One memorable evening when I climbed the hill to reach my van I found that one of the safety divers still hadn't departed. His old car wouldn't start even after he had worked on it for an hour, so he hitched his car to my vehicle by means of two nylon towropes and I pulled him into town, but nothing was open. There was a garage several miles down the road and since there wasn't much traffic on the divided highway at that time of the evening we started out toward it, but as we came down a hill he picked up speed and thought he was going to rear-end me. He applied the brakes so suddenly that both tow ropes snapped and he drifted to the side of the highway. Those ropes were now useless and all he had left was a long, heavy single towline which he didn't want to cut to make a pair of tows. Since we were only a few miles from the gas station we secured his car to mine using the long towline and started out slowly again. When we were only a short distance from the garage I noticed that a car was trying to pass me, and as it drew alongside a quick glance showed that it was the safety diver, head bent over the steering wheel, fast asleep. By the grace of God we had just reached the base of a hill and were starting up the slope, and his car slowed down enough for the slack in the towline to be taken up. As soon as it had, I started blowing the horn incessantly and he woke in time to steer in behind the van. Breathlessly we stopped and shortened the line and crept the rest of the way to the garage where we were finally able to get his old car running. He left before I did, for it took some time for me to stop shaking from the near-death experience, and all the way home I was looking for a wrecked car in the ditch with an injured sleeping driver at its wheel, but somehow he managed to stay awake and live to dive another day.

Gary taught geography and I taught biology and the idea came to construct a senior level course in zoogeography and do some field work in it. We approached a young professor in marine biology at the university and sold him on the idea that our students would spend a series of Saturdays with him during the winter and then do our field work in the Caribbean, with him as the resident guru, during the March Break. Naturally, there would be no cost to him and we would arrange for a substantial honorarium as well. We then approached the School Board and got permission to run the course for a full senior academic credit. When the school had also given permission and a dozen students had signed up we began the Saturday sessions. As spring drew near our young professor surprised us by getting three professors from the University of the West Indies to come along at their own expense. He said it was not difficult to convince them to come once they learned that we had reserved a sixty-foot sailing barque with only a captain, a first mate and a cook. We were to be the crew. It was to be a grand adventure.

We flew to St. Vincent and spent a day doing research at a marine ecological station where they were experimenting with oyster beds to produce cultured pearls, then picked up our ship and sailed toward the Lesser Antilles. With twenty people on board space was at a premium below deck and we remained topside as long as possible, for down below the bunks lined both sides of the ship and a central table took up most of the remaining area. Gary and I were assigned a tiny cabin in one half of the bow, with bunks scarcely two feet high and three feet wide. For some reason the Captain decided that we should sail to the next island that evening, although the weather was getting rough. We were ordered below decks and lay on our bunks watching the water squeeze through the caulking and trickle down into the bilges, causing the warning bell to ring continuously. The Captain worked furiously to keep the pumps alive and ran back and forth from the bilges to the helm station to check on the compass setting with the First Mate. For several hours the students lay round-eyed and quiet on their beds, but we finally found the harbour, dropped anchor and took the punt to the dock. As soon as they were ashore the students wandered the town looking for a non existent pizza parlour or burger stand and came back with some island pop and local munches. It was their introduction to culture shock.

Perhaps to make up for the harrowing passage, the Captain arranges the next day for two high powered motor launches to take us to the far side of the island where the reef was alive with multicoloured fish swimming on the shelf close to a six thousand foot drop off to the ocean bottom. One of the professors from the West Indies was familiar with the dive area and led us in a long line across the shelf and down to the one hundred and ten foot depth along the wall where large pelagic fish below us were just visible in the indigo blue of the disappearing light. At that depth divers can absorb too much nitrogen from their tanks and a condition known as 'rapture of the deep' usually develops. It is a feeling of euphoria, similar to the buzz caused by two stiff drinks, and a trained diver can recognize it and begin to ascend to a shallower depth where the intoxication will vanish. I was swimming 'shotgun', the last position, to make sure that the students all stayed in line, and Tom, our cerebral palsy buddy, was swimming beside me.

The final two girls in the scuba line stopped, adjusted their buoyancy jackets so they were weightless at that depth, and began pushing one another. As I swam closer their laughter could be heard through their regulators; it was obvious they were 'narked', drunk with the excess of nitrogen gas (once called 'laughing gas') in their systems. They couldn't have cared less that they were hanging over a bottomless abyss, nor that at any moment they might start to believe they could breath underwater without the tank and regulator. I grabbed them both, shook them and tapped them on the forehead to indicate narcosis, then pointed sternly to the rest of the group calmly swimming up to shallower water through a cut in the shelf. Begrudgingly they obeyed and I turned back to join Tom, only he wasn't there. He was twenty feet below me and dropping!

Tom had learned to clears small amounts of water out of his mask by tilting the mask upward and breathing out through his nose. The procedure worked, but the loss of air created a negative buoyancy and Tom hadn't adjusted for that. He was on his way to the bottom. Up until then I'd never been below one hundred and ten feet and Tom was nearly twenty feet deeper than that, but I knew I couldn't face his mother if I let him sink all the way to the ocean floor so I dove down to him, inflated his jacket and accompanied him up to the group. In my dreams I still see that yawning darkness and I must confess, there was a moment that I didn't think I had the courage to chase him. Later I dove much deeper than that, but the first time is a challenge. It was a marvellous trip and now, some fifteen years later, I still get calls from certain of the students that were on that excursion; one lad even turned it into a life's work and ended up living in the Caribbean, running dives and selling scuba equipment.

We built a house in a small town near the city and began to teach scuba in the evening, twice weekly, for a local Community College, a part-time arrangement that was to last for over ten years. Two of my divers, Glenn and Larry, had progressed through the ranks and eventually had become instructors themselves, and it was only with their support and effort we were able to enlarge the Halcyon Dive Club. Over the years we must have introduced a thousand people to the sport and several went on to set up their own dive store or teaching facility, including Glenn who eventually took over the Club, formed his own company and has continued to instruct new candidates right up to the present time. But Glenn always had a romantic attachment to the sport having married one of the girls he taught to scuba. Larry has stayed in diving in spite of the fact that he detests cold water and consequently had earned the nickname 'Shakey', yet he loved the sport so much he became a leading figure in the annual Underwater Show that was one of the largest gatherings of divers and their wares in North America.

Chapter 14
More Stories

A few years ago one of the director of the scuba agency met me at the underwater show and asked me to take over the agency, since he was ready to retire. By this time it had become the giant in the industry, and the offer was tempting, but the children were small, we would have had to move to the west coast and I'd be spending a great deal of time away from home. It was a lovely offer but I had to refuse, but he appointed me the local agency representative which meant that I handled local complaints against instructors and appeared as a special witness at court cases involving drownings related to scuba. One such case concerned the death of two men who had drowned while doing an ice dive, a specialized type of diving that our Club had done for many winters. The coroner had no knowledge of such dives and requested instruction on how such dives could be done safely. We used roped divers who enter through one of several holes cut in the ice and who are secured on a hundred foot line to a surface tender, with another tender and secured rescue diver stationed nearby in case of some mishap. In this tragic case, the divers after a few minutes underwater had unhooked themselves in order to explore a mineshaft and when they exited the shaft they couldn't find the safety line and had wandered farther down the lake and eventually run out of air. Unfortunately any opening in the ice is not visible underwater from more than five feet away and their neglect of the safety rules had cost them their lives.

One elderly couple that we had taught in the Community College program planned to do their diving in the Caribbean, but agreed to do their open water in a local quarry before heading south. When they returned they dropped in one evening while we were running another course to thank us for the training we had given them in 'buddy breathing', a way of sharing air when one partner runs out under water. They had gone to the Cayman Islands and asked the local dive shop if they could do a single dive on the reef, which was about three hundred yards off shore. Unfortunately, the dive boat had already left for the day's dives and the only suggestion the shop could offer was to ask one of the local fishermen to take them out to the reef in his fishing boat. They left the shop and walked the beach until they found a captain who said he would take them out for fifty dollars for a half hour dive, which was about all they wanted to do that day. The captain rounded up an assistant after the couple stowed their rented gear in the small boat and they started out on a calm sea, with a light off shore breeze.

By the time they arrived at the reef the elderly man had donned his mask, buoyancy vest, flippers, tank and regulator and was ready to enter the water. The captain asked the assistant to throw in the anchor, which he did without noticing that the end of the rope had not been secured to the bow, so the whole thing went twenty feet down to the bottom. Our diver agreed to retrieve the end of the rope but when he returned to the surface the boat had drifted farther away than the rope would reach and he was left on the surface holding on to the rope that was anchored on the reef. The captain shouted, "Don't worry! I'll restart the engine and come and pick you up!"

Then in disbelief, the diver watched as the captain continued to pull at the starter cord on the outboard while the boat gently drifted off the reef and out into the deep, and when it had gone a fair distance he called to his wife to jump overboard. Luckily, she already had on her mask and flippers and was able to swim to where her husband was still anchored to the reef. They stayed on the surface, holding on to the anchor line, until the boat drifted out of sight. It was a lovely day and except for small ripples caused by the offshore breeze, the ocean was quiet; still they had a long way to swim to the beach and discovered that if they shared air and swam just beneath the water they made better time than on the breezy surface. He said it took them over an hour to reach safety and by the time they crawled up on the sand they were both exhausted.

When they finally got their wind back they found they couldn't get any of the other fishermen to be concerned for their captain, since his friends said he was a good mechanic and would soon get the engine fixed and head back to land. The couple went back to their hotel, showered and had a leisurely lunch before heading back to the beach and still there was no sign of the missing boat. By late afternoon they had reported the event to the local police and a search was begun, but to no avail. The small boat and its occupants were finally picked up by a passing ship three days later, some sixty miles from the island, and our divers had come to thank us for the scuba training they had received, for they were confident that they would have perished without it.

We had built our new home in the small town and come to know the friendly neighbours. The man next to us turned out to be amazing fellow and eventually a close friend. John was born in 1920 and had enlisted in the British Air Force when he was twenty, just at the start of the Second World War. He was bright and slight and eager and fit nicely into the tail gunner's spot in the Lancaster Bomber where he flew bombing raids over occupied Europe for the entire duration of the war. Bombing crews never lasted very long against the Luftwaufa and the German ack-ack guns, yet John survived more than the required number of runs needed for 'rotation', making twenty seven bombing raids, two more than the rotation number of twenty-five. He had made more than a dozen runs with his first crew but when he went out to get in the turret one night for the next run the captain realized that John was running a high fever and ordered him to the camp hospital. That was the last run for his crew; they were shot down over Berlin and none of the crew survived.

With another crew he was battling his way over Berlin one night when he suddenly was hit with shrapnel from a German ack-ack burst. The shrapnel came in one side, sliced through his oxygen hose and exited out the Plexiglas on the other side of the turret, missing him by inches. He realized that he was dizzy from lack of oxygen since they were at twenty thousand feet and radioed the captain to request that on the way home they drop down to six thousand feet where the oxygen was more plentiful, but the captain only replied,

"Sorry, John. At that altitude we're sitting ducks for the German gunners. You'll have to make out as best you can."

Then in spite of John's frequent requests to drop down, the radio remained dead.

"That's it." thought John, but when he bent over he found that he could just squeeze the severed end of the hose into his mouth and get some life sustaining oxygen. When they landed back in England he was so cold from being stuck in the shattered turret he couldn't talk, and when the crew pulled apart the tail gunner's bubble they laid him in the foetal position on the tarmac. Then they called for the 'meat wagon' for they were convinced he had frozen to death. Only when they lifted him up to put him in the mortuary truck and he groaned did they realize that he was still alive. To this day he still has trouble with the nerves in his hands where frostbite had injured them.

For his many raids, his tending to a wounded upper turret gunner during one battle, and his coolness and accuracy under fire he was awarded the Distinguished Flying Cross, one of the top military awards given out during the war. When he returned after the war was over he joined the fire department, married his childhood sweetheart, raised two children and earned several more commendations for his rescue work in fire fighting. He ended his career as lead fireman at our local airport, where they now have the National Warplane Heritage exhibit. We went there one day and he crawled up inside a restored Lancaster bomber but refused to squeeze into the tail gunner's turret. It brought back too many bad memories, he said. Now he is retired and sometimes over a beer he'll confess that he still has bad dreams about the bombing raids and all the bombs they dropped. Although John feels some guilt over his part in the devastation caused by the bombing raids, he still insists that the war was a grand adventure for many of the young people who took part.

That sense of adventure is the same thing that leads divers to push the limits of their ability, sometimes with fatal results, as in the case of the ice divers who perished, and another case we still speak about. Bobby was one of our better divers but he took a unwarranted chance and paid the ultimate price. It was on one of the dive weekends I couldn't attend, and was set up only for qualified divers who had a number of deep dives already in their dive books. Behind the large house they rented on the shore of Georgian Bay there is a fall-off that reached down to over a hundred feet in depth. It is an area that we frequently dive, so there was nothing unusual about Bobby's plan to dive it with a friend, except that he had less than half a tank of air when he entered, but his buddy later said, "We only intended to make one quick dive to the bottom and out again."

On the bottom Bobby ran out of air and tried to share air with his friend but must have swallowed water, for he suddenly bolted for the surface and died of embolism as the air in his lung expanded past their breaking point. As a club we have logged thousands of dives without mishap, but unless the divers are always aware of the inherent dangers, there are bound to be accidents.

There are as many scuba stories as there are dives, for each dive is a step out into the unknown where anything can happen. We've had divers who got lost in wrecks and had to be rescued, divers who were attacked by large fish that were cornered in a sunken boat, confused divers who insisted on swimming down instead of up to exit on night dives until they ran into the ooze on the bottom, dive boats that sunk under us, divers who over inflated their dry suits and popped to the surface like the Balloon Man, and even a couple who rented a small boat in October to go diving off a channel island and had the anchor lift off and their small boat drift away while they were down. They knew they wouldn't be missed until the next day, long enough for them to perish in the freezing cold of the night, so they elected to swim after the boat which continued to drift further out into the lake. It took them three hours to reach the boat and another half hour before they could find the strength to get on board. Luckily the trailing anchor hooked on to the bottom while they chased the boat or they would have made their last dive.

But there also have been strange and funny things happen, like the time I found a human head at fifty feet. We had run an advanced course, and the last dive was a fast water dive, just below the spill gate of the dam on the picturesque Moon River. By the end of the day I'd had enough of protecting the divers and as they took off their suits I went for a relaxing short dive in the deepest part below the dam. The light was not good at that depth but the current wasn't too strong and the bottom was as smooth as a marble floor. I was just heading back when I came upon it. There was no body attached, just the head and some of what looked like the muscles of the neck drifting out behind it. It couldn't be left because there was no way to mark the spot and no landmarks to indicate the exact spot for the police divers. Holding it at arms length and trying not to look into the empty eye sockets, my ascent was straight up. As the light increased it showed itself not to be a human head after all but a football helmet with a goggled bee keeper's face mask inside; the neck muscles were really strings of torn green netting that draped over the helmet and fell down below it. About ten feet from the surface I cleaned it out, stuck my hand inside and couldn't resist the impulse to come up beside a young woman swimmer and raise the artifact slowly out of the water. By the time I had crawled up on shore a crowd was gathering as she told her friends of her horrible encounter with the swamp monster. That's probably how most myths get started.

Of all the adventures scuba presented to us, the most memorable was our search for a sunken fur trading boat used to carry beaver pelts from a 'carrying place' to a Hudson Bay outpost in the eighteenth century. We were just finishing up an Open Water certification course at Tobermory, just off Lake

Michigan, when two commercial diver friends dropped in on their way home from repairing a northern town's water intake pipes, and enchanted us with a description of the artifact they had seen in the home of one of the bush pilots. He had shown them small artifacts, flintlock rifles, axe heads, pots and kettles, and asked if they would do a dive on the shallow wreck he had seem from the air since it was too deep for him to fully explore. The stuff he showed them came from a few breath-holding dives he had made to the deck, but he was sure there was much more in the hold. When they showed up at the floatplane dock the next day he had changed his mind and called off the trip. Still he had given them enough information about the wreck's location that they decided to try to reach the magical lake themselves by way of the logging roads, but the bridges were out, removed to keep campers out because of the high danger of forest fires at that time of the summer and they had to abandon their plans.

A group of us thought about it all winter, and explored what information the university library had to offer about the possibility of a fur trading fort being in the area described, in the late 1700's. Indeed, it had been one of the earliest and most successful fur trading areas in North America, and the historic records sang with the music of Indian names, like Assinogamy, Michipicoten and Capoonicagomie. It was enough to convince us, and early the next summer three of us loaded two twelve foot aluminum boats and small outboard engines, ten full scuba tanks and all our scuba and camping gear into a heavy-duty trailer and pulled it with a four-by-four the seven hundred miles to the northern town of Hearst. Our maps showed logging roads running from that town to a place called Oba on the Oba River, a river that ran straight to our destination! After we had loaded up with gas and food we madly rushed down into the primal Boreal forest confident that the first timber road would quickly lead us to our river of dreams. The word 'road' when speaking of timber-runs is as misleading as their direction, for they wander, split and often disappear entirely leaving the driver to park and walk on ahead to see which direction the way ambled over some rock face. Often a deep rain gully had to be filled in with dead trees and rocks before the 4 x 4 could proceed, but we had to keep going for reversing with the trailer on that narrow pathway was impossible. After hours of labour we pulled into Oba, much to the disbelief of the occupants who insisted that the only way into their town was by rail. We stayed at one of the town's three hotels, sleeping on the floor in a store room, for the 'hotels' existed only for the beer trade generated by the railway section gangs that were stationed there. It was a desolate place and a sign on the wall in our hotel described its isolation. The sign read simply: 'Booze is the answer.'

Next morning we parked our 4 x 4 and trailer on the riverbank and loaded our two small boats to their gunnels and proceeded down the river's serpentine back, expecting any moment to hear the lilting paddle song of an early French-Canadian trapper. We camped at the mouth of Lake Kabinacagami where the Oba River enters and dove repeatedly at all the probable spots for a week. We came closer to nature than we ever thought possible, for by day there is something about the Canadian North that mimics the vastness of the universe, and at night in the glow of the campfire the dark trees seemed to round themselves upward to greet the stars. The treasure hunt became secondary as the stillness of the Northern Pines mesmerized us, and by the end of the week we had to admit that the haunting mystery of the sunken ship remained. When we returned with our graphic stories of this adventure they fired up the imaginations of many of our compatriots, who insisted that we all return the next summer. We needed more accurate records of those early days, and got permission from the Canadian Government to research some of their historical records before making a second attempt. In the National Archives of Ottawa we came across the actual factor's daily journals for the area and even found a teasing notation, written in a hodgepodge of English, French and Indian tongues, with a generous helping of misspelled terms, that directed the factor to abandon the post and sink the boat! Then we realized that the declination of magnetic North in the late seventeen hundreds would be different from our present compass readings, making the opposite shore the more logical point for the site of the original outpost and the sunken vessel.

This time six of us went in, and by rail, with a small portable compressor for refilling the tanks, and found treasures enough to satisfy our souls. The lake yielded up a carved stone totem shaped like a loon, a stone axe head, square green bottles, old axe handles, square nails and old pieces of pots. We located the spot of the old trading post complete with its large hearthstone and stood on the lookout point where the post factor had watched for the appearance of the Indian canoes or his own trading boat. We had been met at the mouth of the Oba River by a launch from an expensive lodge on the lake. They loaded all six of us, and our gear, including the compressor and our tanks, into their large boat and whisked us to their wilderness camp in a quarter of the time it had taken us on our first trip. We stayed for a week in a small cabin at this fly-in northern fishing camp and used their new sixteen-foot aluminum boats, each with its own twenty-five horse-powered outboard engine, to dive all the sites indicated by our research. The lake had much to offer us. At the south end of this twenty-mile lake there was an abandoned gold mine whose slag pile towered a hundred feet above the lake, and underwater we discovered three great ore cars that had made a final journey across the slag tracks and plunged into the dark brown waters, where they will rest forever. We dove in the clear, rushing waters of the rivers that empty into this long lake and found fishing lures that sport fishermen had travelled thousand of miles to lose, and at the north end of the lake, where the river flows toward James Bay, we found a wooden skid way around a deep waterfall. At the river end of the skid way a great, rusting steel boiler rose fifteen feet above the marsh grass, abandoned when it proved too heavy to be moved to the gold mine. A hundred years from now it will still startle the unsuspecting hiker who walks along the old skid way. But we never found the boat. It is still there and is still calling us, and perhaps someday we'll try again, foraging once more into that land untouched by time.

The adventure had a final bonding of the six of us in an activity not related to diving. We were in the habit of eating supper in the dining hall of the lodge and often would head there immediately after dropping off our diving equipment in our cabin at the end of our day's search. Naturally we looked pretty dowdy in T-shirts and torn jeans as we entered to sit among the sport fishermen, dressed in the latest styles from the outfitter's store, and eventually were asked by the manager of the lodge to wear more suitable clothes so not to upset the other patrons. And the next day we did. Max spent extra long time in preparing, dressing himself in the best of his clothes and even using some of our better pieces, probably so that he could circulate among the rich patrons and engage them in spirited conversation just to show them that although he was only a house painter, he was very well educated and every bit as good they were, in spite of all their money. Our cabin was the last in the line of cabins, and we had found it easier to go by boat across the curve of the beach than to walk that distance. That evening we used two of the boats, but as we docked at the lodge Max stood up to exit from his boat and suddenly lost his footing, falling backwards into the lake. But that didn't stop him! He was still well dressed and he was going to supper! And he marched, head held high, dripping wet into the dining room and while the rest of us couldn't contain our laughter, he sat there and ate his meal, glaring at any guest who happened to glance his way. None of the guests seemed offended and even the manager left us alone.

The next day it turned out that two of the sport fishermen who were guests at the lodge had not returned by nightfall and there was some concern that they might have run into trouble. Perhaps even serious trouble, for it is a wild land with untamed animals who view people as lower on the food chain than themselves. Because we knew the lake well, having dove most of its bays, three of our group were sent out the next morning to search and others climbed into one of the float planes to act as look-outs for the pilot. We covered the lake several times, once spotting a floating outboard engine gas container, but no sign of the missing fishermen. After an hour in the air we returned to the dock and were met by the two rescued and tired lost men. Their engine had failed and they had spent the night shivering on top of a small rock outcrop on the edge of the lake until found that morning by one of the search boats. They were hungry and they were still cold and they couldn't wait to take a hot shower and head for the dining room. They were also thankful that our group had taken part in the search and when it came time to leave we had the feeling that in spite of their comments on our lack of a dress code, they really had enjoyed our company. Later that afternoon the owner piled us all into his large launch and returned us down that magic river to Oba where we waited for the next milk train to take us south. We spent some hours in one of the three 'hotels', which are actually only beer halls, along with members of the railroad section gang and gradually began to believe that the sign on the wall was not just clever, but accurate as well for it still read, 'Beer is the answer.' By the time the train arrived the town of Oba was beginning to look pretty good, and once on board we slept most of the way home.

After we returned from this adventure one of our members phoned me one day and asked if he could borrow the large topographical map we had been using to dive our northern lake. He had a new girlfriend whose father was a diviner, using willow sticks to find lost objects, and wanted to show him the map of our search area to see if he could 'devine' the place where the ancient ship lay. Later he said that the sticks had gone down on the map in the one part of the lake we had neglected. More reason to plan a third trip to that undisturbed and beautiful boreal landscape. When we returned we heard that the *Waome* had claimed a victim, but not from our club. A qualified diver, who had not been underwater for over two years, went with his buddies into the dark wreck and became disoriented in the murky water when his flashlight failed. Surrendering to panic he dropped his weight belt believing that he would ascend to the surface from the air in his buoyancy compensator but instead became stuck to the ceiling of the deck above him. Although his buddies did a search for him in those ghostly waters they never thought to look upwards, and eventually he ran out of air and drowned.

Our scuba club had all the usual safety regulations in place, but because of such tragedies we became even more concerned that all the members, and those in training, were aware of the saying, "There are *old* divers, and there are *bold* divers, but there are *no* old, bold divers."

Scuba deaths are lower on the mortality scale than most other sports, but the difference is that in most sports the death is cause by an accident rather than by the onset of panic. A panicking diver ascending from deeper than fifteen feet will likely suffer an embolism if he is holding his breath as he surfaces, and if he or she runs into trouble at more than sixty feet there is only about one minute's time to overcome the feeling of panic, release the weight belt and do a controlled exhalation all the way to the surface. It is a strange feeling to be able to breathe out continually for the minute it takes to ascend as the air expands inside the lungs, without any sensation of being out of breath. We made sure our divers knew and practiced this drill.

One of the deepest wrecks we occasionally dove was the *Forest City* whose fantail rested on the bottom at about one hundred and eighty feet. By the time we started diving on the wreck it had already claimed several lives, so our preparation was always thorough. We dove in groups of four, all highly trained and each diver with a large number of dives at other sites. Our dive plan was to follow the dive boat's anchor line down and spend a few minutes around the fantail before swimming upward along its broken back to view the rest of the wreck, which started at about sixty feet, the boat having been originally sunk by running into a large island in heavy fog. On one particular dive we had stayed longer around the fantail than usual but finally started up, then I found myself yanked backward as if my extra regulator had caught on a piece of the ship. Turning around to set it free it showed no entanglement, so I started up again, only to be pulled once more; after the third pull I grabbed the trailing regulator and drew it toward me. On the end of the regulator was a fellow diver who had run out of air and was using my trailing one, and who had turned behind me every time I checked so that the extra regulator wouldn't get pulled out of his mouth. Sharing air at one hundred and sixty feet was not my idea of a perfect dive, and at that point we carefully rose to the surface. When I checked his tank it was almost full; what had happened was that his regulator malfunctioned and stopped delivering air on the bottom and so he had immediately used my secondary one. No panic in that diver.

Several police divers that we had instructed in the methods of underwater Search and Recovery invited me to an international conference on body and evidence recovery, which is a specialty work among police and commercial divers. Police from all over the English speaking world attended with their slide shows and video clips taken from the actual scenes of such recoveries in lakes, oceans and rivers. One was even of a small commercial plane that crashed into a frozen lake leaving some of the dead right on the thick ice and others in the waters below. Some were half in both, and frozen where they lay, necessitating the use of welding torches to free them. It was, these divers admitted, the most difficult task they had ever done in years of recovery, for their working temperature was ten below zero on the ice and nearly freezing underneath. They were unable to cut holes in the ice near the crash site for fear that the major parts of the plane that had not sunk would crash through the weakened ice and rain down on them as they searched for the other missing bodies. The divers entered a hundred feet away through holes cut in the ten inches of ice, then had to string marker lines from their entry points to the wreckage sixty feet below in order to bring the bodies out. Each diver was fastened to a safety line, held by a topside tender, and the lines often got snagged on the rocky bottom or on the forward parts of the aircraft. All the bodies were recovered within two days but the surface wreckage was allowed to sink in the spring and the plane was not raised until the next summer.

Some police units are not allowed to remove the bodies from within cars or trucks before the vehicles are raised out of the water, which caused quite a sensation in one case that was videotaped by a State Trooper. A car had driven off the rim of a deep and murky quarry and the police divers who attached the tow line to the axle of the sunken auto couldn't tell if there were bodies inside or not. A brand new super-heavyweight tow truck had been brought to the scene and the divers had taken down its towline and put it in place. The tow truck driver stood at the tail of the truck where the winching levers were and watched as the rear of the car became visible. Everyone was craning their necks to see if the bodies were present, including the trucker on the winching controls, who was so fascinated by the occasion that he didn't notice he had begun to walk slowly toward the edge of the quarry as his new tow truck quietly rolled backwards. By the time he realized that the towline was not moving but the truck was, it was too late to stop the inevitable and the great machine slid over the lip and disappeared. The Trooper said that a week later they had to bring in a heavy crane to drag both vehicles out of the quarry. Another film showed two English police divers recovering evidence from the Thames River in London, England. As they exited the defiled water they were hosed down with a strong disinfectant, then undressed and placed in an ambulance and taken for a day's stay in the isolation wing of a nearby hospital. Because the River Thames is one of the most polluted rivers in the world police divers are not released until all necessary tests and observations are concluded.

The California State Police used large blown-up pictures to show us the case of a woman's faceless body that had been found wedged under a tangle of logs in a local lake. They described the body as being supple and intact except that the face was imploded inwards. At first they thought the murdered person had been killed only a short time before being found, but the coroner concluded that the body was five years old and almost perfectly preserved by the tannic acid from the logs that hid it. Her biker boyfriend eventually admitted to using a shotgun to send her away.

We continued to dive wherever there was a large enough puddle to allow us to submerge: Gary excelled in underwater photography and won a trip to the Red Sea from one of the contests he entered and met Jacques Cousteau on board his dive ship 'Calypso'; I got to dive in the Atlantic, Cuba and other islands in the West dies; but it was Max who put us all to shame. As a house painter he buys all his supplies on Visa and earns oodles of frequent flier points, allowing him to dive not only in Cuba but Australia, Japan and many of the Indonesian Islands, not once but several times. The only unfulfilled dream place that the three of us shared was to dive the Truk Lagoon where much of the Japanese fleet was sunk during the Pacific War. So far even Max has not settled that yearning, and none of us likely will, in this life.

The divers in the club included doctors, dentists, police, most other occupations and even one millionaire. Joe 'Tech' was a construction engineer who started with a business partner buying up and improving large apartment buildings. When one was largely rented they would use the building collateral, float a new loan and purchase another apartment, until they eventually owned seven modern high rise dwellings, each one paying off its own loan and upkeep through the rental income. They were so successful that Joe found that he didn't have to go into the office often and became one of our most active instructors. But he should have spent more of his time attending to work, for his business partner, who had scant knowledge of building codes, signed a contract to purchase a large apartment right on the shore of one of the Great Lakes. When Joe eventually did the inspection of the building the first thing he noticed was that the elevators were not working properly. Further inspection revealed that his partner had bought a 'pig-in-a-poke', for the building was actually sinking and as the renters began moving out the interest on the loan could not be met. The domino effect set in and within a year the company went bankrupt losing all seven of the buildings. Things went from bad to worse. Joe's lovely wife developed cancer, his country estate was seized along with his five-car garage full of vintage autos, and all his personal assets were confiscated. After his wife died I saw him off to his boyhood home in Florida, and later learned that he had gone into real estate and had become a certified cave-diving instructor.

It would be remiss not to mention our other instructors: Gary, Glenn and Larry, W.T., a professional welder who taught all five of his children to scuba and who recently signed on as crew on a year's sail around the world on a Tall Ship; Dan, who spent so much time diving his wife divorced him; Janet, who fell in love with a different 'hunk' at every Open Water session and who, after all her scuba romances, married a non diver and never put on a scuba tank again; Doctor Bill who kept us healthy; Big John who had a bit of a weight problem and never complained about how cold the water was; Dixie and Rob who started their own dive shop; and Hugh and Doug and Laurent and Ronn and David; and finally Donna, our lovely Indian princess, whose father was an Iroquois Band Chief, and who was the most gentle and successful of all the instructors when it came to dealing with nervous candidates. And of course there was Max; indefatigable, irrepressible Max who one evening was chatting-up some lovely young thing as we all set around in the main room of the cottage after a night dive. With a wink to us he excused himself to go to the washroom. Max *loved* cooked German sausages and often brought several with him on a dive. When he re-entered the room one was hanging loosely from the fly of his pants and when his new friend yelled "Max!!" and pointed he replied, "Oh, is that out again?" and pulled it out of his pants and devoured it on the spot. Eventually his new friend recovered and we all marked it down as another victory for Max over the conventions of society.

We began to dive the *Waome* wreck in the early 1970's and sold the cottage at the beginning of 1990, which effectively ended those halcyon days that had lasted for some twenty years. Then one evening in late June, as we gathered in a restaurant after a training session with a new group of students, a sense of nostalgia seemed to overflow from all of the instructors and we decided to have one more go at the 'old lady'. The following weekend turned out to be available for many of the instructors and senior club members simply because the new class wouldn't be ready for their open water sessions until mid July. The only problem was that our dive boat, the Manatee, had been sold and converted into a cargo barge for taking building materials to the various islands that dotted the long lake. Nevertheless the next Saturday we loaded our tanks and scuba gear into our vehicles and headed north, overcome by a yearning for the deep dark waters that surrounded 'our' wreck.

Much to our surprise, when we arrived at the marina we found our old dive boat right there, empty of cargo and ready to go. The new owner was not to be found but the proprietor of the local hotel had the key and when we offered him $100 he felt that the owner wouldn't mind seeing how we were the original builders of the craft and knew how to care for it. We loaded our tanks and gear onto its deck and after gassing up set out for yesterday, laughing and reminiscing about when we were younger and the things that had happened then. When we arrived at the dive site we saw that the markers were still floating on the surface, tied to the bow and fantail by 100 foot lines, and under the watchful eyes of the appointed rescue divers who were dressed and ready to enter but saved their dive until all the others had completed their time on the bottom, we buddied-up and entered in pairs.

I first dove the wreck in the late 1960's when it was in pristine condition: all the glass was still in the wheelhouse, the white-painted canvas covering the roof of the upper deck glowed eerily in the flashlight's beam, the ship's name glistened on the sides of the bow, collapsible chairs littered the observation deck, the ship's smokestack was still black and stood upright, and the shoes of the drowned minister, who had been asleep when the ship suddenly plunged to the bottom in the mid 1930's, were to be seen underneath his bunk. Even the ice-box, an early form of today's refrigerator, was closed and when opened revealed to the flashlight's probing eye tins of foodstuff and glass bottles, some unbroken. A local diver who had gone down in the 1950's had brought up two unbroken bottles of milk and after exiting the water poured the soured milk into the lake not realizing that there would have been value in analyzing the contents of the bottles to determine the radiation level of Strontium 90 that was present in those early days.

Now our wreck was in its last days. Gone was not only the top canvas but many of the roof boards themselves; no glass remained in the wheelhouse, the ice-box and deck chairs had disappeared, the smokestack had collapsed and was just a tangle of rusted metal and only one of the minister's shoes had escaped pillage. Even some of the partitions had been torn down by divers whose aim seemed to have been to destroy rather than enjoy. We penetrated inside and dove down its collapsing stairway, circled it slowly and soon returned to the surface. Our trip back to the marina was done in silence, and no one has asked to dive it since. We had seen it in its glory and could not face it in its decay.

Chapter 15
Another Job Change

One of the teachers at the private school, where I had taught for the past twelve years, approached me one day asking that I attend a meeting to get our teachers unionized. His cousin was an employee of the Teacher Union and they had recently unionized another large private school and had chosen our school as the next one to canvas. Some eight of us attended Jack's meeting in late June and at the end of the meeting agreed to hold a second meeting, with even more of our confreres, early in September. During the holidays Jack asked me to act as secretary for the second meeting and we set it up, again at his place. This time there were more than a dozen present and one young woman seemed enthralled by the prospect of a union in the school and insisted on taking over the task of secretary, taking down the minutes of the meeting and offering suggestions about how and when we would get the union organizer to hold a general meeting in the school, as the Labour Laws outlined.

Shortly after the second meeting Jack told me sadly that his marriage had failed and that he was quitting teaching in order to play semi-pro hockey in Europe, and asked that I take on his position as union organizer. After he left I contacted the secretary several times about a date for the next meeting, where we would officially canvass the whole school and put the idea of unionization to a vote, but for one reason or another each suggested date was deferred. Suddenly she was given a promotion and I was fired; she had been the informer in our midst, sent by the Headmaster to get the names of all participants. The Teacher's Union took the school to Court and they had to pay my whole year's salary, even though I was dismissed at Christmas.

The ironic thing was that the students and I had already set up a scuba course and booked a Caribbean trip for the March Break, and the parents wouldn't let the school cancel the function. So twice a week I'd show up at the school at two-thirty in the afternoon and take the students to a downtown pool for training, even though I was a 'persona non grata' with the administration.

In the meantime I applied to a Catholic Board and was hired on the spot for the following September. Fifteen years later I'm still there and still thankful. You never know when a kick is really a boost. The Caribbean trip was one to remember; we went back to Bonaire and my young son and I liked it so much we purchased a time-share at the main resort. The beaches there were quite special: it was the first time our boys had been introduced to a nude beach and it was difficult to get them to concentrate on the diving. But they recovered and did everything: diving on an untouched reef, cave diving, and even drift diving along the shoreline. We rented a van and followed the safety divers and students by road until near the end of the island. After they were all safely on shore Tom and I went in and did the last half-mile of the shore line and almost got swept out to sea, the current near the end was so strong. The trip was a grand adventure and at our last meal on the island the congeniality award was given to Ian, a sensitive, fun loving grade 12 student, who stepped off the school bus a week after we returned and was instantly killed by a young driver who went through a stop sign. At his funeral his mother read from Ian's journal where he had written the day before his death, "Life is beautiful, too beautiful not to be infinite, and I have seen that beauty and felt the infinite."

The new school was my first introduction to immigrant working class families with strong cultural bonds, where the girls began thinking of marriage as soon as they turned sixteen, and the boys put school lessons secondary to their after-school work. On a survey it was learned that the boys worked an average of twenty hours a week on evenings and weekends, which left them scant time for homework and school projects. Still they managed to pass their subjects and get their twelve diploma but it meant that the teacher had to make the subject as practical as possible, concentrating on the important topics and building into the curriculum lots of classroom review. Their emotions lay quite close to the surface and they could flare up at any time, but they had great hearts and seldom carried grudges. What you saw was what you got, for they were not pretentious, and overall had great affection for their teachers.

One young grade ten student was an exception; he hated all teachers, including the school social worker who tried to help him adjust to the school, but who gave up after he threatened her. I don't think he hated me any more than any other teacher, but one spring day he walked into my grade 12 Applied

English class and challenged me to step outside the portable classroom and settle our differences. He only weighed about a hundred and twenty pounds soaking wet, and I started to laugh seeing the humour in the situation and knowing that it was a lose-lose situation on my part if I left the room, in spite of the cat calls from the other students who were electrified by the prospect of a teacher-student fight. Suddenly one of the larger grade 12 boys had enough of the youngster's bravado. He got up and walked to the back of the room where the small student stood, spun him around and actually pitched him out the door onto the grass in front of the portable, then came back up and sat down. When I got to the door the young student was running away, scared but apparently none the worse for wear. When I sat down at the front of the class, the grade twelve student bent over and whispered, "That'll cost you an extra 10% on my essay."

The teachers at that Catholic school were unique in their attitude toward administration, for there was no sense of servitude in their position. They accepted the Board, the Principal and Vice Principals as necessary parts in the smooth running of the school and who could deal with truant students or ones who acted out too much in their search for identity, but these teachers did not look to administration for methodology in teaching their disciplines. They were well read in their individual subjects, discussed options and problems with their confreres, related to the new 'insights' from the Board, and loved to teach. The vast majority of the students saw how knowledgeable and dedicated these teachers were and found them approachable and friendly. There was a give-and-take attitude in the classrooms, which was a welcome relief from the 'spit and polish' upper class belief of the private school. They were bonded together in their acceptance of the importance of education, including religious education, and all the teachers taught a religion course at some point in their career, yet their interpretation of Catholic dogma was as unique as their teaching method. They believed in the universality of the Church, and the teachings on the Eucharist and the value of morality, but 'small' points, such as the infallibility of the Pope, or the absolute need for weekly Mass, or the concept that marriage was always permanent, were subjects open to discussion. The vast majority of them were Catholic to the core and good hearted, but no more inclined to servitude in religion than they were to servitude to administration.

One of the most unique teachers was Martin, the mechanic who ran the auto technology courses at the school. He had taken up teaching after spending several years as an artist and mechanic for Ford, General Motors and other majors in the field. There wasn't a nut or bolt on any car that he hadn't seen and modified, but he had a fatal weakness: he couldn't pass a 'for sale' sign on any car without making an offer on it. Consequently, his classes were always working on some ancient vehicle that he had bought, and his yard and large shop at his home were filled with a wonderful variety of cars and trucks in various stages of repair. On most of them some particular piece was missing and he was ordering it on the Internet or from some auto magazine, and someday it would be completed. One of the things that kept this large array of vehicles in the incomplete mode was that he was generous to a fault. If someone had a problem, or was poor and needed some work done on their car, Martin would leave whatever he was doing and solve their problem first, even to the point of buying them an old wreck and refurbishing it completely at very little cost to themselves. He always felt that the skill that he had acquired over the years belonged more to those who asked for his assistance than to himself, and so he was constantly living just above the debt line. Those who knew him loved him for his outgoing spirit and marvellous generous nature.

On his fiftieth birthday his sister held a surprise party for him at her house and enough people showed up to fill a banquet hall. Those who couldn't attend sent messages of good wishes. At about 11:00 p.m. when the party was in full swing a female police officer showed up to arrest him for some vague offence, and placed him in handcuffs. She then seated him in the main chair in the living room and began to remove her clothes. Of course it was a set up, arranged by a few of his buddies, but there wasn't even standing space left in the living room by the time she began to unbutton her shirt. One older gentleman who was seated across from her made an off-colour remark just she removed her bra and she said, "Shut up or I'll give you a bust in the mouth!"

And he immediately replied," Oh, Please! Please!"

Because by this time our children were grown up and no longer our full responsibility, both he and I bought motorcycles and began a series of adventures that hasn't ended yet. We spent a part of one winter planning an excursion to Newfoundland where he owned a summer home, and talked three other riders to throw in with us, but as spring approached and the bikes were put back on the road, the thrill of the chase began to dull in the minds of the other three, and when Martin himself backed out because of more recent commitments it remained a solitary venture. The roads were good and the weather was agreeable until the end of the second day on 'The Rock', when the rains fell and the winds blew and threatened to sink the entire island. He had told me to stay at his summerhouse, giving me easy directions to arrive there by following the highway to Trout River where his house was the last one before the road ended in the sea.

However he had forgotten to tell me that there was *one turn* before the road ended, and the house I tried to sleep in didn't belong to him. Since the house was empty and there was no way of getting in, it turned out to be a cold night in the travel tent I had brought. In the morning the first thing to be faced was a long ride up a *wet, steep* hill back to the main highway. On the way back from Corner Brook it rained so hard it was difficult to tell if I was still on the road or had ridden off into the sea, and to add to the excitement a 16-wheel 'semi' transport allowed me to stay ahead of it only if my speed didn't drop below 70 mph. Newfoundland truckers only stop for moose and beer, and frequently don't bother to stop for the moose. Then a lonely truck stop showed up on the horizon and after I dismounted from the bike a waitress kindly led me to a booth close to the door so the water damage would be minimal. At Port-aux-Basques, where the ferry docks, they have no storm sewers and the water cascades down the steep streets using the asphalt as a pathway. That night it was almost a flood and in many places the water reached up to the foot pegs on the bike. Once back on the mainland the overcast sky found the sun again and the ride home through the North-Eastern States was exceptionally beautiful.

And there have been other rides, some with Martin or Rick, another teacher, who has an amazing gift for planning and finding every unknown road in our area. When Steve reached adulthood I bought him a motorcycle and one summer we rode together to the Bike Week at Sturgis in South Dakota, and the next summer to see my daughter, his sister, who was working in Oregon. That ride was certainly the longest and most demanding of all, for my bike broke down and had to be jury-rigged in a small town in Washington in order for us to get to Portland, where it was repaired at a cost of over a thousand dollars. The trip out had been so sunny we often rode with only jeans and boots, but on the way back the gods of weather made it up to us by having their storm clouds rain on us right up to our home driveway. Later I rode alone to Laconia in New Hampshire, and more recently to the northern section of the Blue Ridge Parkway in Virginia where there are at least thirty curves in every mile. They have been wonderful rides with wonderful friends, and more are planned if God extends my life for a few more years.

Eventually we sold the cottage and the boats and did our Open Waters training sessions in local quarries or lakes. It was my pleasure to teach Martin to scuba, and in exchange he has taught me how to do body work on old cars. Steve needed one to attend university so an old station wagon was put back in shape and lasted until I rebuilt a newer sports car for Beth, which she adamantly refused to drive because it had a gear shift. Then Steve gave the old station wagon to his uncle and raced around in the sport car until it finally fell apart and he was able to buy himself a new one. Beth by then was in high school and secretly I had arranged to lease her an automatic from a dealership that happened to be on the main road on our way into the city. On a Saturday morning I invited her to come for a ride in the truck so we could go shopping at the Mall, a 'given' way of getting her consent to spend some time with her old man. As we rode toward the city I told her that the warning light on the dashboard had suddenly lit up and we would have to pull into the garage at the nearby dealer. The salesman was ready for us and acted as if he was trying to sell *me* a new car, and asked Beth if she would like to go for a ride in their latest small, automatic, front-wheel drive vehicle. She was delighted and during the drive tried to 'sell' me on the idea of getting this new car by trading in my old truck, which was a standard drive. But when we returned and the salesman gave her the car in *her* name she was speechless. Even the euphoria felt by divers at the close of a harrowing adventure was nothing when compared to hers, when her voice finally returned. Bonding with Steve had been easy, but this was a step in the right direction with Beth.

Steve didn't like university and finally went off to work on his own, selling goods on e-bay, and eventually did so poorly he had to turn the business over to another and take out a substantial bank loan to pay off his suppliers. He got a job in an upscale restaurant where he met a couple of men who suggested ways of making money quickly to pay off the loan, and he almost went with them but stepped back in time to stay on the straight and narrow for our sake. But Beth stuck to the books, received her undergraduate degree, and graduated in Law from Notre Dame University in South Bend, Indiana, then moved to Oregon and married a fellow lawyer. He's a nice person and bright, but why did she need *him* when she could have just remained *my* daughter? We attended her wedding in Oregon, and it was better than even the ones on television; another bright spot along the way. I often wonder if Steve had the same problem that I had when I was his age: trying to live up to a successful father image, which of course is an impossible and castrating task.

It had been my intention to sign the scuba business over to Steve when he reached the instructor level and although he became an excellent diver and a club Dive Master he didn't want to proceed any further in the ranks. But he turned some of his intentions to body building, and now outranks us all. He has continued to dive and several times Max and his son, Tyson, and Steve and I have gone off as a foursome and explored some hidden area. Whenever their work allowed, Steve and Tyson would come along with Max and Gary and the other instructors on our group training dives, especially on our weekend at Tobermory where it was possible to do both shore diving on nearby wrecks *and* deeper diving on the offshore wrecks using a converted fishing trawler, rented as a dive boat for the occasion.

We frequently rented a large shoreline house that had sixteen bedroom, some very small, for the entire weekend and as many as thirty divers, beginner to instructor, would show up with all their gear and try to find a spot somewhere near a bed. Both groups, beginner and advanced, dove Friday; a wade-in dive for the beginners in the late afternoon and a night dive in the black waters for those who were already certified. Saturday was a busy day and by the end of the day the instructors with the new candidates would have a pretty good idea of who would pass the course and who would have to return at a later date to complete the drills they had failed that weekend. The euphoria of the successful or attempted dives of that first full day always turned Saturday night into party-time with everyone sitting around with a beer trying to tell the others about some amusing or scary incident that had happened that day.

Max couldn't allow such a captive audience to escape his hairy-dog stories or his mimicry of certain British sit-coms, often interspersed with solos on his golden trumpet. And any one of those activities usually sent the instructors and most of the certified divers out into the kitchen where they continued their *own* party. But his repertoire always delighted the new divers, often to the point of their *insisting* on giving him another beer. Yet even here he was a champion; his years as a sailor had developed an impossible ability for clear headedness even after the first keg. Only once did I hear him ask for consideration when the duty of instructor fell upon him. He had stayed up until four in the morning having found a small group of nighthawks intent on draining just one more story from him. When I woke him at six in the morning and shook him out of his odiferous slumber he looked at me out of morning-after eyes and said simply, "Oh my God". It was a prayer, not a curse, for Max is very religious in his own way.

After that prayer of petition I didn't have the heart to make him face the reality of a cold plunge into the bay with his students that morning. But he was back for the afternoon dives and did his usual masterful magic with his students, and all of them passed with flying colours.

Linda's parents often spent part of the summer with us. Gordon had been a truck driver after his service in the Second World War and had no end of fascinating stories, always punctuated with his infectious laugh, and his wife, Gladys, was a cook from the old school whose baking is still legendary with family and friends. They spent a good deal of time with our family at the cottage during the month of July or August, depending on which month was reserved for the exclusive use of my sister and her family. There were no divers ever invited during those sacred months, and pity the poor one that mistakenly showed up unannounced at our door. To say that the ladies were unforgivingly annoyed would be an understatement. Outside of those two months we had the boats in the lake by late April and didn't pull them out until late November or early December, depending on when the snow arrived.

During the sacred clan-only months our cottage and my brother's next door, rocked with the intensity of family trips and games. The dive barge Manatee was used for outings and picnics into the hidden and forgotten bays in the large sequence of lakes nearby, and such trips have remained as memories of being able to once again become a child with our children when they were small, and to play 'Who can push Papa Bear off the barge?' when they were older. Chris and Becky are the children of close friends and the same age as our two and often shared a part of the summer with us. These four grown-up children have remained so close in friendship that each has vowed to be the Best Man or Bridesmaid at the other's wedding, with Becky leading the way at Beth's recent one.

After the children grew up and Glenn took over the diving I was left with some free summer time. A national charity organization asked if I would spend a part of a summer building houses on a Dakota First Nation reservation and I agreed. My job was to act as an assistant plumber, having spent some time with my uncle who had his own plumbing business, but when I arrived at the site it presented itself as an untouched grassy field, the other volunteers not having shown up. Luckily the earlier training in surveying proved useful and the dimensions of the small house were soon staked out and waiting for the arrival of the excavation crew. They showed up and carved a depression of thirteen inches in the soft soil; it was to be a house with no basement, beginning with an eight inch layer of crushed gravel, on top of which the plumbing pipes were to be laid before being covered over by five inches of concrete. There was no room for error once the concrete was down, so I began carefully and with some trepidation. As I laid the pipes a Gray Jay (Perisoreus Canadensis) showed up and perched on a fencepost, but began his chattering alarm cry only when I connected a piece of the of main drain line together. And he was right, for it was a 'T' connection and I'd placed it in backwards. In the following days he always showed up and always complained when I had done something wrong or done it poorly. On the day before the concrete was to be poured he was quiet all day until near the end, then started such a ruckus that I shooed him away, but that night in bed as I went over the final layout in my mind it became clear that there was a water trap in every line but the one from the laundry room. If the concrete had been poured the smell from the septic tank would have come up that solitary pipe and made the house uninhabitable. Early next morning the oversight was corrected and although I stayed another week he never returned. Was it just another coincidence in a long life of coincidences, or had the little bird been sent?

I've often been asked if I would return to the active priesthood if the Church allowed such a move, and my answer has always been the same: 'in a heartbeat.' I loved the priestly life as much as I love the family life, but so far a married clergy in the Roman Catholic faith is not permitted and I respect and understand the Church's decision. None of the priestly abilities such as hearing confessions, saying the words of consecration or administering the Sacrament of Healing (the Last Rites) are lost when a priest is released from his vows. These faculties are only suspended, and revive in extreme circumstances when no other priest is available. Several times during the family years I have come upon a serious accident or life threatening situation when I was the only priest anywhere in the vicinity: two sisters apparently dead in their mangled car at a 'T' junction in the road; an unconscious patient waiting to be air lifted to a hospital; a young teenager hanging upside down by her seatbelt in the family overturned van, bleeding profusely from her mouth and who squeezed my hand when I asked if she loved Jesus; her father in the driver's seat already apparently dead; a friend's dying wife who had fallen away from the Church and who wouldn't see anyone but me; and my long-time friend, Danny, who had his aortic operation moved ahead when a surgery theatre became available and who lay in an induced coma for six weeks before completely recovering. All these received conditional absolution and the prayers for the dying in their moment of extreme necessity.

As well as these there are two others that have their claim to a place in my memory. The first involved a horrific crash of two cars on a country crossroad. I was waiting at a stop sign behind a tiny two door foreign car when it suddenly accelerated right into the path of a speeding heavy car travelling down the main road. The small car became airborne and ended up in the corn field on the opposite side of the road, while the heavier car skidded a hundred yards down the through way and stopped at the side of the road. The driver of the heavier car exited and waved that he was not badly hurt, but the young woman in the smaller car was obviously dying. I had the impression that she also squeezed my hand as I gave her absolution. Her car was totalled. All the windows were smashed but the rear one. It had popped right out of its frame, and in the back seat were a broken baby carrier and a multitude of scattered diapers. We searched among the cornrows until the police brought in a canine unit but the baby was not found. The next day the newspaper carried an account of the accident, reporting that the mother had been on her way for a job interview after dropping the baby off at the sitters. Those who had been at the scene of the crash were both saddened at the loss of the young mother and relieved at the escape of the infant.

The second one resulted when a motorcycle with an inebriated handler flashed by me at midnight on one of the city's perimeter highways. It was a blur as it passed and I was probably well over the speed limit myself. Within the next quarter mile it developed a wobble in the front wheel, then dropped tumultuously to the roadbed in a shower of sparks and bits of fibreglass fairings. The driver went belly-down and spun like a giant pinwheel, ending up against the massive concrete barrier in the middle of the divided highway, while I braked hard and stopped behind his 700 pound bike, resting in the centre of the road. Leaving the flashers on in my truck I ran to where he lay and after checking for bleeding gave him conditional absolution. Almost immediately a station wagon pulled up against the barrier on the opposite side of the highway and two men vaulted over the wall and began examining the victim. One went to his feet and worked upwards checking for wounds and broken bones, and the other took out a pencil and poked around his neck and spinal cord asking the semi-conscious man if he felt the pressure.

By luck, or God's intervention, they were ambulance attendants on their way home after their shift and knew exactly how manage the injury and control all aspects of the accident area. They called for police and back-up medical coverage, and unable to find any injury on the motorcyclist still kept him restrained and comfortable. When the police arrived we pulled the touring bike to the side of the road, and after answering questions I went on my way home. Next day when I called the police station they said that his motorcycle was in the repair shop and the driver had been released after being charged with 'Driving Under the Influence.' It was the opinion of the officer that the bike had *not* developed a high speed wobble that caused the accident, but rather that the driver had just passed out and lost control. One of the doctors had told him that if the motorcyclist had not been so relaxed when he fell from the bike *he would have tumbled* and certainly been killed. God takes care even of fools.

After nine years at the Catholic high school I was officially retired from the Board and began to do supply work when other teachers were away. One of the schools on my coverage was an all-girls' school, aptly named Holy Name of Mary, and when a position to cover an extended leave of absence opened up I applied as a Long Term Occasional teacher, and have been at that school for the past seven years, filling all and every spot that became available, even that of Latin teacher! How unbelieving my old seminary Latin teacher would have been, but then I have always believed in miracles, and to be quite honest, my lovely students were so good they really didn't need me. Our experience with the girls is that they do much better scholastically when the boys are not around, and in standard competitions our school always scores in the top percentages in Math, Science, and Literature. Unfortunately the school was only rented by the Board and we were informed last March that its administrators had decided to turn it into an exclusive private school with a large annual admission fee. So this is our final time in the old building and its beautiful grounds. It is quite possibly my last school as well.

Another of my friends retired from teaching when he had reached the magic age of sixty-five, but continued to work as an officer in the Teachers' Union for several more years. Quite to his surprise he found out one day that he had an advanced form of cancer, although up until that time the only thing he had noticed was that he didn't have his usual energy for doing repairs around the house. Within a month he was bed-ridden almost every day, but occasionally could have a 'good' day and get out for a walk or a visit. He showed up one morning on my doorstep to ask me to be one of the pallbearers at his funeral, which was quite an honour for he was well known and highly respected in the community. I went to see him a few days later just after returning from a shrine some hundred miles distant from our town, and both he and his wife were very interested in going there themselves, if at all possible. The next week his wife phoned me with the news that they had indeed gone, but when they arrived he became so ill that she started to rush him to the nearest hospital. They had to stop for gas and the older lady attendant noticed how ill he was, because she was a retired nurse, and had him taken in and placed in a bed in her home where he immediately fell into a deep, peaceful sleep. They decided to watch him rather than rush him to the hospital, and when the wife awoke in the morning he was already outside in the fresh summer air and asking for his breakfast.

They returned to the 'shrine' which was actually a series of crosses set up in a farmer's field with a meditation station at each cross. The crosses ran in a pattern, first half way around the perimeter of the field, then up the escarpment by a series of stone steps before turning again on a downward slope to rejoin the original cross. The overall distance was close to a mile. His wife told me that he had *run* up the steps like a young child and completed the course without losing his breath. He had no pain and said he felt renewed. On the way home he soon fell asleep and then, said the wife, the most amazing thing happened. Because it was the end of a summer weekend the highway was crowded and they drove bumper to bumper for several miles until a long, black limousine pulled in front of them and another grey car pulled in behind them. Then all the other cars on the road parted to let them through. They were home in forty minutes, an impossibly short time, and as they turned onto their own street the two cars vanished.

She simply said, "For those who believe in miracles no explanation is necessary, and for those who don't, no explanation is possible."

My friend died the next week and I was thankful to have known him.

The divers from the original gang still meet annually at Donna's place and reminisce about earlier days, such as the time we dove the *Waome* at midnight, or tied plastic roses on its bow on the fiftieth anniversary of its sinking, or dove in December water so cold it froze on our masks when we surfaced, or kissed Janet underwater, or lost our way in underwater shafts, or barfed over the side on pitching dive boats, or took trips anywhere whenever possible, or recalled Max's exploits, or a thousand other things never to be forgotten.

Not everyone gets the opportunity to get paid for something they like doing but of all the jobs that have been available throughout my career there have been really none that were not enjoyable in one way or another. Some were physically difficult but the fellow workers turned the tedium into fun. Others were exciting in their own right, and such was scuba. Still others allowed me to watch anguished minds become peaceful, whether in counselling or in the administration of the sacraments. But of all the joys nothing surpasses those of teaching, whether it was in literature or religion or scuba or any of the other subjects I have taught over the past thirty-five years. It would be difficult to say which subject was the most pleasing for each had its own nuances and rewards, but truthfully I must say that the past seven years at Holy Name girls' school have certainly ended my teaching career on a high note. And what has been so special about teaching those young ladies? Well, they were bright and dedicated and spirited and more than anything else, they were fun to teach. A thousand faces pass through my mind at this writing, each one smiling or challenging or kidding and always with an underlying note of kindness and eagerness to learn, and I am reminded of how Mr. Chips in the famous novel must have felt as his teaching career came to a close. And for them and all the others I have had the privilege to teach, I breathe a silent prayer of gratitude.

Now nearing my eightieth year there are still roads to ride down and perhaps still time for an occasional dive or two. Steve is already talking about us retracing my ride down to Newfoundland and the Atlantic seaboard and maybe even a trip up the Alaska highway. My other two cycle buddies, Martin and Rick, seem to believe that anything over a three day jaunt is just asking for trouble, so Steve and I will probably do a couple of shorter rides with them just to warm up for a longer adventure. With God's blessing there is still time for a few more adventures in the grand and painful adventure of life. Belief and hope from my faith have always been present and I look forward to when the last ride or the last dive beckons me into eternity.